# THE
# GREAT
# WHEN

# THE
# GREAT
# WHEN

# ALAN
# MOORE

BLOOMSBURY PUBLISHING

LONDON · OXFORD · NEW YORK · NEW DELHI · SYDNEY

BLOOMSBURY PUBLISHING
Bloomsbury Publishing Plc
50 Bedford Square, London, WC1B 3DP, UK
29 Earlsfort Terrace, Dublin 2, Ireland

BLOOMSBURY, BLOOMSBURY PUBLISHING and the Diana logo
are trademarks of Bloomsbury Publishing Plc

First published in Great Britain 2024

A catalogue record for this book is available from the British Library

ISBN: HB: 978-1-5266-4322-3; TPB: 978-1-5266-4323-0; SPECIAL EDITION: 978-1-5266-8288-8;
SIGNED SPECIAL EDITION: 978-1-5266-8287-1; GOLDSBORO: 978-1-5266-8286-4;
EBOOK: 978-1-5266-4321-6; EPDF: 978-1-5266-4319-3

2 4 6 8 10 9 7 5 3

Typeset by Integra Software Services Pvt. Ltd.
Printed and bound in Australia by Griffin Press

To find out more about our authors and books visit www.bloomsbury.com
and sign up for our newsletters

For Michael Moorcock and Iain Sinclair, both longer
in London and there before me

# Contents

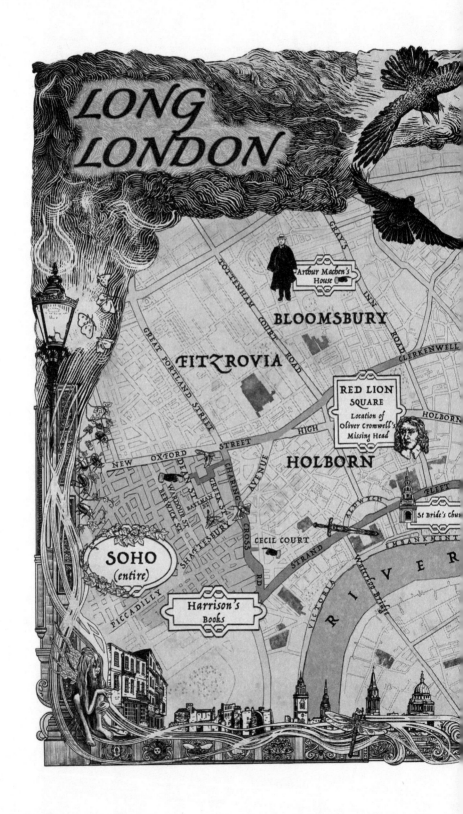

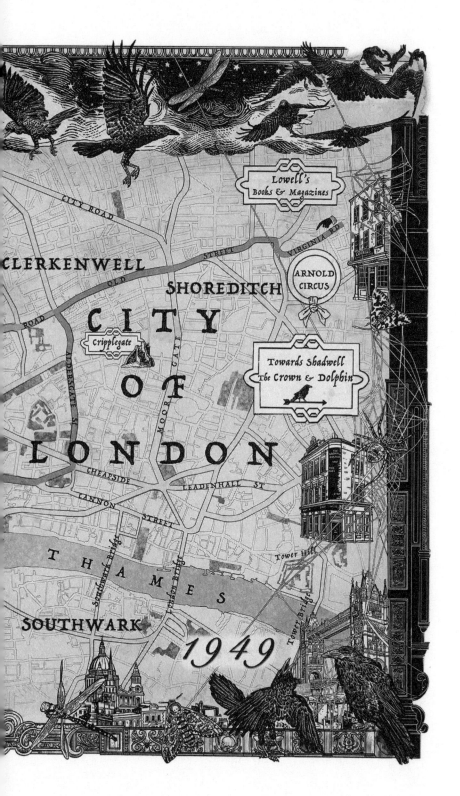

Lowell's
Books & Magazines

CITY ROAD

CLERKENWELL

SHOREDITCH

STREET

VIRGINIA RD

ARNOLD
CIRCUS

OLD

ROAD

CITY

Cripplegate

OF

Towards Shadwell
The Crown & Dolphin

MOOR GATE

ALDERSGATE ST.

LONDON

CHEAPSIDE

LEADENHALL ST

CANNON

STREET

Tower Hill

THAMES

Southwark Bridge

London Bridge

Tower Bridge

SOUTHWARK

1949

## The Music at the Beginning

Woodwind: out behind the boarding house, where a low winter sun has spattered gold on towering weeds, two sorcerers are dying over tea and biscuits.

The old boy is birdlike, almost dainty with the neat white Van Dyke beard. Having lost several stone and much of his studied monstrosity, he sits with a plaid blanket draped across his knees, recalling nothing quite so much as a retired art teacher, perhaps one who dreamed himself another Sargent in his youth. Across a folding table and the tea service thereon, his guest restrains a breeze-borne strand from her somehow heroic brow. Near fifteen years his junior, she watches as he pours the steaming twist of burnt sienna into mismatched china cups, hands quaking visibly where was he once the terror of his age.

He passes her the laden saucer, jingling like a milk cart, and regards her quizzically.

'My dear girl. You are very ill, I take it?'

The high, lilting voice is always a surprise. She narrows her perennially disappointed eyes, impressed despite herself by her host's divinatory skills, and then at length she laughs.

'That's rather good. I almost thought you were a real magician for a moment. But, of course, you know that you are literally the last person I'd want asking me how many sugars.'

Glancing down at the delinquent lawn, he smiles apologetically. She stares at him for a few moments more, broad bulldog features settling into a pensive frown as she considers.

'Although, following that logic … oh, dear. You as well?'

Above, winds at high altitude drag crumpled bedsheets from an unmade Hastings sky. He shrugs regretfully, deteriorated saint of a rained-off apocalypse.

'Afraid so. Nothing definite, and if the universe is willing, I might have another year or two. At least, that's what the cards and coins inform me, but, then, I'm an ancient ruin and such setbacks are to be expected. What of you, though? You're a mere child, barely in your middle fifties. It just seems such rotten luck.'

Off in the house's kitchen, the diabolist's latest and last apprentice anxiously prepares egg and cress sandwiches, all but the bread and cress obtained off-ration, and fastidiously slices them on the diagonal. Outside, the high priestess wrinkles her nose, declining sympathy.

'Mm. Or possibly the spite of the Almighty. Deo, non Fortuna. God, not luck. A nice thought if you're doing well, but if not, it's a bloody stupid motto, and a bloody stupid name. I'm suffering from an incurable disease, apparently. Something to do with bone marrow, I'm told, although I'd never heard of it before. Leukaemia could have been a handmaiden to Hera for all I knew. Now, though, I've got a few months for putting my affairs in order, then I'm off to find how much was only theory after all. I hope to last the war, but not unless we're going to win.'

She hunches into her thick overcoat, chin resolutely at a jut that always makes him think of Churchill. Sitting up, he nods in an attempt at reassurance.

'Oh, we'll win. Frankly, I'd be surprised if Germany survives the cricket season. It's a pity, really. I had such high hopes that this was going to be my Aeon of Horus, stern and radiant, all decked in sun wheels, but it's not to be. It seems that I was wrong about a lot of things.'

He sips, then sucks the surplus from his yellowing moustache. The woman snorts.

'Well, as somebody who's spent half her magical career apologising for the hellish mess you've made of yours, I'd say that was a pretty accurate assumption.' Reconsidering, she softens. 'Although I suspect my own Age of Aquarius will soon be following your aeon to the junkyard of the eras. Sometimes the etheric voices spout a lot of frightful twaddle, don't you think?'

Both chuckle at this heresy, surprised to find how much they like each other without all the pantomime of light and darkness getting in the way. Dead-nettles rattle in a brief but sudden gust, with the exhausted whinny of a dray floated from the suburban streets nearby. Feeling an awkward spasm of affection for the quavering devil magnet, she leans in to touch him lightly on the arm.

'Despite our differences, you're still the most experienced magician that I've ever read. You know that, don't you? Morally, of course, you're quite the vilest creature that can be imagined, but in matters of enchantment, I have nothing save the greatest of respect for you, old man.'

Beyond all expectation, he finds this absurdly touching. Both their teas are going cold.

'Nor I for you, my cara soror. I have always thought you the most gifted of your generation.'

To their mutual embarrassment and without warning, they are at the brink of tears before the woman saves the situation with a head toss and contemptuous sniff.

'I'm sure that you thought nothing of the sort. What about your "Miss Firth was schooled at Radcliffe Hall" insinuations? And these from a flagrant bugger like yourself! What you are is an awful, awful man who happens to be very good at magic – although a fat lot of good that's done for either of us. All those gorgeous robes and here we are, both looking as if we've been dressed by the Salvation Army. I mean, are you getting by alright down here? How do you pay your rent?'

The innocence of his expression is a small comedic masterpiece.

'Why, magically, of course. I have secured my tenure by providing Netherwood's proprietor with tablets that restore his faltering virility, being infused with my own yogic essence.'

She stares fixedly at him and blinks in puzzlement before unwanted realisation dawns.

'Oh, for God's sake. Tell me they aren't just crushed chalk and your own ejaculate.'

Sheepish, he spreads his hands, skin crinkling like foil and fingernails untrimmed.

'Would that I could, dear girl. Would that I could.'

Everything drips with history beneath the dog-fought heavens, and across the globe fretful uncertainties resolve to sticky ends. She gapes at him in what, if not for his unsavoury reputation, would be disbelief, and then they're snickering: a pair of papery and shopworn children. When their mirth abates, the older conjuror stares rheumily into the middle distance and becomes more sombre. Everything is changed, and even the procession of the aeons stumbles. There will never be an afternoon again of this specific cigarette-card blue. After a time, the woman speaks.

'You know, there's going to be a frightful crack in England when this bun-struggle is over. I'm not sure my angels helped a bit. The V-bombs go straight through them. And there's going to be a bloody awful hole in magic when we're gone. Even if most of our assertions were delusion, we both know of some that weren't. The occultists that will be our successors have spoken convincingly upon the subject, but have never had that subject answer back. They've never had it pulsing right there in the room with them. Their only entities are met in books.'

As if on cue, young Grant emerges from the house's back door with his film-star looks, Macassar glisten and a plate of sandwiches balanced upon one upraised palm. The pastured Beast regards his visitor with eyes unreadable beneath haw-frosted brows.

'Do you remember that appalling cat?'

She stiffens in her seat and shoots him a reproachful look. He notes the brief, involuntary shudder that she's evidently trying to suppress.

'Of course I do. It came into my house, when Moina Mathers set it on me. It was the most terrifying episode of my entire life.'

The eager acolyte approaches, carrying refreshments, paddling in the shaggy lawn. With lowered voice, the woman volunteers a last remark to her moral antithesis and sole surviving peer.

'In fact, the other London is a case in point. That wasn't our imaginations, was it?'

Sharing a rueful gaze, they might be an old married couple. Solemnly, he shakes his head.

'No. No, it wasn't. That was real.'

A picnic neither has the energy to eat arrives, and everybody's shadows are unrolled across the unmown ground, black carpets welcoming midnight celebrities. It's February, 1945, and a lone songbird bounces rhapsody from off a lowering ionosphere as they sit bickering, amiable and intermittent, in the failing light of English magic.

♫

Brass: a river now of shouts and punches, Cable Street smells like a circus in stampede. Bristle of fist, flag, bottle, poker, shovel, people like pushed paint across the flagstones and why, David Gascoyne thinks, is there not poetry that will contain the passion and intensity of this, its snarl, its cauliflower-eared jazz? Suspended in a sea of shoulders, forced against gabardine backs in angry intimacy, he relinquishes volition to the furious animal in which he has become a component. He can only go where it goes, scuffed shoes commandeered into its millipedal shove, a passenger of the affray.

Surrendering to brute consensus brings an unexpected sensuality – excited human heat and movement rubbing up against his own, the colour-flood of an October palette smearing on overcast doorsteps, symphony of boot-stamp, beaten dustbin lid and florid Yiddish curse. 'Hang yourself with a sugar rope and have a sweet death!' He's nineteen until next Saturday, had his third book out just a month or two ago, and brimming with the moment; jittery with history. Howling women, nippers flinging bricks, but mostly a determined crush of men in their cologne of cigarettes and haircut rum and Sunday dinner, up for trouble. He has never felt more Jewish in his life than in this pungent rush of elbows, and the one thing he's afraid of here is an erection.

With the uproar's crunch perhaps a hundred yards ahead, his chest's a ringing anvil. Past the tide of shaved necks and turned heads in front of him, he sees the scuffers in their navy greatcoats, some of them on horseback, swinging truncheons through skull-cracking arcs into the ancient face of the East End. This storm of bruises has its purpling and half-closed eye right outside Gardiner's department store, which seems to have already lost one of its sheet-glass panes. Here are the boys in blue with boiled-ham jaws, gazes like marbles pressed in lard, concussing schoolteachers and haberdashers to protect the chinless thoroughbreds a little further down the road: the boys in black.

Pallid as ghosts, these flinch from every clatter, startled and incredulous at their Whitechapel welcome, the heart-stopping scale of it. By David's reckoning, there look to be a thousand or two fascists, although shrinking in together like they're doing makes it seem like fewer. Perhaps twice that many bludgeoning police, but even if you count the black shirts with the blue shirts, dirty shirts have them outnumbered ten to one. From upstairs windows either side, mothers and wives hurl chilling epithets; coal; putrid vegetables; boiled water; turds from chamber pots or chamber pots themselves; a weather front of missiles. With all things considered, 1936 has been a funny year.

Amongst the thrust and clamour, he remembers Dalí's frantic mugging through the dusty faceplate, terrified and suffocating with his moustache bent, during the London International Surrealist Exhibition that David had helped to organise this June just gone. The artist had insisted on appearing in a deep-sea diving suit, then realised he could neither get the helmet off nor breathe. Only by David's intervention with a spanner were burning giraffe herds and inverted elephant-swans spared extinction. Looking at the mortal boil about him now, his luminous moth eyes incredulous, the poet wonders if surrealism tries too hard, or doesn't try enough. A furious young girl who only has one arm is brandishing the limb of a shop manikin in her remaining hand,

and there's some toothless alter kocker with an evil eye, dragging a sack of lion shit cadged from the zoo to bolt the coppers' horses. Breeze blocks and bowel movements hang suspended in the autumn air. This is above real, *sur*-real, what the word meant before André Breton fiddled with it. This, he thinks, is the true fire that melts the clocks. This is the memory that persists.

Something is happening near the epicentre, some new current spiralling into the maelstrom. From torn scraps of dialogue blowing through the crowd, he pastes together what is going on. 'It's Spotty!' 'Spotty's coming!' 'Here comes Spotty and his lads!' This, he presumes, is local mauler Spotty Comer with his kosher cosh-boys, lending a veneer of anti-fascism to the horrific violence that they'd have been perpetrating anyway. Glancing above the struggling statuary busts surrounding him, he sees the frighteners steaming in with cloth caps, crowbars, anthracite expressions; getting on a hundred of them; a grey wedge of noisy damage hurtling at the police with Comer roaring at its sharp end, swinging something heavy and ornate that David will learn later is a lead-filled sofa leg. The bellowing meat locomotive throws its weight into the wall of constables, with as much blood as possible its only politics. This is a thrilling if uncomfortable allegiance, all its ethics in explosion.

Either the unstable atmosphere or David's brain ignites. The trampling squeeze he's in slops forward and then back, a shifting fluid mass that takes him with it, gasps its terror and excitement. Placards dip and slice around him, cutting vision, time and continuity to coarse-grained photos from tomorrow's newspapers, inexpertly collaged and difficult to make much sense of. Someone's broken the police line, could be Spotty Comer, and is caving in the ribs of the six-foot gorilla next to Oswald Mosley. A police horse rears to split the head of a tailor's apprentice, and for no apparent reason a soiled bedsheet has been set alight. He's lost in the cascading images, as in a poem without discipline. The year, the day, the instant swell up like a heart attack or chord inside him, and the snapshot swirl kaleidoscopes against his assailed retina: a small boy limping with one shoe gone, hurtling furniture, the burning sheet reflecting filthy orange from the upper glazing, shock-haired cats, knocked-over braziers spilling rubies to the dusk, an obscure viscount cowering and weeping, fish-gut rain, the giant woman, apoplectic rabbis, hard-faced little girls with billhooks, sparking hobnails, military veterans, frantic dogs, birds flying the wrong way as though through an eclipse …

The giant woman.

Moving through the mob, she's nine or ten feet high at least, and nobody is seeing her. They turn away right on the brink of apprehension to look somewhere else, appearing vaguely troubled. The horde parts to let her through, and does not seem to be aware that it is doing this. It is as if the world cannot allow her. Belly-deep in communists and paupers, she steps unconcerned amid the multitude, where David reels and thinks he might be dying. A bright scarlet cap atop the molten copper of her tumbling hair, a garment crumpling white and red across one shoulder – scarf or sash or toga, he can't make it out – so that her breasts are bare, not as a provocation but as token of unanswerable authority. Above the highest lamp-posts that beatific countenance, fond eyes demurely downcast at the baying insurrectionaries that brush her skirts, smiling and dimpling with maternal pride at all the wound and weapon. On her coral flesh, the shadows shifting in her motion appear steel-engraved and, God, she's taller than a house! Why isn't anybody screaming, running, worshipping? Why doesn't anybody notice? The barrage of pelting debris all sails wide of her. She wades a tide of fistfight, where the screwed-up faces are preoccupied by their fierce effort to remain oblivious to what's amongst them, holy and unbearable, so lovely that even the blazing linen dare not touch her.

Doubling over, David spews into his turn-ups. He's seen meta-phor itself, enormous in a London lane and now his ears are ringing, his eyes watering the world into a squirming blur. From lips once slick with lyric, bile depends in tensile threads, and when he lifts his head again she's gone, perhaps a trick of light on the soot-mottled walls; perhaps continuing her promenade down the hysterically blind avenue. In the months following the riot, he joins the Communists, he goes to Spain and more than ever is convinced in poetry, but on sanity's floorboards is thereafter apprehensive, having felt their sag and heard their threatening splinter.

♪

Timpani: 'Black man for luck, white man for pluck,' he yells, his voice like church bells, the imaginary African. A schoolboy sun is crayoning the downs with simple, happy colours as he navigates the Epsom throng, a piece of solid music chiming in the titfers and the toppers by the track. The titfers offer cheers of recognition and the toppers condescending smiles, but all of them are marvelstruck as if he was to English eyes a rhino, or an orchid, or a continent. 'Spion Kop first, the others nowhere,' he proclaims, this teak flamingo, and a June breeze lifts the roquelaure trimmings of his waistcoat in embroidered wings.

They touch him as he passes, rub the horseshoe or the lion's claw he wears around his neck and stroke the suns, moons, stars and shamrocks stitched into his robe, the turf messiah come to cure a leprosy of poor equestrian decisions. He'll profess to reading certainties in tea leaves, stars or zebra entrails if that's what's required, then cheerfully admit it's nonsense and that inside knowledge is his only spirit guide, though this admission is, of course, itself a lie. 'Whoh-hoh-hoh-hoh,' he booms from leather lungs amid the pretty frocks and pinstripes. 'Spion Kop to win the Derby!' White blouse like a swollen sail and lurid ostrich feathers at his masthead, he parades from out of the empire's dreams across the course's crew-cut margins, tilts or sways or quicksteps through the tinkling conversation and the summer mumbles.

His celebrity precedes him, just as surely as his creditors come after. Everywhere is his tumultuous legend known – the Abyssinian prince shanghaied aboard a British boat, shipwrecked in Portugal, arrived at Tilbury Docks, the greatest racing forecaster this land had ever seen. St Croix in the Danish West Indies and a runaway horse-breeder's son called Peter Carl McKay are dull inclusions that have no real bearing, best forgotten and why even mention them? 'Whoh-hoh-hoh-hoh,' he foghorns to the baggy-suited punters at the rail, the toffs clutching binoculars. 'I got a horse!' And yes, he has, but where he got it is another story.

It was, what, eight years ago? A thin patch, where his many skills had failed to keep wolves from his door; indeed, had even failed to keep his door. His tips would limp home if they made it that far, and his fortune-telling sideline plunged into an unforeseen decline. His trade in self-invented medicines looked not long for this world, and following the failure of his kerbside dentist business – with a deafening 'Whoh-hoh-hoh-hoh' to drown the screaming when he pulled a healthy tooth – only his wallet faced painful extractions. Hence, a touring Negro show bound for St Petersburg had seemed the very breath of opportunity, for a theatrical engagement of that kind would surely be another feather in his cap, if there was room. He shimmies in the trackside sunshine now, a fountain of volcanic laughter and outrageous hues, uttering priceless oracles to his delighted subjects. The great European adventure is not long ago but everything in life, he thinks, is changed. He is a different man, astride a different nag, a different world.

In Russia, self-described as Abyssinian royalty, he'd been presented to his fellow head of state, Czar Nicholas. Although perhaps bewildered by his visitor, the czar seemed a kind-hearted chap and not at all the sort to be so soon thereafter murdered as a frightful tyrant. When the Negro show at last packed up its ridiculous paraphernalia, he had roamed the continent from Italy to France to Switzerland, using undignified expulsion as a means of international transport. This was the unfortunate itinerary that delivered him to shitting Germany in that eventful year, 1914. When the authorities there soon contrived the rounding up of coloured men, he had been sent to an internment camp called Ruhleben outside Berlin, for who knew how long. He processions through the racegoers, advancing without hurry on his favoured spot beside the finish line, and as he goes he thunders his free prophecy, 'Spion Kop for best, and damn the rest! Whoh-hoh-hoh-hoh!' He grins to think that by an almost comical coincidence, Ruhleben had been built upon a racetrack. With the other prisoners, he'd slept in filthy stables, which had much increased his sympathy for those proud beasts who were the usual occupants, as well as his abiding hatred of the Germans.

In that cold, malodorous place he'd shared his straw cot with an older coloured gent from London, who had been a railway stoker in the reign of Queen Victoria. Before pneumonia took him, he had whispered many confidences to his bedfellow, remarking on their native city's more elusive lengths and how these might be utilised by someone of sufficient foolishness or knowledge. This had been an entertaining yarn, although he'd thought it probable that the old fellow was a crackpot, or else one of those infuriating fellows who make up unlikely stories for the fun of it. But then, with the war's end and his eventual return to Blighty just last year, he had been given cause to reconsider this unkind assessment. He'd gone to the Seven Sisters Road and done the things that he'd been told, performed the cockney obeah, and then he'd seen with his own eyes the unbelievable extension.

He breathes deep of the invigorating Epsom air – he will not make some crack about the salts – and savours its enticing redolence of grass, of clothing laundered or unlaundered, with a base of underarm sweat and sweet accents of manure. He struts between the bookies' trestles to admire the blurring semaphore of pallid hands, their tic-tac-toe unreadable until one knows its alphabet, much like that stretch of the metropolis he'd found near Highbury on the advice of the dead stoker. There he had encountered something called the Inferred Saracen, and similarly a fine gentlewoman with a most extraordinary steed. She'd said to him that he had flair, but that success would be the one who followed flair. He did not properly absorb the lady's wisdom at that time, being preoccupied with screaming at her terrifying mount and hurriedly departing those intolerable extremities, but has since come to know her quip for the best tip of his part-fabricated life.

As near the winning post as he is likely to attain, he makes his stand. At almost seven feet if one includes the plumes, the lucky charms on his billowing drapes will be the only view for those luckless enough to stand behind him, and his voice the only rumbling they'll hear. 'Put all you've got on Spion Kop! Black man for luck!' Some months after his meeting with the memorable rider, which he had by then dismissed as a result of undigested food, he had been loitering at Peter Gilpin's stables, listening out for useful news, as was his habit. When a stable-lad had asked his boss, 'Is Flair alright, d'you think?', receiving the response, 'Oh, she'll be fine. She beat that colt, and she's the best we've got,' the name had struck the quietest of notes. Flair was a filly owned by Major Giles Loder, an exquisite specimen that had outpaced promising colt Spion Kop, and was the major's entry for the Derby. But why had the boy sounded concerned? He'd quickly launched into his loud, distracting patter, then had managed in mid-flourish to spill all the sealed envelopes containing forecasts on the cobblestones outside Flair's stall. In the ensuing mockery, assuming his most woebegone visage, the self-styled poor, uneducated darkie squatted to retrieve his errant packets while examining more closely the prospective champion. She'd made a funny ducking motion with her head, repetitively; to his eye an indication if a horse was going barmy. That was when he'd understood.

This wasn't going to get better. Flair would be withdrawn, and the next-best contender substituted. Spion Kop would have the training and attention necessary to alleviate Major Loder's disappointment. Spion Kop would be 'the one who follows flair'. So, he'd put every penny on the 100–6 outsider and, without charge, had encouraged everybody else to do the same. Along the track where he can't see, a thousand-throated monster roars the words, 'They're off!'

Time crumples like a losing ticket, and the race is starting, happening, ending all at once. Faces in the surrounding jostle flicker through fifteen expressions in an eye-blink – hope, anxiety, wild triumph and despair – as they attempt to read their next month's rent into the smearing blurs. He catches sight of Flair's successor with the yellow-, blue- and black-clad form of Frank

O'Neill stood in the stirrups, then can't see a thing as those about him try to howl their preferred outcomes into being: 'Come on, Archaic!' 'You can do it, Orpheus!' Peering around a hat more ostentatious than his own, he shrieks with joy to glimpse O'Neill, a crouching incubus, propelling Spion Kop in first position past the post. The day explodes in a confetti of congratulation. He runs back and forth, stamping his feet, throwing his arms up in the air and barking, 'What I told you? What I told you?'

Everything becomes a splendid dream. Touring the Epsom bookies to collect his winnings, wading through a sea of jubilation and remorse, he finds that grateful beneficiaries of his advice are pressing notes and coins into his hands, his pockets. He is rich beyond his wildest hopes, and though he will no doubt have lost it all before the year is out, that does not rob this perfect moment of its shine. Receiving ten-bob notes and backslaps with an earthquake chuckle, he can't help but think of the illustrious patroness who'd given him her cryptic tip, and who might well be due some favour in return. He pictures her, side-saddle on her thing of polished and articulated bones, that rattled as it shook its head and fixed him with its staring sockets. Now, *she'd* got a horse.

♫

Strings: the decrepit rents back on to one of London's vanished Liberties, and that's how it got in. Ingeniously hinged, a slotted and indented central mass hangs in the firelight almost motionless, just under the low ceiling. Three of its extensions with their numberless points of articulation are supporting it – one by the door, one by the spitting hearth, one at the bed's foot where a pisspot is knocked over – while the other two are lifted, mantid-still, in contemplative pause. The glasswork of an optical arrangement in its thorax sparkles with reflected nineteenth-century flame as it surveys the detailed artistry beneath, ratcheting, clicking, swivelling appropriate magnifiers into place with lurching shadow vast against the flaking plaster overhead.

After some several minutes of deliberation, delicate adjustments are performed. Sticky and glistening in the infernal pink, the worst thing is its inappropriate beauty. All five many-jointed limbs have curling arabesques of chitin; poppy-stem hydraulics; troubling decorations that encroach on the Nouveau and gesture to a hideous aesthetic. Limp black membranes droop in folds between the quintuped's splaying extremities, theatre curtains fluttering at each infrequent breath. Craned over bold impastos on the mattress canvas, dipping and rotating, pecking, calibrating, every movement is balletic. Both superior arms are armoured swans' necks in their motion, plunging and retracting with appalling grace through rubicund miasma. Tilting, cutting, click-click-click-click-click.

A little after two o'clock, when finally the image cannot be improved, it carefully manoeuvres itself down to a more manageable shape and size. Four of the thing's appendages are folded up into themselves, becoming thicker and considerably shorter. It stands balanced now on two of these, its fifth protrusion curling up to wind into a tight, flat disc, approximately head-sized, at the top of the assemblage. Settling with a repellent shiver to the contours of this new configuration, its funereal membranes do not seem dissimilar to the falling pleats of a long overcoat, save at closer quarters where their beads of milky perspiration are made visible. With gait that of a rearing centipede, it crosses to the poorly fitted door, unlocks it with one razor finger and slides out into the cobbled cold.

In the adjacent district that it hails from, it is called a Pope of Blades, and isn't meant to come anywhere near Commercial Street.

♫

Percussion: four days after Christmas and he's cracking gas meters in Aldersgate, or trying to. The way it works, you wait until you hear the sirens, then when everybody's in the shelters, you can nip in through the cellar window and have all the shillings. Dennis, though, has messed it up: he couldn't force the meter open, and he's even having trouble clambering back up the coal chute to get out the way he came. His mates would laugh if they could see him, trying to haul himself up on his belly, coal dust everywhere, coughing and wheezing. He's a dead loss as a crook, he's cottoned on to that alright, but then, he's only nine.

He's got his fingers hooked on the wood frame he took the wire-mesh panel from when he broke in, dog-paddling on the rough slant for a foothold, rubbing all the scabs and skin from his bare knees. He's starting to feel a bit frightened, to be honest. If he can't get out before they sound the all-clear and whoever's house this is comes back, they'll fetch the coppers, and his mum will find out, and he might be put in prison. Panicked by this thought, his toecap finally finds purchase on the chute's brick sides, and with a desperate heave he flops his upper half nose-down on to the chilly pavement of the street outside. The sirens have packed up, but now it sounds as if the sky is shaking – angels moving furniture, according to old ladies when it thunders – so it's only just occurring to him that there's worse things than the coppers, prison or his mum, and then the bombing starts.

More fire than he has ever seen shoots up into the dark, it might be over Moorgate, and a second later it's not even noise; it's like the world is being punched. Then there's another one, and then another. After that he isn't counting. Making sounds that he can't even hear, he's halfway to his feet when they're slapped out from under him and he just misses being flung back down the coal-hole. Face first on the slabs again and crying now despite himself, he struggles on his elbows like a caterpillar, staying flat as possible. He crawls quick as he can towards the nearest turning, and with every second there's another roaring flash, so he can see his shadow in the middle of a Sunday night. Squirming around the corner into what he thinks is Glasshouse Yard, surprised to find he's still alive with nothing hanging off, he slithers underneath a gate into some funny-smelling area open to the rowdy night. A leather business, where he curls into a ball behind a pallet stacked with slippery pelts and he can't tell if everything is shrivelling up inside itself, or if it's only him.

And BOOMBOOMBOOMBOOMBOOMBOOMBOOM why is he here? He doesn't even BOOMBOOMBOOMBOOM doesn't even know what he was BOOMBOOMBOOM was going to spend it on, his BOOMBOOMBOOMBOOMBOOMBOOM BOOM his loot, probably sweets and BOOMBOOM sweets and comics, something for his mum, and BOOMBOOMBOOM and now BOOMBOOMBOOMBOOMBOOMBOOM and now he's going to be dead, he reckons.

How long it goes on for, he's got no idea, like it's a small forever on its own. At any moment, he's afraid one's going to come down right on top of him, right on his head, since that's about the worst thing that he can imagine. He begins his prayers, because, well, you're supposed to, but he only gets as far as 'hallowed be thy name' before he feels all daft and realises that he doesn't properly believe in God. The thumping great explosions and the somewhere–up–there Jerry bombers, they're the only things in heaven that he knows are real. At last, after a minute or two's silence when he dares to let himself think that it's finished, he gets up and makes his way on jelly legs between the trolleys and the hides, back underneath the gate and round the corner on to the main road. Where he sits down on someone's icy doorstep and just stares.

Cripplegate's gone.

It's not ... but how can ... it's not just blown up, it's gone. There's nothing there. No streets, no buildings. All the way to Moorgate, it's like one enormous sloping field that's growing fire instead of grass. It's like the devil's football pitch. It's gone. But, like, hundreds of years it must have been there. Since the Romans, didn't someone say? And now, it can't have been a half hour, and it's all been scrubbed away. The barbers' shops, the washing lines, the drapers, everybody's houses, places that he's known since he was little, all of it a burning nothing; a big empty hole in London that he can't believe he's looking at.

He stands up, sits back down and then stands up again. He doesn't know what he's supposed to do, or even what he's doing. For no earthly reason, he starts heading down in the direction of St Paul's, when he lives up the other way, off along Old Street in Shoreditch. For quite a while he thinks the ground's still shaking, but it's just the way he's walking. He can't take his eyes off all the blazing rubble not ten yards away across the road, the sheets of flame shifting and blowing in the wind, like laundry. Splitting, spitting, cracking noises and he can hear fire-engine bells but doesn't know where from. In glimpses through the billows and the showers of sparks, he can make out four buildings just about still standing in the whole of Cripplegate.

The nearest, some way up the red-hot oven that he thinks used to be Beech Street, is the fire station. It strikes him as funny that it's not been touched. There's something going on there, when the thick theatre curtains of black smoke lift out the way, but it's not where the bells are coming from, because the bells, he figures out belatedly, are only in his head. Past that – is it called Chiswell Street? – there's somewhere else that's not been flattened, by the look of it. It might be the old brewery. He's not scared any more, although he isn't really anything, to tell the truth. All of it's too much to do any more than gawp at. Furthest off, right down the bottom, there's a church that's had a bomb go through its roof, with all fire belching from the blown-out shell, then closer by there's ... what is it, exactly? Through the blaze, it's hard to make it out.

It's like an archway or a gate, a tall shape in the rolling clouds and bursts of flame, but then the top of it, it's more a normal building with a row or two of tiny windows. Eyes stinging like mad, he strains to have a gander but keeps losing sight of it amongst the black drifts and the orange flares. There's something that's not right about it, where he's not sure if it's really there or if he's made it up out of the lights and lurching shadows. It's the arch that's wrong, he finally decides: it's open, with no gate across it, but when you look through it to the other side, it's only dark. You can't see any fire or anything, when everywhere around has gone up like a Roman candle. Squinting, blurring, trying to understand what he is getting wrong about the picture, in a sudden gout of firelight Dennis spots that there's a figure in the opening, a man stood looking back at him.

Wearing a long coat or a cloak or something, he leans with one hand against the archway's wall to steady himself and the other up over his mouth, as if the sight has knocked the wind out of him. He's a bald bloke, with what hair he's got in greasy rat-tails hanging down the sides. Not what you'd call a big chap, and he doesn't look like he'd be much good in a scrap, but it's the eyes that he's got on him, massive like an owl's. He's sagging, staring out at all the fires, the neighbourhood that's disappeared, and Dennis can't remember ever seeing anyone look that upset. The man's expression stops him in his tracks. Now that he thinks about it, he supposes that this is an awful thing he's in the middle of. He feels all weak, and starts to turn so that he can head back up Aldersgate, but when he looks around, the lofty gatehouse and the grief-struck man are gone. There's only burning wreckage. He's not even mystified. He wouldn't be surprised if people saw all sorts of things after an air raid. He hears urgent grown-up voices, all-clear sirens and fire engines that aren't just the ringing in his ears. It starts to tipple down with rain and he wants only to get home, if home's still there.

Over the next few weeks he tells his pals the story until even he's not listening, leaving out the archway that he has by now put down to shell shock. After that he more or less forgets the whole experience. Two years later, when the amputated stump of Cripplegate becomes a pink expanse of rosebay willowherb, what they call London rocket, he's eleven and they've started learning about plays in school. He's sitting frowning at an illustration of the playwright in a fancy oval on the title page, trying to think who it reminds him of, but doesn't have sufficient interest to pursue the thought.

In fact, not until 1949 when he's eighteen does Dennis Knuckleyard have cause to think about what happened to him on that night, and after that he doesn't have a choice. By then, the city's secret vertebrae have made their own decision.

♫

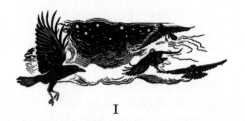

# I

## *The Best Way to Start a Book*

'It was a bright cold day in April, and the clocks were striking thirteen' was, in Dennis Knuckleyard's opinion, the best way to start a book he'd ever heard of. Inconveniently, this insight had occurred at an inopportune point in the eighteen-year-old's morning regimen of exercise, where a distressed copy of *Picture Show* from 1920 was the only apparatus. With a stifled groan, he realised that an Orwellgasm wasn't going to be possible and, after three or four despondent tugs, abandoned the whole enterprise. He was the dead.

It was a bloody miserable day in Shoreditch and the clocks weren't striking anything, most nearby churches having broken in the clumsy hands of the preceding decade. Something after seven, judging by the tinge of Reckitt's Blue to the October light, decanted into Coffin Ada's spare room through disheartened curtains. In the halo of a nursery-size lamp, flypaper yellow, he allowed his cancelled date on page sixteen of *Picture Show* a last apologetic glance before ungallantly consigning her to the debris that topped the bedside table. She was maddeningly beautiful, black hair like lustrous petals in an inky bob that kissed her pewter neck, mascara as a soot of filings caught in the magnetic field of her unanswerable eyes. Licentious smirk, only its pout adorned by a dark dot of lipstick letting the observer know that here was everything he'd ever wanted while also informing him he didn't stand a chance. The wavering, liquid brush-stroke of her body line. She'd probably died elegantly through some Isadora Duncan balls-up, strung pearls caught in the propeller of a Spitfire and 'If You Knew Susie' crackling on the wind-up gramophone.

From downstairs, he heard the ongoing fury of the hounds that were his elderly landlady's lungs, which meant that Ada was already up and facing down the leaden day with her superior unpleasantness. Landlady and employer, he supposed, and possibly disturbing mother-substitute into the bargain: he'd been twelve when first he started running errands round at Ada Benson's bookshop – Lowell's Books & Magazines according to the sign, although nobody ever called it that, and he'd always assumed the name to be that of a previous owner. Then, when he was four-teen and his mum had died, Ada had let him come and stop with her, provided that he earned his fucking keep and didn't mistake Ada for his fucking mother, as she'd put it. Not that there was any chance of that. Dennis's mother had been nice, unlike the wheezing engine of contempt and malice that was Coffin Ada.

There were benefits, though. During uneventful stretches at the till he was permitted to read what he wanted from the wildly various stock, as long as he did not remove it from the confines of the shop itself. This would have constituted borrowing, and Ada had on numerous occasions made it clear that she was not a fucking library. The tattered *Picture Show*, plucked from a nonde-script stack by the counter with a dozen like it in the last-gasp thrupenny pile, was obviously not included in this stricture, which presumably only applied to books. He'd had to read the Orwell novel in instalments, perched behind the register, when the shop had acquired a copy that August just gone. Near mint, barely two months since it was published, with its green Secker & Warburg wraps still pristine, brought in by an outraged communist or outraged Tory who had taken it all personally. Dennis wouldn't dream of spiriting a thing like that back to his room. Even safely lodged on the New Fiction shelf downstairs it had already spoiled his morning.

Grudgingly, he crawled from a warm bed into cold clothes and a still colder day, where he could see his breath. Knuckling a residue of dream from clotted sockets, he somnambulated his way down the stairs into the shop's rear rooms, relieved to find that Ada and her bronchial cannonade were up front, tidying or counting change. He went through to the backyard for a Jimmy Riddle in the outside lav, numbly absorbing fortnight-old torn headlines from the scraps of newspaper on their bent nail, then hurriedly retreated to the kitchen, gasping *Comic Cuts* balloons of fog. His strip-wash at the cracked stone sink was a perfunctory nod in hygiene's general direction, while his subsequent thin smear of margarine on a grey noggin-end of ration bread gestured at breakfast. When she heard him fill the kettle and swill out the teapot, Ada somehow simultaneously coughed and shouted from the shop with her upsetting voice like fifty crows; at least four murders.

'You can make us one as well, you useless little toerag,' was approximately what she said, but with dislodged phlegm substituting for the comma.

Dennis grunted in assent then made them both a cup of tea, milk and two sugars, before carrying one in each hand through to the shop and Ada, opening the intervening door using an elbow. Mercifully, his employer was already dressed, in that her horrible pink dressing-gown was knotted at the waist, and she already had the half-smoked Park Drive Plain glued to her curling lower lip. It was what Coffin Ada looked like, all the time. It was her uniform.

Her unimpressed eyes glanced down at the steaming cup, then back at her already flinching shop assistant. They were mottled green and grey, like sunken marble colonised by algae.

'Well, half of it's in the fucking saucer and it looks as though the cow's dead, but cough cough cough it'll have to do.' Not enough milk then, but otherwise satisfactory. Good, even. Dennis concealed his relief with an apologetic shrug and asked if she was going to want him serving in the shop that day. Sipping her tea, she skewered him with a pitying expression.

'Dennis, love, if I weren't desperate and near death, I wouldn't want you in my fucking shop this day or any other. I can't stand the sight of you. Cough cough cough cough. No, where you

21

are today's up Charing Cross, hole in the wall place, Harrison's Books. I've heard there's a chap there with some cough cough Arthur Machen bits and bobs he's having trouble getting rid of.'

Setting cup and saucer on the counter, she commenced a shuffling circuit of the premises in slippers which were either tartan or elaborately stained. Audibly tutting, back towards him, she returned books that had wandered to their designated shelves, wiping the covers with one matted cuff. Atop her thinly papered skull stood the stiff mass that had once been a hairstyle, before decades of neglect compacted it to off-white rhino horn. Regretting it immediately, Dennis risked a question.

'Who's this Machen bloke, then?'

Ada stopped what she was doing and rotated slowly to appraise him with the kind of look one might give dog shit. Shaking both her head and driftwood crust of once-was-hair, she turned back to her rearrangements before venturing a curdled-milk reply.

'He was a proper writer who weren't nothing like Hank Janson, so you won't have heard of him. Cough cough cough cough. He came from Wales, went barmy over London and put out some holy terrors in the nineties. Died a year or two back, somewhere up near Buckingham. Turned a bit fascist at the end, but, still, he had a fucking lovely way with cough cough cough cough words.'

Slender diagonals of light leaned in through the front window, so that all the flecks of dust showed off like ballerinas. There were a few people passing by outside now, fellers mostly, on their way to work, which meant it must be getting on for eight and Ada would be opening soon. The sun, unseen for days, crept furtive on worn spines or the gilt names of vanished authors, burnishing the typefaces and titles to a coppered mausoleum of unwanted sentences. Remembering to stir his tea when he'd already drunk three-quarters of it, turning the remainder into barely moving diabetic silt, Dennis attempted to learn more of that day's salvage mission.

'So, the fascist business, is that why this bloke wants shot of Machen's books, you think?'

Paused between Medical and Ghosts, Ada considered for a moment.

'No, I shouldn't think so. That were one book in the thirties, writers putting their two penn'orth in about the Spanish Civil War, and he came out for cough cough Franco. No, more likely it's that no one these days gives a toss about him either way. Dead stock you couldn't even donate to a fucking cough cough cough cough orphanage is my best guess.'

In the mostly erased sketch of a street outside, there were already two or three prospective customers who squinted through the mildly dirty pane at all the mildly dirty books that were Ada's front-window strategy: *Walter – My Secret Life. The Well of Loneliness. Rape of the Lock*. Dennis's benefactress gave her would-be clientele a long, unblinking stare out through the half-glass door which said that, yes, she knew that they were there and, no, she wasn't going to let them in before the stroke of eight because she didn't like the look of them. Peering disconsolately down into his cup where tea leaves swam in torpid circles through the glucose sludge, he cautiously enquired as to why Ada wanted the forgotten works of a Welsh fascist that were, by her own account, unsaleable.

Off in the battered distance a surviving clock began to chime the hour, but Ada gladly interrupted her unhurried totter in the door's direction, while she both replied to her assistant's query and exacerbated the annoyance of the reading public shivering outside.

'Because I know a cough cough cough fucking investment when I hear it. All signed books and rarities, this Charing Cross Road pillock said. Give it enough time, that'll be gold fucking cough cough dust, you mark my words. It's like with all this occult rubbish – hardly anybody wants it, but the ones who do will have your hand off for it, and they're rolling in cough money, most of 'em.'

Rotating the bleached cardboard sign from LOSED to PEN, she next pretended not to know which key of several would unlock the shop and so tried all of them, baggy eyes glittering with evil glee as the short queue outside gave up the will to live. In Dennis's unvoiced opinion, Coffin Ada was most probably a Dracula who feasted on human discomfort. Finally, the door was PEN. Finding herself in mid-paroxysm, she greeted those seeking admission with a hostile semaphore, waving them irritably in through a damp haze of pulmonary spindrift. Thus, reduced to herded livestock, the quartet of middle-aged men slouched resentfully to their desired shelves while Ada – stockings corrugating at the ankles; still trying to smoke even as she was coughing – made her way back to the counter and the conversation with her cringing underling. Congealing custard eyes surveyed the crystallising mess in her employee's cup. She pointedly restirred her own, then took a noisy slurp before springing the till and taking out two fivers with a handful of pound notes.

'This cough cough cough cough Harrison, he reckons they're worth twenty quid, his Machen items. So do I, but he can cough cough whistle for it. Fifteen's what I'm giving you. Talk him down any further, you can keep the cough cough cough cough change.'

She pressed the money with a pencilled list of required books into his palm, and Dennis stuck it in his jacket's inside pocket, where there were no holes. The bell above the door jingled reproachfully as one of the four men and the briefly intruding sun both exited together without making any purchase. Dennis couldn't tell if Ada's strychnine sneer was meant for the non-customer or the departing daylight. After what seemed an interminable paragraph of coughs, she carried on with her wheeze of instructions.

'Listen, keep your eye out for scarce occult stuff as well. I'm thinking there might be a craze. And put a coat on or you'll catch your cough cough cough cough cough cough death.'

He nodded, usually a safer bet than saying anything, and took his sugar-varnished cup through to the kitchen, picking up a gabardine mac on the way. Back in the shop, still pulling on his raincoat, Dennis noticed that one of the three remaining customers was sidling towards the counter with a fair-condition copy of

Sax Rohmer's *Dope* and a superior expression. This, in Dennis's experience, might not make for the smoothest of transactions. Hurriedly, he did his buttons up and edged towards the front door, anxious to be on his way before Ada was given opportunity to show her still-worse side, but wasn't quick enough. The doomed man had by then reached the cash register, and greeted the shop's owner with a condescending smirk that he perhaps believed to be intimidating. Ada ran a rosebud tongue tip around desiccated lips, and Dennis struggled to remember if he'd ever seen her blink. He wasn't even sure that she had eyelids.

'Ooh, Sax cough cough cough cough Rohmer, is it? Very good choice, that. Very popular. Cough cough cough. Should you like it in a paper bag cough cough?'

Lapels now twinkling with sputum, the surprised man – possibly a teacher, doctor, somebody accustomed to authority – attempted to repeat his strategy of seeming loftily amused.

'Ha ha. Yes, I was looking at the cover …'

'Mm. Very attractive. Lovely olive-green cough cough cloth boards, you'll notice. Cassell first edition, that is, 1919, and at seven shillings very reasonably cough cough cough cough priced.'

'Ha ha. No, I was looking more at where it's rubbed, and how the spine's cracked. What d'you say we call it five bob?'

Still without a flicker of expression in her lithic features, Ada held the man's gaze for a moment, then looked down at the scuffed volume in her hand, as if uncomprehending. Finally, she tilted back her petrified coiffure and once again stared into his increasingly uncertain eyes.

'Oh. Cough cough cough. You want to haggle.'

That was it for Dennis. Uttering a hasty, 'Right, I'm off, then. See you later,' he made for the exit past the brace of other customers, who both stood rooted to the spot as they watched the unfolding ugly situation at the counter. Ada's kippered voice, behind him, notched the volume up.

'You want to fucking cough cough haggle, do you? Is that it, you cough cough cough cough cough cough cough cough haggling little cunt?'

Lent speed by cowardice, Dennis burst jingling through the door into the petrol, brick dust, coal smoke, horse muck, cooking offal, reeking tanneries, glue-factory particulates, urine that smelled of beer, medical ointments and fresh air outside. Despite his urgent pace and stork-legged stride, he was barely halfway across Gibraltar Walk when the shop's doorbell tolled again. He had no need to ask for whom, but craned his head around and peered over his shoulder anyway.

Lowell's Books & Magazines stood at the top end of Gibraltar Walk, a single carious tooth somehow protruding from a jaw that was no longer there, punched clean off in the recently concluded prizefight. All of the street's other houses and therefore the street itself were gone to lumpy pumice, likewise the adjacent parts of Gossett Street and Satchwell Road. The luckless customer was backing from the open shop door, where stood his tormentor in her morbid dressing-gown and slippers, skeletal and rattling like a woman made of coat hangers. She brandished the Sax Rohmer book in front of her, as if repelling heretics with a witchfinder's Bible.

'Five cough cough cough fucking bob? I'll give you fucking haggle. Cough cough cough. I'll fucking haggle you in a cough minute. Here, you want five fucking bobs' worth, do you, you cough cough cough jumped-up splash of spunk? Well, how about this for a cough cough bargain?'

In a storm of mucus and exertion, Ada tore the book's front cover off and flung it at the stammering, retreating miscreant. She did the same with the ripped spine and, in an emphysemic frenzy, clawed the innards of the tome into bold-headed signatures: **Kerry Consults the Oracle**, **Night-Life of Soho**, **The Black Smoke**, most of them flapping down the empty memory of Gibraltar Walk after the frightened and now sprinting man. Spitting at where a gutter used to be, the nastiest old woman in the world went back into her musty bunker while the curtain-twitchers on the other side of Gossett Street gaped in appalled surprise, as if this didn't happen every other morning.

Overhead, in an enormous grubby fleece of sky, the sun briefly apparent from inside the shop was nowhere to be seen. Regretting that he shared a species let alone a house with Ada Benson, Dennis turned his collar up, so that he looked more like someone mysterious and violent, from a film. With what he thought might be construed as a detective's or a secret agent's gait, he hunched off moodily through the remains of Shoreditch, heading towards Old Street and the shattered city piled beyond, humming the 'Harry Lime Theme'.

Dennis dum-badum-badum-badummed his way to Clerkenwell and over Gray's Inn Road, thinking haphazardly of sex, books, Orwell, Coffin Ada, finding somewhere else to live, sex again, money, and the relative attractions of a lonely but dramatic death in the Vienna sewers, being meanwhile largely unaware of his material surroundings. Unseen stagehands wound a canvas backdrop past, a crawling frieze of buildings hyphenated here and there by rubble. Chimneys that exhaled an early midnight were cranked by unnoticed, as were horses, carts, bikes, barrows, a few motors and the trudging multitude of strangers. This oblivious trance was only interrupted when he crossed the entrance to Red Lion Square in Holborn, the supposed location of Oliver Cromwell's missing head, so he'd been told, stolen when Charles the Second had the erstwhile Lord Protector dug up and dragged through the lanes of London, with his putrefied cadaver having spent the night before laid out in the eponymous Red Lion Inn. As rumours went, it was a memorably ghastly one.

Deciding that he'd probably have been a Roundhead but would have denied it later when the monarchy was back, Dennis continued past a soot-skinned church in Bloomsbury Way and then, before he got to Oxford Street, banked into Charing Cross Road on his left.

The occident of London crowded in, with signboard lettering and garish product names as make-up compensating for a ruined complexion. Ravelling away downhill towards the river, the bookseller's thoroughfare was an Afghani mountain pass between steep cliffs of retail, shopfronts crammed like tattered spines into a too short shelf space, jumbled architectures making the cropped sky above a pallid strip with jigsaw-puzzle edges. Armed with nothing but the name 'Harrison's Books' when a house number would have been more use, Dennis resigned himself to the ordeal of door-to-door investigation. Grudgingly, he slouched down the long avenue and sank into its clumsy melody of clopping hooves and shouts and motor hooters, throaty engines shifting their catarrh.

It took some time. He made his way along the street's east face, squinting at painted signs where English words had peeled or faded to the foreign lexicon of an exotic land; this other, post-war planet everyone had ended up on. Hopping quickly over Shaftsbury Avenue to dodge a lorry, Dennis carried on down the junction's left trouser leg, past Leicester Square's demoralised theatres and the slightly unreal alleyway of Cecil Court, self-consciously enchanting. True, there was an occult bookshop halfway up it, Watkins, and Ada had told him to be on the lookout for that kind of thing, but she wouldn't be wanting stuff already marked up by a rival business. She'd want rare, unheard-of novelties, where she could price them in accordance with her own unfathomable esoteric principles. Crossing the busy road, he went back up the street's far side, no longer sure of Harrison's' existence.

Patiently decoding leprous painted scripts, at last he found the place that he was looking for, back at the top end, not far down from Foyles, between two larger shops and scarcely thicker than a generous sandwich. It was shut. 'Closed until further not ice,' read the poorly spaced note sticky-papered to the inside of a half-glazed door. Beyond this aperture, the clumped interior dark was undisturbed. No lights on out the back. Nobody there. Well, that was that. There wasn't anything that could be done, as far as he could see. A stranger to persistence, he gave up immediately, unused to falling back upon his own resources. He had no resources. Falling back on them could only lead to serious injury. At eighteen, this conveniently undemanding self-assessment was the closest Dennis got to a philosophy. The best way not to fail was, obviously, not to try.

On this occasion, though, he thought at least to enquire at the place next door, if only so he could tell his employer that he'd made the effort when, by any valid definition of 'the effort', he'd done no such thing. The neighbouring establishment, which specialised in dull-looking religious books, was staffed by a surprisingly concerned and helpful woman in late middle age who Dennis thought might be the Anti-Ada. Constantly apologising for her less than perfect memory, she said that Mr Harrison hadn't been near his premises for the last day or two, but that she thought he had a flat in Berwick Street, perhaps above a wool shop, all this without once characterising Dennis as a halfwit, bastard, shifty little arsehole, work-shy ponce or failed abortion. Stammering his gratitude, he got out of the place as quickly as he could, startled by common decency and worried that he might propose.

Back on the blustery main road, he essayed a left turn to Manette Street and slipped down the hoarse throat of Soho. London's other districts, as he saw them, had a tendency to merge into each other without any necessary change of atmosphere. With Soho, on the other hand, you knew when you were there and when you weren't. The intestinal knot of shady doorways seemed to have acquired collective intellect and personality the way that anthills were supposed to do, if ants had coloured lightbulbs. Soho's ravaged spirit was possessed of a cold-eyed congeniality – that air of saucy fun which always drew a flock of the unhappy – and seemed to assume it knew the sordid bottom line of everyone. Perhaps it did. He'd never spent a lot of his time in the area, so that it still felt foreign in the sense of being threatening and exciting both at once. Hands deep in his coat pockets, he crossed Soho Square, then threaded himself through the needle's eye of St Anne's Court and into Wardour Street. The dustbins here once brimmed with unused filmstock, so he'd heard, though since the war you didn't see that sort of thing so much. No one had any money.

You could read the economic news from people's faces and the boarded eyes of private businesses. Just days after the war, the Yanks had ended the Lend-Lease arrangement, forcing Britain into crippling debt for who knew how long. 'Shabby money-lenders,' one of the MPs had called them. It had been four years now since the bombs stopped, and most things were still on ration. So, liver and onion roll it was, kids bandy-legged from rickets, demobbed soldiers with nowhere to live and young lads his age pulling stick-ups with the Lugers that their dads brought home as souvenirs. If this was winning, he decided, then thank Christ, we didn't lose.

Before he knew it, he was at the foot of Berwick Street, the landslide rubbish from its market spreading across Broadwick Street down at the bottom in an odorous surf of empty Woodbine packets, trampled haddock, here and there a Savoy cabbage leaf like puckered emerald. Kicking his way through the detritus, looking for the rumour of a wool shop, he slogged up a narrow incline crammed with barrows, stalls and people in thick coats comparing carrots. Crowd sounds swelled about him as he shouldered between plaid caps and funereal bonnets, scraps of 'Go on, then' and 'Bloody cheek' and 'Well, I never' tangling with the arias of an opinionated dog, a wailing baby and the traders' bellowed innuendo. Stood beside a folding table bearing trinkets worth less than the velvet they were glinting on, a little man with a great big man's upper half seemed to gaze quizzically, one eyebrow raised, but then, with Dennis being tall, he was self-conscious and thought everyone was looking at him, often balefully. Excursions were spent inwardly rehearsing fights that didn't happen.

E. J. Tate ~ Knitting Supplies, the only place that seemed to be providing wool, was halfway up on the east side. Next to its recessed customer door was another entrance, opening directly on to Berwick Street and probably allowing access to whatever rooms might be above. It was at this that Dennis tapped politely, knocked, rapped urgently, shouted 'Hello?' and hammered like a bailiff before he elicited a quavering and spinsterish reply; a tremulous falsetto from the door's far side.

'Who is it, please? I'm an old lady and I don't take callers.'

Dennis sighed. This wasn't going well, by which he meant his day or possibly his whole life. Struggling to be heard above a nearby stallholder promoting whelks, he offered his credentials.

'Sorry, love. I might not WHELKS! the right address. I'm here from Ada Benson's bookshop LOVELY WHELKS! in Shoreditch, looking for a Mr Harrison. She'd heard he'd got some Arthur GET YOUR WHELKS HERE! that he wanted rid of.'

From beyond the peeling wooden panels came a silence freighted with deliberation, finally replaced by almost a full minute of keys turning in reluctant locks, chains rattling on their catches and bolts sliding back. At last the frail old woman creaked the portal open and, unnervingly, became a tubby and moustachioed fellow in a sleeveless mustard pullover, his forties and a state of evident anxiety. The man's small, darting eyes were chocolate drops floating in semolina.

'Sorry about that. Can't be too careful. Come in quick, I'm letting all the warm out.'

Undisguised, the voice was low and rasping. Dennis let himself be hurried into a cramped passageway that smelled faintly of gin and armpit, where the warm had already escaped or else had never been there. While the clearly worried little chap rebolted and relocked the door, his already unsettled visitor examined the hall carpet, trying to determine if its worn-out pattern had been previously composed of splayed ferns or enormous spiders. Door secured, the resident female impersonator guided Dennis up the stairs to which the hall and its ambiguous flooring led, making the necessary introductions as they climbed.

'I'm Flabby Harrison. I didn't catch who you were.'

'Dennis. Dennis Knuckleyard. Like I was saying, Ada Benson sent me here.'

'Yes. Yes, I've heard of Ada Benson. Knuckleyard, though. That's a funny name.'

They were now both on the perfunctory landing that preceded Harrison's stale first-floor lodgings. Dennis grunted in agreement. Yes, it was a funny name. There didn't seem to be another person in the whole of human history called Knuckleyard. Over the course of many mutually puzzled chats with his late mother, they'd concluded that his even-later father must have simply made the surname up, either for laughs or to replace an uglier-sounding one, if such a thing was possible.

In the grey daylight falling from the morning going on outside, Harrison's kitchen-dining room was vanishing, turning into the overexposed photo of a place. A shade more pallid and it wouldn't have been there at all. Perfectly neat, except for getting on a dozen model aircraft sculpted lovingly from balsa and suspended from the ceiling. These were high enough for Harrison to wander comfortably beneath, but hazardous for the more lofty Dennis. Some of them had plainly hung there for so long that dust had made them into dangling, shapeless mysteries which could have been dead bats for all that anybody knew.

Harrison nodded to a prolapsed armchair for his guest, sitting himself upon the ottoman trunk opposite, after first taking from its depths a cardboard box with the soap-powder brand name 'Oxydol' stamped on two sides. His rudimentary eyes constantly twitching towards Dennis's attempt at impassivity, the older man set the receptacle down on the fraying rug between them with exaggerated care as though it were a fragile child or unexploded bomb.

'There. Twenty quid for the whole lot. Can't say fairer than that.'

Preserving what he hoped might seem an aura of intelligence, Dennis said nothing. From his inside jacket pocket he retrieved the jotted list that Ada had provided, folding back the top flaps of the box in order to appraise its contents.

Which were marvellous. He hadn't worked for Coffin Ada long enough to be described as anything remotely like a bibliophile, but long enough to recognise the thrill such souls were seeking when a wholesale carton full of it erupted in his face. It wasn't just the heady scent of vintage paper – which was anyway masked by a memory of soap flakes – but rather the radiant glamour of the books within that rose about him in an exhalation of desires hitherto unacknowledged. It was a charisma wrought of lovely and forgotten lettering styles inlaid on wan cloth boards, pervaded by implicit histories of publishing or personality and sodden with the ghost of a dead writer.

Reaching into the container, he removed the topmost volume from the tidy stack inside, its plain black cover cross-scored in a diamond pattern and its title in a paper strip glued to the narrow backbone. *Ornaments in Jade.* Yes, it was there on Ada's list, with an appended note to say it was one of a thousand copies, signed and numbered. Dennis dutifully checked the book's interior to foster the impression that he knew what he was doing. There were hand-cut pages and a title sheet embellished with green curlicues that bore the imprint of Alfred A. Knopf, New York, dated to 1924. Flipping through the collection of short stories to its rear, he found the number in jade-coloured ink, 673, and under that the greying signature, its line making a sprightly bound from the tail end of Arthur to the opening upstroke of Machen. Disappearing particles of powdered shellac tracked the moving hand, and prised a spectral crack through twenty years to a few seconds of the author's intimate reality, their fleeting aches, their momentary notions when they were alive. It muddily occurred to Dennis that all autographs were haunted, written on a heavier stock of time.

The next book down was thicker, older, eerier: *The House of Souls*, published in London, a Grant Richards first edition from 1906. Boards of diluted sea spray sported one of the most startling cover illustrations that he'd ever seen, a black and bristling form somewhere between a human being and a housefly or horned beetle, sitting cross-legged in a patch of lethal-looking toadstools. Temple bells in brilliant cyan hung from the monstrosity's raised antlers. Dennis struggled to hold down his eyebrows and look unimpressed, the hardest work he'd done for days. His face studiedly glum, he shot a glance at Harrison, by now crouched tense and nervous on the front edge of his ottoman.

'Mm.Very nice stuff. Nice condition. It's a pity that there's not much call for his work these days, what with, you know, all the fascism and that.'

Harrison frowned, plainly bewildered, and his pursed lips turned the arms of his moustache into convulsing caterpillars. Realising that he was on risky ground with his political improvisations, Dennis ploughed on into less contentious territory.

'Although, what makes his titles difficult to shift, it's more he's been forgotten by the readership. I know it's shocking, but the younger folk, a lot of them, they've never heard of him.'

He shook his head regretfully, ruing the Machen-ignorant youth of those times which, until ten to eight that morning, had included him. Looking uneasy, Harrison offered a throaty interjection.

'Alright, fifteen nicker. This is daylight bleeding robbery.'

On this occasion Dennis found a deadpan manner easier to maintain, his features paralysed by shock from having stumbled on somebody even worse at bargaining than him. Suppressing his euphoria, he carried on with an inspection of the Oxydol box and the trove contained therein, pretending that he hadn't heard the vendor's fire-sale price reduction. Each fresh tome he lifted from the cloistered pile to check against his boss's list was more mysterious and alluring than the last – *The Cosy Room*, in wraps adorned by marbling like peacock feathers, Rich & Cowan, 1936; *The Great God Pan*, in the original John Lane Keynote edition, 1894; a copy of *The Three Impostors*, signed and dedicated to Max Beerbohm – until he came to a scruffy and unprepossessing item that was not on Ada's roster nor, apparently, by Arthur Machen. Clothbound, brown boards badly rubbed, publisher's name illegible on the cracked spine but an interior date of 1853. *A London Walk: Meditations in the Streets of the Metropolis*, its author someone called the Reverend Thomas Hampole. Dennis held it, quizzically, in Flabby Harrison's direction.

'Should this one be in here? I can't find it on Miss Benson's list.'

The absentee bookshop proprietor regarded the proffered anomaly with a resentful and unblinking gaze, milky complexion yellowing to complement his pullover.

'Five quid. Take it or leave it.'

This was frankly unbelievable. While not the sharpest knife to be found in a kitchen drawer, Dennis knew better than to twist on nineteen. Hurriedly returning the inspected goods to their detergent packaging, he stood to shake hands on the deal and found himself assailed by a de Havilland Mosquito and a fluff-covered Bristol Beaufort, battering his forehead as if Dennis was a more easily cowed King Kong. Embroidering the moment's awkwardness, Harrison pointedly ignored the taller man's extended digits until they were holding one of Ada's big white fivers.

With a genuinely odd transaction thus resolved, the agitated shopkeeper seemed eager to have both his customer and sagging Oxydol box gone from the immediate environment as soon as possible. Still dumbstruck by his first ever experience of success, Dennis allowed himself to be rushed back along the landing, down the staircase and across the might-be-spiders in the hall, holding the bulky carton in both hands before him like an overdue and rectangular pregnancy. Only when Harrison had unlocked, unchained and unbolted his front door, with the two standing on the open threshold and mercantile chatter all about, did he find anything to say to his ungainly caller.

'So, you reckon Machen was a fascist?'

Trying to keep the box of books from slipping, Dennis wished he'd listened to what Ada had to say upon that subject, but he always found her voice unbearable and didn't tend to take much in. Recalling what he could, he bluffed authoritatively.

'Yeah. Yeah, he fought for Franco in the Spanish Civil War, so I was told.'

Brows knit, Harrison stared perplexedly at empty air, moustache contorting around muttered calculations. Having seemingly reached a conclusion, he transferred his puzzled scowl to Dennis.

'But he would have been in his late sixties.'

Patently out of his depth, Dennis was trying to disengage, backing away downhill as he reversed out of the floundering conversation.

'Yeah, well, that's a Welshman for you. Hard as nails.'

Nodding a silent cheerio, he turned away from the confounded bookseller and fumbled off into the market's push and shove, with his soapbox encumbrance jostling before him. Possibly because he didn't have to keep his eyes peeled for a wool shop any longer, Dennis noticed a lot more of Berwick Street on his way down than he had done on his way up. He spotted the same strangely built chap who'd been giving him the eye when he was heading towards Harrison's place half an hour ago, still standing there behind his spread of shiny magpie tat, still tracking Dennis with his fed-up, melancholy eyes. He looked to be the over-literal result of some circus romance between a lady dwarf and the World's Strongest Man, his barrel chest and dreadnought shoulders stacked precariously on jockey's legs. From this fresh angle, Dennis realised that the cause of the disparity between the tradesman's two halves was one lower limb being a good five inches shorter than the other, this divergence compensated for by means of a huge, built-up iron shoe. A little over five foot in his heavy overcoat and homburg hat, incongruous cravat bunched in a silver ring at his thick throat, he looked less born than fashioned by a blacksmith.

Dragging on a dog-end, he returned Dennis's gaze, unblinking, unembarrassed, and clearly without a monkey's fuck if anybody saw him looking. Despite being younger, taller and not crippled, Dennis was the first to glance away, intimidated by the other man's superior gravity. He shrugged off his discomfort through immersion in the difficulties of manhandling his burden through the press of worsted elbows, fraying raffia baskets, and the steep street's other down-at-heel distractions.

These were myriad. Trestle tables fluttered horror comics of outlandish hue, and non-specific fish displayed resentful profiles against white slabs, as though posed for police photos. Tumbril cabbage crates brimmed with the heads of slain vegetable royalty.

Towards the bottom of the crowded gradient, pausing to adjust his grip on the ungovernable box, he spotted somebody he knew – if not to talk to, then at least by reputation. Maurice Calendar, who stood beside a fruit and veg stand, chatting to its owner, was widely considered the most fashionable man in London, although nobody would think that looking at him here. Around his middle twenties, black hair neatly Brylcreemed, Calendar had on the same ubiquitous fawn raincoat worn by all the city's decently paid younger blokes, the same starched shirt and neutral tie, the same smoke-coloured trilby. There were those who said he'd been the first to dress like that, long before anybody else had, but it didn't look to Dennis as if there'd been many major innovations since. It wasn't just the run-of-the-mill clothing, either. Calendar seemed somehow puffier and more swollen, slower in his movements than the last time Dennis had run into him. Appearing short of breath, the flagging trendsetter leaned heavy on a corner post of M. Blincoe & Son Fresh Fruit and Vegetables, regaling the stall's hulking monolith of a proprietor. This latter's face was like the flat side of a split log, having a nose so broken it was barely three-dimensional, whorls that with imagination might almost resemble eyes, and enough wrinkles to suggest a grain.

Having regained control of his oblong obstruction, Dennis soldiered on through Soho, heading back towards the Charing Cross Road and then possibly a bite to eat and cup of tea somewhere along the Strand. That would be nice. He might see his mate Clive. Retracing his steps over Broadwick Street triggered a random landmine-burst of history and disconnected semi-facts. Wasn't it somewhere along here that a Victorian doctor stopped a cholera epidemic in its tracks, just by having the handle taken off a sewage-tainted water pump? Morosely, Dennis speculated that there was most likely a bad-news pump somewhere, letting all the shit in, and that England's miseries might be alleviated by somebody qualified in medicine, with a sufficiently large spanner.

Dennis didn't have an avalanche of friends, and 'not an avalanche' meant less than three. He'd lost touch with the other kids from school around the time he'd gone to live at Coffin Ada's, which was understandable. He bore no grudges for the way his classmates had abandoned him, and would have steered clear of himself in their position. All the same, lacking romantic interest other than the girl in *Picture Show*, that only left him with Clive Amery and Tolerable John McAllister. Ironically, he'd met both these enduring pals through the same situation that had lost him all his others, which was his proximity to Ada Benson. Tolerable John was a reporter for the *Daily Express*, who would sometimes drop by Lowell's Books & Magazines to draw on Ada's talent for uncommon gossip, and if Dennis got the chance, he'd look in on John later when he headed back to Shoreditch. Clive, contrastingly, had been a punter fortunate enough to call at the establishment while its repellent manager was out spoiling a church-hall beetle drive and Dennis was alone at the cash register. The dazzlingly funny trainee lawyer had been looking for William Le Queux's *Things I Know About Kings, Celebrities and Crooks*, and he and Dennis had immediately hit it off. It was Clive Amery that Dennis hoped he might bump into as he manhandled his clunking soap container down the Strand.

He clutched and cursed his way along the ancient boulevard that still recalled a Roman occupation and had barely registered the buzz bombs, flinching every few steps as he reached the next shop window and was shocked anew by his reflection. Dennis was a thing made out of string with lumpy knots to represent his knees and elbows, bending slightly backwards under the encumbering box as though some sort of hunch-front. The short back and sides that left a bristling chestnut lawn atop his shaved suede skull made him look like a wilted thistle. He conceded it was little wonder, given his appearance, that at eighteen years of age he was still technically a virgin. Yes, he'd been tossed off by Susan Garrett when he was fourteen, but that was true of most people.

The firm Clive worked for had their offices down at the Strand's eastern extremity, near the Royal Courts of Justice, so that the young legal eagle often spent his lunch break at Bond's Coffee House, roughly halfway along. It was to this that Dennis veered his barely manageable load, turning around to shunt the front door open with his arse and backing in as if arriving for a papal audience. Although its management appeared uncertain of the new arrival and his hefty inconvenience, the place itself embraced him with aroma, steam and more warmth than he'd felt in weeks. A halting series of apologies led Dennis to the cafeteria's rear, where he was instantly relieved to see Clive lounging at an otherwise unoccupied table for four, jotting down memos on a notepad between careful sips of black and steaming coffee.

Seemingly oblivious to admiring glances from a clutch of office girls across the aisle, Clive swept the fine blond hair out of his eyes, tapped thoughtfully upon his lower front teeth with a pencil, and was everything that Dennis wasn't. Clive was funny by intention rather than anatomy; talked comfortably with everyone; could charm a breeze block. And while Dennis was a problematic shape that clothing happened to, Clive wore his glad rags beautifully – only an ordinary chalk-stripe navy number, but it hung like silk, and close up you could see the cut, the quality. Well-polished shoes. Smart wristwatch. Horse-head cufflinks. Grunting with exertion, Dennis dumped himself on the chair facing the apprentice barrister, and his debilitating box on the one next to it. Amery glanced up with annoyance, which immediately transubstantiated into unalloyed delight.

'Stone me, it's Knuckleyard. What's up, chum? Did you finally take a blunt bread knife to that horrible old woman who you work for? And that's why you're looking for a brilliant lawyer, who can get you off with a life sentence rather than the rope.' He nodded at the box. 'Is that her head?'

It was a lovely thought that started Dennis laughing down his nose. 'Got it in one. So, anyway, this brilliant lawyer that I'm looking for – d'you know one?'

Clive smiled at him fondly. 'Why, you cheeky bugger. Just for that, I'm going to let them hang you. Draw and quarter you, if they've a mind to. Would you like a cup of tea?'

Dennis was part-way through informing Clive that, yes, he'd love a cup of tea and possibly a piece of cake if one was going spare, when an offended-looking man with sleeves rolled up and managerial manner stormed the coffee house's length to pull in at their table, snorting like a train.

'These seats are for my customers, son, not your rubbish. Come on, get it off that chair and then be on your way.'

As a first step to his surely immemorable reply, Dennis had let his mouth sag open idiotically, when Clive leaned forward and held up a manicured forefinger in the restauranteur's direction.

'Perhaps if I could just stop you there.'

Surprised, the man switched his unfriendly gaze to Dennis's much more presentable companion, who returned it calmly as he flipped a business card from his breast pocket with a practised gesture, holding it aloft for the irate proprietor to read.

'Clive Amery, Jessop & Wilks. I'd hoped that meeting with my client here at your establishment might spare him any more undue publicity, but it seems not. This man is Sir Dennis Compton-Knuckleyard, the fifth Lord Oxydol. You have heard of the Oxydol soap dynasty, I take it?'

Looking on amazed, Dennis wished that his own voice was as middle class as Clive's, and had the ring of someone used to being listened to. Given the right enunciation, you could get away with anything. The manager, if that was what he was, now seemed uncertain and increasingly alarmed. Responding to the lawyer's question, he bobbed his perspiring head in affirmation, mumbling something that to Dennis's ear sounded very much like the word mumble. Clive went on.

'I don't know if you follow any of the quality newspapers, but if so, his lordship's plight can hardly have escaped your notice. I'll be blunt. It's squatters – rough types who've been in the army, and who think that just because their houses have all been blown up, they can live anywhere they want, whether it be in disused army barracks, or the mansions of our most revered detergent tycoons. Strictly between us, a mob of them have commandeered my client's stately home. As you can see, they've taken all his decent clothes and left him with the hairstyle of a convict. That, and those few heirlooms he could haul in this dilapidated box, marked with the emblem of a once proud family. For pity's sake, I ask that you might reconsider your previous assessment of his character, and unless you yourself happen to be the fourth Lord Oxydol, that you do not refer to him as "son".'

Halfway through this, Dennis was forced to clap a hand across his mouth and turn his face away, hoping the gesture could be taken for a pang of reawakened grief. Similarly, perhaps his shaking shoulders might pass as a bout of stifled weeping. By this point the putative coffee house owner was apologising unreservedly. He even tried to bow to Dennis, although the resultant ducking of his torso and accompanying sideways movement of his arms made the whole thing look like a constipated curtsey. Squirming with remorse, the man asked Clive if there was anything that he could do, and was told in reply that with a cup of tea, a wedge of fruitcake and another coffee for himself, the whole unfortunate affair would be forgotten. Mopping his damp jowls, the chastened cafeteria boss trundled away, returning presently with the requested fare and more apologies. Benevolently, Clive waved these aside, pressing a florin on the poor chap – 'for your trouble' – and assuring him that in his modest way he was assisting in the battle against communism.

When they were once more alone except for the admiring giggles of the nearby secretaries, the two settled to a lively and digressive chat, Dennis's half delivered in a spray of masticated fruitcake. He told Clive about the Machen books, making the other young man grin with his somewhat embroidered sketch of Flabby Harrison and the bookseller's dusty air-armada. 'No, I'm serious. It was the whole Battle of Britain, mummified and hanging from his ceiling.' Amery, in turn, discoursed amusingly upon some recent cases at his place of work, which led on naturally to an appraisal of the striking post-war surge in London's criminal activities.

'Most of the plain, straightforward theft, that's soldiers who've come home accustomed to the military attitude regarding property, where if you're short some piece of kit, you swipe it from the fellow five bunks down. It's just the way that life works in the army. Sanctioned larceny is part of the supply chain, but apparently, if you apply that principle on civvy street, you're looking at a year or two inside. Who could have known? Armed robbery, now that's a different kettle of catastrophes. With that, it's largely mouthy little berks who've not seen combat save for at the pictures, and who've got an arsenal available at every junk shop. So, they do a jeweller in broad daylight with no getaway car, shoot a bystander and end up swinging for it. No, all this, it's something anyone could have seen coming half a mile away. The only new thing since the war, to my mind, it's these crackpot killers.'

He sipped at his black and steaming beverage, then went on.

'You know. The nutcases. The ones who kill people because they're wearing brown shoes, or because it's Tuesday. There was Neville Heath, who murdered those two girls while living under half a dozen aliases, including "Rupert Brooke". Or look at Haigh, two or three months back. Nine, they reckon he did. More than Jack the Ripper. Drank their blood out of a mug, dissolved the lot in drums of acid and laughed fit to burst when he was sentenced. Mark my words, young Knuckleyard, we're going to be seeing a lot more charmers like that in future, raving mad and killing for the fun of it. You'd almost think that there were people who took being bombed for five years rather poorly.'

At this juncture, Clive excused himself to visit the toilet facilities out in the coffee house's rear yard, winking at the office women as he passed their table and reducing them to whispering jelly. Dennis whiled away his time by dabbing up stray cake crumbs with a moistened forefinger, and tried to read the pencil jottings in Clive's open notepad upside down. Up at the page's top was what appeared to be another legal practice – Dolden, Green, Dorland & Lockart – and then under that what he imagined were reminders for appointments, scheduled conversations and the like: 'Talk Harwell Wednesday, Collins case'; 'Vaughn's statement eight years old – no libel action at the time?'; 'Malcolm and Paul, drinks Friday' and a host of suchlike stultifying memoranda. Dennis was surprisingly uplifted to find out that even someone like his mate was capable of being really, really dull. Of course, no sooner had said mate returned and sat back down, than he said something funny that dispelled Dennis's fleeting brush with self-esteem.

'Of course, the man that I blame for this awful violence is Dick Barton, special agent.'

Dennis spluttered over the last tepid mouthful of his tea. There'd been a lot of talk in newspapers that credited the bloody mess, from Heath to Haigh and all points in between, to the titular tough guy of the fast-paced wireless serial. Clive sighed reproachfully at Dennis's amusement.

'You may laugh. I only know that when I hear the theme music, it makes me want to kill somebody, usually myself. I'm sure that I can't be the only one.'

The pair expanded on this notion, entertainingly, for a good fifteen minutes: 'So, then, what you're saying is that John Haigh only had to hear that dum-diddlum-diddlum-diddlum, and he'd think, "Right, it's time to order in another drum of hydrochloric."' This subsided into a more general interchange where Clive, remarking on the vast amount of post his job entailed, impressed his younger friend by citing a Moroccan letter opener he called a kris that he'd bought in a Portobello junk shop. His seemingly effortless exotic style would surely have made anybody envious. In the end, with Clive considering a third coffee and with Dennis sort of eager to get back and crow to Ada over his remarkable success, the two shook hands and parted ways.

Manoeuvring out of his seat, Dennis once more took up a
load like Sisyphus's boulder but with corners, and then made
his clumsy and protracted exit from Bond's Coffee House. This
took him past the hypothetical proprietor at the front counter,
who seemed both uncertain as to whether he should bow, and
how to do it if he did. On this occasion, he opted for the back-
and-forth sway of a startled metronome, curtailing his obeisance
only to rush from behind the till and hold the glass door open
for his burdened customer. Allowing the intimidated serf what
he thought was a passable aristocratic nod, the fifth Lord Oxydol
and his heraldic cardboard box continued up the Strand towards
the inky latitudes of Fleet Street.

Stumbling his lumber down a highway that was famously all
gutter, Dennis noted that Fleet Street's mystique of flashbulbs and
last-minute drama wasn't to be seen from pavement level, and
supposed that this was simply how it went. Mythology was only
visible from far away. The place that people conjured when
they thought about the city and its landmarks was nowhere in
evidence; a phosphorous idea of London that had either been
demolished in the war, or else was hiding.

As he'd hoped he might do, he bumped into Tolerable John
McAllister. This was outside the alley mouth that granted access
to the Cheshire Cheese, from which the fatalistic newshound
was emerging just as Dennis and his obstacle went by, although
their interaction was unfortunately brief.

'John. How's things?'

'Ah, well, you know – tolerable. Listen, Dennis, I can't chat,
mate. All us lot are off to Westminster, to see what Attlee's got to
say with China gone red as a beetroot. Probably "Oh dear". Why
don't you look us up tomorrow, when I should be here all day?
Cheers, Dennis. Love to Ada.'

Glumly, Dennis watched the journalist barrel away into a
background clamour of lugubrious pedestrians and petulant
Ford Populars, sleek and black like tadpole taxis. Peering at the

dwindling figure over the top flaps of his increasingly unwieldy carton, he began to worry that he might resemble Kilroy, scribbled on a bog door underneath the legend 'Wot? No prospects?' Suddenly self-conscious, he turned and resumed his overladen journey to the east. Down at the street's far end, the blanched dome of St Paul's swelled up above the gap-toothed skyline, a crash-landed moon.

He got almost as far as Ludgate Circus without incident, but when he passed Bride Lane, his luck, such as it was, deserted him. The steep street wound away and to his right, with near the top a lamppost just across from St Bride's churchyard, against which was propped a woman who was lovelier than any met in magazines, and also in full colour. She stopped Dennis in his tracks halfway across the road, where he stood thunderstruck and struggling to accept that she was real.

It was the hair that first seized the attention, roughly, by the eyeballs. Guy Fawkes Night come early, it spilled down in bonfire waves to set the tatty collar of her short black coat alight, conflagrant orange, startling against the stony palette of the overcast printworkers' passage. Somewhere around five foot six and beautifully rounded, a lit cigarette in one hand, she faced slightly off from Dennis as she lounged so that he only caught her quarter profile, strong, and serious of intent. High heels and stockings. He could see one clip-on earring in the same electrifying green as her visible eye, and was belatedly assessing her most likely occupation when, alerted by his halting footsteps, she looked round and flattened him with her incurious green gaze.

'Yeah?'

Her face was exquisite – possibly a little younger than he'd first assumed – betraying not the slightest trace of interest in her uninvited audience. As she turned, he noticed with surprise that in the hand without a smouldering cigarette she held an open book. She was a reader, then; perhaps a student. His unworthy preconceptions suddenly in disarray, Dennis was lost for all but fatuous words.

'I'm sorry. I saw you were reading.' This was untrue. 'I like books. This is a box of books I'm carrying here. Work in a book-shop.' This was true, but made Dennis sound simple. The young woman, or perhaps girl, it was hard to tell, was now regarding him with an expression of concern.

'That's nice.'

Anxious to put right the half-sharp impression he was foster-ing and before he could help it, Dennis came out with the most unhelpful, unconvincing thing that he had ever said to an attractive woman, or an unattractive woman, or a man, or anything.

'Haha. No, it's alright, there's nothing wrong with me.' Realising how this sounded, albeit too late, he added, 'What's the book, then?'

She stared at him for too long in silence, as if trying to make him out, glanced at the cover of the volume she was hold-ing, drew deep on her fag, exhaled, and then looked back to Dennis.

'*London Churches.*'

Oh. She was religious. That was why she stood here leaning up against this lamppost opposite St Bride's, the printer's chapel. Feeling more ashamed than ever of his prior assumptions, he jiggled his brow in obvious confusion until she put him out of his misery.

'I was up here a week ago, and thought I spotted something in the churchyard over there. That's why I'm reading up on it.'

'So, what, you thought you'd seen a ghost?'

Brushing stray flames of hair out of her bottomless eyes, she regarded him with almost tangible indifference.

'No. No, not a ghost. Can you remind me why I'm talking to you?'

Clutching at his load to stop it sliding, Dennis ducked his head uncomfortably.

'No, I, I just, I saw you standing there, reading your book, and I thought, well …'

Slowly, a smile began to spread across her perfect face.

'You thought I was a prostitute.'

Caught bang to rights and stumped for anything to say, he laughed self-deprecatingly, which was as good as a confession. The girl's smile evaporated, leaving in its place the patient, sympathetic countenance that's necessary when explaining matters to a four-year-old.

'Well, funnily enough, I am. I'm just one who can read. You have a nice night.'

And with that, as if he wasn't there, the precious balm of her attention was returned to a disintegrating book on churches that could not know its good fortune, or be troubled by inopportune erections. Grateful at last for his all-concealing Oxydol container, Dennis at least had the self-awareness to know that he'd made himself appear ridiculous. When Bride Lane failed to open up and swallow him, he did his best to follow the red-headed girl's example and pretend that their exchange had never happened. With his every cell attempting to cringe from its neighbours in embarrassment, he lugged his stupid-looking box down Ludgate Hill, and never dreamed that the foregoing incident would prove to be only the second-worst encounter with a woman that he'd have that day.

Off Warwick Lane he found a fish and chip shop where he got himself cod and four penn'orth, setting down his load so he could sit crouched on a partially dismantled wall to eat the only hot meal he'd been near for days, out of a week-old *Daily Telegraph*. He'd paid for it with his remaining pocket change: he was aware that Ada had said he could keep the difference if he managed to talk Harrison down under fifteen quid, but he was equally aware that since the difference had turned out to be a tenner, she would have his guts for garters if he took her literally.

Squatting on blown-down brickwork, he exulted in the chewy dough of skin and batter, in the glossy chunks that slid apart like pages in a poorly stapled magazine. Eyes watering from the acetic overdose he'd lavished on his chips, he peered at the surrounding street through rationed daylight that was gradually abandoning its day. Everything had been knocked about, and in the middle of the road there stood an obsolete Anderson shelter, gaping empty and no longer plump with frightened families. Up on a corrugated-iron fence, old home-front propaganda posters lingered, half erased by rust. London was haunted by six years of burning sky, tongue sandwiches and rained-on slogans. Staring gas masks under everybody's sideboards. Dennis scoffed his grub, then licked his fingers and deposited the crumpled rose of newspaper, glassy with grease, in someone's dustbin. Once more taking up his crate of woes, he carried on with the return to Shoreditch.

He made hard work of ascending Aldersgate, up into settling dusk and more people than usual coming in the opposite direction. He excused his way through crowds at studded crossings, egg-yolk light from a Belisha beacon dribbling on faces with expression all but worn away. Across the road and its occasional rush of vehicles, the nothingness of Cripplegate blazed pink with London rocket in defiance of encroaching twilight. Out amongst the weed-bound hollows and the absences, he could make out the cordoned sites of archaeologists, white ribbons shying from a risen breeze.

Adjusting his grip on the box at every other drainpipe, he recalled the finds he'd read about or picked up from the gossip washing in and out of Ada's shop: it seemed the Luftwaffe had turned out to be keen historians, helpfully excavating parts of London that had not been seen for centuries. By London Wall, the boundary of the Roman city, fragments of the gatehouse for which Cripplegate was named had been unearthed; an archway – fortified, imposing and with upper storeys – giving access to a round fort situated here before Rome stumbled and the ages suddenly went dark. It had been pulled down getting on two centuries ago when the road needed widening, and then wiped from the lapsing memory of the metropolis until this year, hauled from the ruins of the vanished neighbourhood.

Characteristically, Dennis did not link these retrievals with the thing that he may or may not have seen when he was nine. He'd edited that otherworldly glimpse out of the story of himself almost as soon as it had happened, relegated it to a concussion and effectively suppressed it. As for all the other moments of that thunderous night, they too were lost, buried beneath the mountainous embroidery that Dennis had adorned his tale with in its numerous playground retellings, so that many of his memories were simply things that he'd forgotten making up. At nine, as he remembered, he'd been a case-hardened crook who'd screw a gas meter as soon as draw breath, rather than someone who'd done it once because an older kid said it was easy, and who'd nearly got himself killed as a consequence. And as for what had happened when the fireworks stopped, all that he knew was that he'd saved a kitten; no, a frightened dog; no, a small girl who couldn't find her parents; and as such he'd had no time to witness visions in the crumpling smoke, the spouting flame.

He carried on past Glasshouse Yard without a thought for how he'd sheltered from the air raid there, preoccupied with the increasingly unmanageable box and his increasingly unmanageable life. He wasn't certain of his hold on either of these things, and felt like both could slip at any minute. What kind of a future had he got, or how was he supposed to build one for himself with just these bombed and bankrupt raw materials to hand? Gloomily taking in the blushing acreage of rosebay willowherb across the road, it struck him that both he and London shared the same predicament, with neither able to imagine anything beyond the bombsites; beyond the paralysis and life arrest of shell shock; beyond being Coffin Ada's live-in servant until you yourself were spent and hideous, although this last anxiety was Dennis's alone and London didn't seem so bothered by it.

Feeling old, he staggered along Old Street, groaning with cardboard arthritis, unsure how he'd fill the time between now and his death. The only two jobs that he could imagine himself doing were, first, secret agent, and, then, writer as a distant second. Dennis thought he'd make a decent spy because at over six foot, and with a head like a plucked chicken from the rear, he felt he was unnoticeable. Writing, on the other hand, was a transparent fantasy that he would hopefully grow out of. At school, he'd liked doing composition, but the one or two things that he'd tried since then had fizzled out and not gone anywhere. He was eighteen. He had nothing to write about because nothing had happened to him yet, except the firebombing of Cripplegate and that bit after where he'd rescued the blind nun. He obviously had no aptitude for fiction, creativity or anything like that. So, espionage it was.

Passing the gutted remnant of St Luke's, its roof gone and the cenotaph thing that was its peculiar steeple rearing against falling dark, Dennis reflected how it was most probably his childish literary ambitions which had made him think that working in a bookshop might be a step in the right direction, as if being a gravedigger could lead naturally to a career as a professional assassin. Hadn't he heard that his early-morning bromide, Orwell, had once worked at W. H. Smith's and, for a period, had loathed the whole idea of books as a result? Dennis continued to love books with all his heart – they were a sole escape hatch from the depth-charged submarine of his existence – but feared he was coming to detest old women.

Veering as the load inside the Oxydol container slid from one side to the other, he went past the busy station and then over the main road to Austin Street. Along the home stretch of Virginia Road, he found that he was studying the pavement underfoot as best he could around the intervening box, attempting to discern through the declining light how much of what he trod was fallen leaves and how much litter, litter being less hospitable to surreptitious dog mess. As he neared Gibraltar Walk, he was obscurely gratified to spot a few bold-headlined pages from Sax Rohmer's *Dope* amongst the disparate fluttering from the gutter – **The Cigarettes from Buenos Ayres**, **The Dream of Sin Sin Wa**, **The Strangle-Hold**, flavorous shreds snagged in the gobs of drains.

Electric lamps, few as there were around those parts, were lighting up one at a time and looked the way that a descending run of notes played on a xylophone would sound, bright peals of amber ringing from a deepening violet. Lowell's Books & Magazines hulked lonely in the murk up at what once had been the top end of Gibraltar Walk but which was now, effectively, Gibraltar Walk. He failed to see how the five paces it would take to pass the shopfront could be construed as a walk, unless by someone even more averse to exercise than Dennis was. The relic structure stood heading a queue where everything in line behind it had died waiting, given up the ghost and blown away. It was as if the German High Command had left just this one place alone, perhaps deferring to a greater evil.

From the LOSED sign hanging in the lightless entrance, he deduced the time to be something past five, and so hefted his cargo through the stretch of slate and nettle that had been next door, around to the back gate. Negotiating this was tricky, what with having to put down the box and pick it up again, at least twice, before he could brave the near-dark deathtrap of the shop's rear yard. It wasn't that the walled concrete enclosure was what you'd call cluttered. There was the collapsing shack of Ada's lavatory, keeping to itself up in one corner, but then there was also Ada's inconvenient flowerbed. Approximately six feet long by three feet wide, it seemed this had been situated with an eye to optimum obstruction, a depressing black dirt barricade that somehow only seemed to produce flowers that were already dead. Tripping and swearing on the feature's raised brick edging, Dennis lurched his way to the back door where he repeated all the putting down and picking up again before gaining admittance. Almost weeping with relief, he finally deposited his Machen horde in the rear passage, where the coat hooks were in better nick than any of the items hung thereon.

Ada was waiting for him in the kitchen.

On a stool, she sat beside the lacerated table where she had a magazine, a half-drunk cup of tea and a chipped willow-pattern bowl of walnuts. Skilfully, she'd cracked the suntanned skulls along their seams before winkling out the shrivelled brains and eating them, crushing their crenellated lobes between her twelve or so remaining teeth. Still in her formerly pink robe and perhaps tartan slippers, still with hair like starched steam and with stockings or sloughed skin around her ankles, Ada stood up as he entered, which confused him and made him feel briefly ladylike.

'Well, I got all the Machen books. You'll never guess how much I—'

Ada threw her half-cup of cold tea, complete with floating doily of coagulated milk, into Dennis's face and his unfortunately open mouth.

'You can get out my house, you cough cough cough cough cough cough thieving little cough cough cough cough fucker.'

This took Dennis rather by surprise. Wide-eyed and spluttering his incomprehension, he fished the remaining fiver and its five green underlings out of his inside pocket, brandishing them at his landlady like a crucifix. 'But, but, but look, I got the lot for five quid. There's a tenner change ...'

Her features crowding to the centre of her head in outrage, Ada hissed, 'I don't cough cough cough want your fucking money,' even as she grabbed it with a raptor swipe and stuffed it into a marsupial pocket of her gown. Stepping forward until her sulphuric gaze was level with his chin, she issued her consumptive verdict.

'Cough cough cough cough cough cough fucking cough cough sling your hook, you cough cough cough ungrateful little shit. Pinching my cough cough cough cough fucking stock ...'

Dripping and disoriented, terror-stricken by the thought of being suddenly without a job or home, Dennis had no idea what he'd done or what was happening to him. Reeling, he clutched desperately for any straw of reason that might help explain his dreadful situation.

'No, no, the George Orwell book, I never took it out the shop. I read it at the counter ...'

She flung her remaining walnuts and the cranial debris of their fallen comrades at him.

'George cough Orwell? George cough cough cough fucking Orwell? I'm not fucking talking about cough cough cough

George Orwell. I'm cough cough cough cough cough talking about this!'

Ada snatched up the magazine, the one thing from the table that she'd yet to hurl at him, and shook it in his trickling face. Until that moment, Dennis hadn't realised there was anything that could be worse than homelessness and unemployment, but then recognised the periodical as the copy of *Picture Show* he'd been perusing earlier. His entire sex life, pretty much, was waving back and forth before his wincing eyes, clutched in the venomous old lady's withered fist. A copper-boiler heat was rising in his cheeks and he knew that he must be blushing, although not that he'd turned bright cerise.

'Look, I was going to put it back. I'd, I'd, I'd only borrowed it because, because I'm interested in films. Lots of chaps my age, we're all interested in films. I wasn't going to nick it.'

Tilting her head like a puzzled dog, she squinted first at Dennis and his vivid colouration, then at *Picture Show*, then from one to the other for a few times more, her homicidal fury gradually subsiding into blank mystification. Finally, deep in the unimaginable stew of Ada's psyche, it appeared an understanding had been reached. She lifted sour-cream eyes to meet his apprehensive gaze, and then did something awful with her face that he had never seen before.

Her smile was sunrise on a renderer's yard, its dire light creeping into every crevice and uncovering each gruesome spectacle. The corners of her mouth crawled back towards pendulous ears, exposing the magnolia cemetery of her dentition. Coffin Ada Benson was quite clearly taking something very much like human pleasure from all this, having the time of her abominable life.

'Cough cough cough ha ha ha ha ha cough cough. Dennis, love, you should have said. Ha ha ha ha cough cough. Course you can ha ha ha cough cough cough you can borrow it. Just give it ha ha cough cough cough cough give it back in fair condition when you're ha ha ha ha cough cough when you're done with it. No hurry. Ha ha ha ha ha ha cough cough. See you in the morning. Ha ha ha ha cough.'

She pressed the dog-eared magazine upon him and, upsettingly, patted his hand before she turned and tottered off in the direction of her room, leaving a stave of barking laughs and coughs strung on the air behind her. With his lodgings and employment both apparently secure for the foreseeable, Dennis was unsure why he wasn't feeling more relieved. He looked down at the shards of walnut shell still clinging to his sodden front, and frowned. He hadn't the remotest understanding of what had just happened, and supposed he never would have. As with most of his defeatist suppositions, this was comprehensively discredited in less than twenty minutes.

He'd wiped himself down, locked the back door, then squeaked his way upstairs, back to his quarters with the recently disputed magazine rolled in one hand. Along the landing, he could still hear Ada laughing between coughs or possibly vice versa. Switching on the table lamp and pulling the heartbroken curtains closed, he sat down on his bed's edge in a great complaint of mattress springs and, lacking any other recreation, opened *Picture Show* to page sixteen.

And there she was, even more irresistible than he recalled. He took her in like a tall drink, commencing at the top: her hair, her face, her modest breasts defined by hanging folds in the sheer fabric of her dress, her poured-out legs, her feet with insteps arching like the backs of hissing cats. Beneath the picture, previously unnoticed, was an almost microscopic credit line. He lifted the page closer, so that he could read the name: 'Ada Mae Lowell, in *Starlight Express*.'

It didn't register immediately, but when it did, he was reduced to mewling paste beneath a rockslide of soul-rending comprehension. Away down the landing, Ada oscillated between choke and cackle, which was more demoralising than George Orwell's rat-cage helmet. Empty-eyed and staring into empty space, Dennis conjectured that it was, by far, the worst day of his life.

This time he had to wait until the following morning to be proven incorrect.

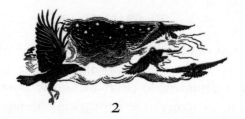

## 2

## *A London Walk*

White as a sheet, she was – whiter than Dennis's – when he crept down the squeeze-box stairs next day and found her sitting at the kitchen table, showing all the animation and complexion of a waxwork. Spread before her were the unpacked contents of the Oxydol container, which itself stood empty and ignored beside her chair, flaps splayed as if for surgery, innards gone.

'Ada?'

He'd writhed through the preceding night, mentally tabulating everything preferable to meeting Ada Benson, stage name Lowell, ever again. The list was mostly modes of death that could conceivably claim either of them before dawn. Or both, although it might look like a lover's pact, but better that than face, the knowing glint in those urinal cakes that his landlady had for eyes. Such, anyway, had been his thoughts during the shame-racked hours of dark, but as she swivelled her meringue-topped skull to look up at him now, it wasn't scorn or lewd amusement nestled in those fissured sockets. If it had been anybody else but Coffin Ada, he'd have said that she looked scared.

'Cough cough cough. Dennis, love, sit down. I think we might be in a bit of trouble.'

Wishing suddenly that this could instead be a conversation about his misguided masturbation aids, he dragged a wooden stool into Ada's proximity and perched precariously, leaning forward with his elbows propped between *The Secret Glory* and *The Hill of Dreams*. 'What's up?'

Her gaze was fixed once more on the scored tabletop and its array of books. He had the worrying impression that his boss was making a considerable effort to remain calm, so much so that she was hardly coughing. Staying calm, though, was for Ada hugely out of character, and Dennis realised with awakening dread that unlike any other exchange that the two of them had ever had, this time she was attempting *not* to frighten him.

'I want you to cough cough cough tell me how you bagged this lot for five quid. And don't say that it's your gift for bargaining, because we both know that you haven't cough cough got one. What was it that happened, between you and Harrison?'

He started chattering about the book-dealer's pretence at being an old lady and the fluffy fighter planes suspended from Harrison's ceiling, trailing off abruptly as she closed her eyes and raised one crinkled palm towards him, wagging it from side to side in weary refutation.

'Dennis, I don't give a cough cough fuck what he had hanging from the rafters. You just tell me how you cough cough cough cough talked him down.'

Himself not fully understanding how he'd managed his impressive price reduction, Dennis shook his head and frowned in the direction of the Oxydol box as he struggled to remember.

'He was asking twenty when I got there, like you'd said. Then when I told him that there's not much call for Machen these days, he dropped straight down to fifteen. I kept on looking through the books, then when I got to one that wasn't on your list and asked about it, he said I could have the lot for five. For five quid, well, I thought I couldn't go far wrong.'

Ada sighed heavily.

'Yes, cough cough cough. Yes, I expect you did. And this book where he dropped his price, the one not on my list – am I cough cough cough right in thinking it was this one here?'

The tallow spearhead of an index fingernail tapped twice on the dilapidated cover of the dullest-looking book in what was otherwise a sumptuous display. This was *A London Walk*, the Reverend Thomas Hampole's *Meditations in the Streets of the*

*Metropolis*, a title so monotonous that Dennis hadn't bothered reading to the end of it. He nodded apprehensively. 'Yeah, that's the one.'

Her saddlebagged eyes now regarded him with something close to sympathy. He was uneasy about all the unfamiliar expressions Ada's face was trotting out. Dennis had known exactly where he stood with caustic and perpetual disdain, but found these new configurations troubling.

'And I don't suppose it cough cough cough occurred to you that this might be the item he was trying to get shot of all along, the shifty little cough cough bastard? No, of course it didn't. I don't cough cough cough know why I'm even asking.'

Dennis screwed his eyes up and stared hard at the unprepossessing volume, brown and battered as though bound in a punchbag, waiting for it to explain itself.

'So ... is there something wrong with it, then?'

His employer didn't answer for a moment, studying the Hampole oddity in quiet deliberation before looking back at him with an expression that he couldn't even guess at.

'Dennis, love, this isn't a real book.'

The sentence hung there in the draughty kitchen air, and nobody knew what to do with it. Dennis would later realise that these few words had allowed the more-than-natural into his life, but at that moment he could only turn them over in his mind uncomprehendingly, this way and that, a baffled monkey with a loaded gun.

'You mean it's, like, a forgery?'

Wearily, Ada shook her floss-encrusted head.

'And why would anybody forge a cough cough fucking piece of junk like that? No, Dennis, you're not listening. When I say this book's not real, I mean it don't cough cough cough cough exist. It's not in catalogues. It's not in libraries. Arthur fucking Machen made it up in a cough cough cough novel, then used it again in a short story, and there's not a trace of it past that, not fucking anywhere. Cough cough. This shouldn't be here. This comes from cough cough cough somewhere else.'

Having comprehended none of this, but at an age where it was crucial Ada think he had, Dennis raised one eyebrow professorially and made what he thought sounded like a pertinent enquiry.

'Where's it from, then?'

This elicited another weighty sigh.

'I don't know as I can explain it in a way you'd cough cough understand. I don't mean this unkindly, Dennis, but you're a cough cough cough fucking halfwit. I don't reckon you can hear a fucking word I'm saying half the cough cough time.'

He nodded faux intelligently, stroking his as-yet-unshaven chin. She went on anyway.

'Look, let me cough cough put it this way. There's another London, Dennis, that nobody knows is there, and that most people never get to cough cough cough cough see.'

At last he had the gist of what Ada was saying, was his dangerous assumption.

'Right. The London underworld. I'm with you now.'

For slightly too long, she gave him a look that held no rancour, but was without hope.

'Mm. Yes, that sort of thing. All that you need to know is that we've got to get this back to where it come from, and then everything will be alright cough cough cough possibly.'

'What, back to Harrison?'

She thought about it.

'If he's still an option, that would be cough cough ideal. It's a good place for you to start, at any rate. Just make sure cough cough cough I never see the fucking thing in here again.'

Dennis had registered her pronoun shift from 'we' to 'you', and, realising that this irksome nonsense was now his responsibility, he did his best to weasel out from under it.

'Couldn't we just, y'know, throw it away, or stick it on the fire?'

'No, Dennis. No, you fucking couldn't. This is from a different part of cough cough London, and it doesn't work like that. Just knowing that it's there is bad enough, without trying to cough cough cough cough burn a bit of it, or flush it down the bog. I've seen this happen once before, to cough cough Teddy Wilson with that Soames book, fucking *Fungoids*, and cough cough cough trust me, you don't want to do that.'

Noticing belatedly that she'd not lit her first snout of the day yet, Dennis was both startled and distracted, failing thus to absorb much of this precautionary advice past the initial 'no'. He'd already decided to interpret everything she said as an old woman's superstitious quirk or mad compulsion which, unfortunately, he would have to humour. He'd do what she told him, to the letter, but he wasn't being paid enough to get caught up in Ada's mental cobwebs.

Ada Benson, for her own part, was of course aware that her employee's rapt attention was a lame pretence, but thought it only proper she should persevere. In what was left of Ada's conscience she felt, well, not bad exactly, but not pleased, put it like that, about what she was getting him involved with. To be fair, it wasn't as if she were sending Dennis to his certain death – uncertain death at very worst, in her experience – but still she thought she should provide him with the basic safety lecture, even though he clearly wasn't taking a blind bit of notice.

'What you've got to do is cough cough cough get Harrison to take this back of his own cough cough cough accord. You can't just shove it through his letterbox. Break all his cough cough fingers if you have to, just so long as he states clearly that he takes it back. Now, if for any reason Harrison is cough cough cough cough no longer available, I'm sure that cough cough something will turn up. Although, if something *should* turn up, it would be better if the book was back with Harrison before that cough cough happened, if you follow me.'

Obviously, Dennis didn't, but was in too deep by that point to admit as much. He did, however, notice Ada's tone of mounting urgency, and asked if he'd got time for a quick wash and shave. Not only did she acquiesce to this without dispute, she also said she'd find him a clean shirt and fry him up some sausage, egg and bacon, 'for a cough cough cough cough treat'. He hadn't been awake long, and found this both touching and appreciative, rather than ominous.

Soon, after Dennis had replaced the bristles on his jaw with grease and yolk, wiped clean by an unlovely handkerchief, he was close to presentable. On the back doorstep, he was much relieved to learn that it was only the presumably cursed Hampole book she wanted taking back to Harrison, and that the Oxydol box wouldn't be required. Instead she let him have a service-able carrier bag, brown paper and string handles, in which she'd secreted both Hampole's *A London Walk* and, for some reason, Arthur Machen's book *The Cosy Room*, wearing its wraps like an embroidered waistcoat.

'That one's not for cough cough Harrison. It's more for you. It's all short cough cough cough cough stories, and there's one called "N" that you might want to take a butcher's at, if you cough cough cough get the chance. It might give you a clue what's going on for once, if things should cough cough cough cough cough cough come to that. Oh, and I want you to have this.'

It was the change he'd brought her home, or at least half of it. She pressed five pound notes, velvety and limp from handling, into his palm.

'I said you could have half the change' – she'd actually said all of it, but Dennis wasn't going to bring that up – 'and I'm a woman of my cough cough word. A bit of lolly might be handy, if the job should end up taking longer than you'd cough cough cough expected. Good luck with all this, love. Alright, I make fun of you behind your back with all the cough cough custom-ers, but underneath it all, I know that being cough cough cough cough useless is a thing that you can't help. You're not a bad lad, Dennis, and I'm sure that you'd have cough cough been a fine young man. Just don't tell anyone about this different London stuff. You'd be as good as cough cough cough cough cough cough dooming the poor fuckers.'

Dennis had tripped over Ada's inconvenient flowerbed, squeaked through the back gate and was already on Virginia

Road before it struck him that, despite her last stern warning with regard to secrecy, she hadn't seemed that bothered about telling him the ins and outs of everything. These inconsistencies were why he took Ada's admonishments about as seriously as instructions not to step on any cracks between Gibraltar Walk and Oxford Street. She'd never worn a bonnet to his knowledge, but this business was quite evidently just another bee in the old woman's rigid hive of hair. His confidence thus buoyed by his contempt for the opinions of the elderly, he Winston Smithed his way into the city, thinking how oppressive cameras and screens everywhere would be. It was the most horrific situation Dennis could imagine, but that was at twenty-five to eight. The day was young.

He'd taken no more than a lungful of the subdued air in Berwick Street, and he already knew things had gone badly wrong. The first thing, unsurprisingly, had been Dennis himself: lost in plans to avoid the Thought Police by the expediency of not thinking, he had automatically repeated his route of the previous morning and was halfway down Charing Cross Road before remembering that he no longer had to find Harrison's bookshop. Forced thus once more to intrude on that congested byway from its lower end, he came upon the second wrong thing, which was Berwick Street.

Braving a spill of broken crate and spoiled tomatoes as he angled through the press of market goers, his immediate impression was that someone had switched off the sound. He could still hear the scuff of feet, the hum of nearby motorcars, the rustling of paper bags, but all the people had gone quiet. No one was saying anything above a murmur. No one was promoting whelks. The customers and traders whispered over purchases, and conversation was conducted through meaningful glances that he didn't know the meaning of. It was as if the motions of the world in this specific stretch of Soho had been paused, or had announced an intermission. It felt wrong.

Whatever its source might be, this uncanny atmosphere had permeated the steep street down to its last subsiding kerbstone, so that every face and every detail seemed to radiate uneasy portent. A dog, perhaps dragging something Dennis couldn't see, was walking backwards. A *Radio Times* front cover, laterally torn, bounced the cold eyes of Arthur Askey down a choking gutter, and from under the striped canvas overhang of M. Blincoe & Son Fresh Fruit and Vegetables, a retinue of Soho apparitions was observing Dennis silently and with apparent interest.

He clocked the watchers straight off but pretended that he hadn't, being already engaged with quite enough activities he didn't understand. One of the group, he thought, had been the disproportioned fellow in the built-up shoe who'd given him the evil eye yesterday morning, while the man beside him looked a bit like Maurice Calendar. He had the brief impression of at least one other figure, standing there beneath the awning with the two of them, but looked away too quickly to be certain. Rattled by the street's prevailing mood, still wondering how he'd make Harrison take back a thing that the book dealer clearly couldn't stand the sight of, Dennis's ability to worry was at full capacity without this cryptic scrutiny. His bag's string handles slithering in a suddenly damp fist, he tucked his head between hunched shoulders and went on up the hushed gradient, insisting to himself that this was just an ordinary thing that he was doing, on an ordinary day.

He kept this up until he saw the ordinary ambulance and the prosaic police cars gathered outside E. J. Tate ~ Knitting Supplies, thereby completely blocking the street's upper reaches. Slowing to a halt, his shoes refused to take him any further and he stood there staring, in amongst a mute and morbid peer of onlookers. The rear doors of the blood bus were wide open and the object being loaded was identifiable, despite a covering sheet, by the taut dome raised from its middle. It was either a scale model of St Paul's or it was Harrison. The ambulance men didn't look as if they were in a terrific hurry. The attending police officers appeared more purposeful, however.

There were half a dozen bobbies, mostly keeping back the subdued crowd with only stillness and an absence of expression, and there were two obvious CID men in grey mackintoshes questioning a badly shaken woman – E. J. Tate, presumably – inside the downstairs wool shop. Also present were what looked like higher-ranking rozzers, one in a superintendent's uniform and two in an expensive cut of plain-clothes, standing back from the near-silent action and conferring grimly. Dennis thought that these might represent Inspector Capstick's Ghost Squad, the new London anti-crime initiative he'd heard about, and reasoned that they weren't there to investigate the death from natural causes of a sickly-looking man in middle age whose intimates knew him as Flabby. As he stood there wide-eyed, trying to take in what he was seeing and what he was meant to do about it, Dennis's shoes came to a decision before he did. Pivoting on worn-through soles, they bore him out of harm's way back down Berwick Street, his gait that of those weighted plastic novelties that seem to walk down slopes but are in truth only obeying gravity.

His adolescent mind, attempting to escape its circumstances in nine ways at once, was paralysed. What did this mean? What was he going to do? Had Harrison been done in? Stomach dropping, he remembered Ada saying that this 'other London' she'd been on about was London's underworld or, anyway, that's what he'd thought she said. This surely wasn't anything to do with the dilapidated volume dangling currently in his brown paper carrier bag, was it? No, it couldn't be, because that would mean he was now entangled in a petrifying murder drama, and he wasn't having that. Like nearly everyone he knew, he much preferred to play his life as a light comedy and didn't think that he could take a shift of genre. Frightened, in internal uproar, Dennis thudded downhill amid speechless shoppers, staring fixedly ahead and trying furiously not to look at anyone. The street blurred past in a peripheral haze of windows, doors and unread hoardings; became an alarming landscape that he desperately didn't want to be a part of or acknowledge. This was why he failed to see the pyrotechnic body hurtling through the market throng until it was on top of him.

'Whoh-hoh-hoh-hoh! White man for pluck, black man for luck!'

The voice was an explosion in the dumbstruck thoroughfare, raucous and prehistoric. In the startle of the moment, Dennis couldn't differentiate between the thunderous sound and equally loud visual appearance of the spectacle confronting him. All of it, the experience, was a terrifying detonation of the inconspicuousness that he imagined he'd achieved.

Blocking his path was an outrageously clad coloured chap, as tall as Dennis but with a good foot of ostrich plumes exploding from his tight-bunched hair that made him seem a giant. Tipping and tilting on the dross-jewelled pavement, zodiac robes constantly in motion, his broad smile invited – or perhaps obliged – observers to delight in simply his existence. Having seen pictures in newspapers, so only black and white ones, Dennis realised, with a mounting sense of all this turning out to be a dream, that he was in the company of auto-legendary racetrack oracle, Prince Monolulu.

Stopped dead by astonishment, Dennis perceived that all around them Berwick Street had come once more to normal, noisy life. People were chattering again as if the self-styled African's stentorian voice somehow permitted theirs. The hapless young man moved his mouth as he attempted to ask questions he could neither formulate nor comprehend, at which the tipster leaned in close with a conspiratorial grin and nodded towards the activity up behind Dennis, at the top end of the street.

'I got a hearse! Whoh-hoh-hoh-hoh!'

Dennis recoiled from this typhoon of mirth at such proximity, but Monolulu checked him with a firm grip on one raincoat shoulder. In his other hand, from nowhere, the implausible pretender brandished now a sealed white envelope, wagging it tantalisingly in Dennis's fear-stricken face.

'I think the starting pistol has made its announcement, sah, and now they're off! No man's posterior enjoys the swift kick of a losing streak, but do not fear! My tip – which is of course entirely free from cost – shall see you past the finish line victorious! Black man for luck!'

A guilty start of the colonial imagination, Monolulu slid his envelope into the boy's unguarded carrier bag with a deft hand, and, once again, that deafening chuckle. Feeling compelled to at least say something, Dennis managed, 'But I'm not a racing man,' which prompted yet another cloudburst of guffaws from the invented Abyssinian.

'You will forgive a poor, uneducated darkie, but the speed with which I saw you racing from a scene of criminal activity had led me to think otherwise! Have courage, sah! White man for pluck!'

At that, the fabulous mirage stepped to one side and, offering an avian flutter of his talismanic garments, allowed his dumbfounded victim to continue down the incline. It was Dennis's first conversation with a foreign person, and he wasn't sure how it had gone. He wasn't sure of anything, except his need to get away from Berwick Street in all its madness, murder, Metropolitan Police and Monolulu. The one plan that he'd come up with so far – waking up in bed, essentially – appeared increasingly unlikely to pay off, and so he hurried out of Soho looking for a quiet spot to panic and miscalculate this whole thing through, with even that district's unusually furtive population thinking he looked like a shady piece of work. Aping the pendulum of a grandfather clock, his fateful carrier bag swung back and forth beside him as he scarpered, ticking off the seconds in a countdown on his life expectancy, or that was how it seemed. When Tolerable John occurred to him, he dug his nails into the concept and clung like a drowning man to crumbling riverbank.

'– bringing the stretcher out, and there were coppers everywhere! I couldn't give the book back, could I, not if he was dead? So, anyway, I bolted back down Berwick Street, but then, down at the bottom, I'm not kidding, out of nowhere was the racing forecaster, you know, Prince Monolulu? It was him, John, no word of a lie. He talked a load of stuff I couldn't make out, palmed one of his tips off on me, and then waved me on my way. I haven't got a clue what's happening or what I should do next, and so I thought I'd come here and find you. What were you going to say?'

A glint-gilded miasma, the unwindowed taproom of the Cheshire Cheese resounded with the clink and mumble of perhaps some half a dozen customers, a not unusual lull for that time on a Tuesday morning. These habitués, gabardine galleons, loomed up from the nicotinic mists now and then on their veering course from bar to chair to toilets, possibly zigzagging to avoid those fifth-pint literary phantoms crowding a half-empty hostelry; swerving the deathless farts of Dickens, Tennyson, Twain, Conan Doyle and Chesterton that shimmered still, in air last ventilated during the Great Fire.

Dennis had burst dramatically into the legendary house of Tudor ill-repute, although the fact he had to do it three times – John not having been there in the first two instances, entailing two anticlimactic exits to a nearby Lyons Corner House – tended to take away from his performance. When he'd burst in on that third occasion, more wet paper-bag than hand grenade, to find the newsman occupying his accustomed chair, the two had both started to speak at once until McAllister had shrugged and said, 'You first.' With the youth's answering tirade of semi-gibberish apparently concluded, Tolerable John leaned forward pessimistically, the only way that he did anything.

'What I was going to say was, I had Ada Benson turn up at the *Express* offices about an hour ago. She had that rancid fur coat on over the dressing-gown, but she was still wearing her slippers. All the older blokes there know her, so it wasn't the professional disaster that it might have been, but it was still a bit of a surprise. More of a shock, thinking about it. Her hair didn't move the whole time I was talking to her. Have you noticed that?'

Dennis, convinced that Ada outdoors in her slippers was a dreadful omen, nodded apprehensively. Voice sounding tremulous and higher than he'd hoped, he asked the older, wiser, and more markedly depressed man what she'd wanted. John shot him an awkward grimace, as if bad news was the last thing that he wanted to pass on, although that was in fact his livelihood.

'She wanted me to tell you something, if I saw you. Said it wouldn't be safe for you going near the bookshop for a little while; a long while, possibly, depending on what happens. What it is, she had some visitors this morning, after you'd gone. Nasty types. What they were after was the book that you tried taking back to Harrison, this *London Walk* thing. God knows why. I'm guessing, from what you just said, that they'd been round to Berwick Street and made Harrison tell them who he'd flogged the book to. So, most probably he gave them Ada's shop address and your unfortunately memorable name.'

Freeze-welded to his seat by fear at this development, the question Dennis needed most to ask was, 'Am I going to be alright?', but, not wanting to sound as callous and self-serving as he knew himself to be, he built up to his selfish query with a display of concern for others first.

'Is Ada going to be alright?'

Scratching his privates, pessimistically, the stocky journalist grunted in affirmation.

'Mm. Yeah, I think she's made sure of that. She told these fellers that she'd never seen the book, because you'd run off with it and the change you owed her. She apparently pulled out that billhook that she keeps beneath the till, and told these bruisers that they'd better find you before she did. Basically, she's dropped you in the shit. It's her reptilian impulse for self-preservation. From what I was told, the billhook put the wind up 'em, and they left her alone to look for you.'

Dennis felt as if somebody had hit him in the breastbone with a pickaxe. Was this, then, what life was really like, a thing that could plunge suddenly into unfathomable nightmare at a moment's notice? Surely it was all a terrible mistake; shouldn't be happening to him when he'd done nothing to invite it. Flailing between dread and outrage, he clutched at irrelevance.

'But, but, but these aren't proper villains, then. I mean, they can't be, not if they're scared off by some old woman on her last legs.'

John, aware that Dennis was attempting to reduce his problem to a manageable size, gave him a long look that made up in pity what it lacked in optimism.

'Dennis, mate, she's Coffin Ada.'

'So, what, were they scared she'd give them pleurisy?'

McAllister looked puzzled for a moment, then caught on to Dennis's misapprehension.

'They don't call her that because she coughs. There was some feller, this was in the thirties, done her out of quite a bit of cash. She had these blokes that she knew find him, chloroform him, tie him down, and when he woke up, he was in a coffin, in a grave, in Ada's backyard. She told him exactly what she thought of him, then her mates put the casket lid on and filled in the hole. They let him have ten minutes down there, just enough to put the fear of God into him, then they dug him up. Although by then, as these things go, he'd snuffed it from a heart attack. Ada and her two henchmen looked at one another, shrugged and buried him again. She didn't start to cough until a good while after that. I'm sorry, mate. I thought you knew.'

He hadn't even known about the billhook kept beneath the till. None of the world was as he thought it, nor, apparently, had ever been so. Dennis sat at the pub table, pale and still as marble, while preoccupied reporters breasted blue-brown surfs of smoke as they passed back and forth behind him. He was lost for anything to say or even think, save for the mortal trouble he was in and a persisting vision of his landlady's poorly positioned flowerbed now blossoming with meaning. Tolerable John went on, filling the huge hole that his comments had made in their conversation with a bigger hole; a gaping abyss so deep nobody would live to hear the splash if you fell in.

'As for them being proper villains, one of them was Jack Spot.'

Dennis laughed, but it was a peculiar, involuntary thing that sounded bad even before he choked it in mid-flow. The city's underworld, as everybody knew, was ruled by Billy Hill. With Hill only just out of prison, though, it was his partner Jack Spot who was seen as working all the blood-scabbed levers and arm-breaking gears of London crime. So, that was why those senior policemen – Capstick's Ghost Squad, as he'd speculated – had been there at Flabby Harrison's, first thing this morning. It was Spot, with Dennis's name and description, who was looking for him and a falling-to-bits book that no one wanted, most especially Dennis. Seriously regretting that he'd jettisoned his waking-up-in-bed idea so early in the game, all he could manage was a repetition of the gangster's name in a flat, hopeless tone.

John sighed in gloomy confirmation.

'Ada recognised him. She's seen him about over the years, and said he still looked like a puffed-up bastard, with that big spot on his cheek. And all these East End cut-throats, deep inside they're all scared of their mums, who Ada probably reminds them of. But don't ask me why Spotty wants this book. She was as in the dark as you are over that. One thing she did say was, you're not to give it to him. She said that would be much worse than all the other things she said you shouldn't do.'

Giving the hellish thing to Spot was the replacement strategy which Dennis was at that moment constructing in his scrabbling mind – perhaps the two of them could meet up in a café: 'Here's the book, Jack. Sorry for the mix-up' – and he greeted this new prohibition with despair.

'Well, what am I supposed to do? John, none of this makes any sense. It's barmy. I mean, have you seen the piece of rubbish that there's people being murdered over? Here …'

He reached towards the carrier bag, but John threw both his mitts up in alarm.

'No. No, no, no. No, Dennis, I don't want to look at it. I don't want anything to do with it, and not because of Jack Spot, either. Him, if I can help you out, find you a place to stay, something like that, I will. But please don't tell me about all the other business. Bad enough that this stuff happens in the book trade every now and then. We don't want it in Fleet Street.'

Still without a clue about the business or the stuff that he was not supposed to mention, Dennis left the carrier bag alone but fixed instead on what John had just said.

'So, what does that mean, "every now and then"?'

Looking uncomfortable, McAllister peered left and right into the Woodbine cloudbank, making sure that no one was in earshot before he leaned forward and replied.

'In our job, us reporters, we hear stories that you won't find in the papers. Mostly that's because they're about people who could make life hard for us, but sometimes it's a different sort of thing, where you just know to leave it well alone. Have you heard the name Teddy Wilson?'

Dennis automatically said that he hadn't, since this was most usually the case, but then recalled that Ada had deployed the name that morning, although for the life of him he was unable to remember what she'd said about it. Bald spot glistening, John filled him in.

'He ran a bookshop out in Lewisham, ten or eleven years back, just before the war, and had the same thing done to him as you had done to you. In his case, it was this nice lady school-teacher who came into his shop with all this nineties poetry for sale, dirt cheap. Good stuff, it was. Richard Le Gallienne, Ernest Dowson, all them. Teddy snapped it up, the same way you did with the Machen books, and then, just like you, he found something unexpected hidden in amongst the bargains. In his case, it was a book called *Fungoids* by this chap named Enoch Soames. The thing is, Enoch Soames doesn't exist. He's from a story by Max Beerbohm, where a disregarded poet from the nineties travels to the future seeking his posterity, only to learn that he's remembered as a story by Max Beerbohm.'

John sipped his half-finished pint of pale ale, where a lacework made of foam hung draped around the glass's unsubmerged interior, and then continued.

'You see Teddy's problem. Then, things started happening, or else he thought they did. To tell the truth, he was unravelling a bit by that point. Said there was a cat that had it in for him, or

sometimes he'd go on about an evil dwarf. He put this down to
being lumbered with the Soames book. He tried giving it back
to the lady teacher, but she'd changed her name and moved. He
tried to flog it, but no one was buying. In the end, he told me
that he'd thrown it on a bonfire but it wouldn't burn, and so
he planned to chuck it in the river. If he did or not, I couldn't
tell you, and when they found Teddy Wilson, well, he was in no
condition to tell anybody anything.'

His voice theatrically low despite there being nobody within
ten feet of them, Dennis asked unnecessarily, 'You mean that he
was dead?'

McAllister gazed heavenward towards the Cheshire Cheese's
kippered ceiling, puffed his cheeks like an aeolian zephyr on a
map and exhaled noisily before looking once more at Dennis.

'He was worse than dead. According to this copper who left
the police force not long after, Teddy Wilson, when they found
him, he was inside out. His skin and face and everything were at
the centre of him, and he was contained in what was left of his
own alimentary canal.'

While this was something of a conversation stopper, after a few
moments Dennis managed to state his response, again unnecessarily. 'But that's not possible.' John nodded in agreement.

'No, it's not, and that's why everybody backs away from incidents like this – police, press, everyone. An inside-out bloke,
that's not possible, and nor is a near-mint edition of Soames's
*Fungoids*, and nor is what you've got in your carrier bag. This is
why I don't want to be involved, not ever. All I'm telling you
for is so you don't try destroying it or throwing it away. You'll
have to think of something else. What was this tip you said that
Monolulu gave you?'

Still trying to let the concept of an inside-out man sink
in, only to discover that he couldn't, Dennis hadn't given any
thought to his encounter with the booming turf Cassandra.
Raising one hand to placate McAllister, he pulled the sealed
white envelope from where it nestled between Machen's *Cosy
Room* and Hampole's *London Walk*, in the unwanted carrier bag

beside his chair. Tearing its top edge open clumsily, he found a second envelope inside the first, this one manila, smaller and unsealed. Across the front, printed or stamped, were seven words: 'SURREALIST RACING FORECAST CARDS – READ INSTRUCTIONS CAREFULLY'. Beneath the wary squint of Tolerable John, he untucked the tea-coloured flap before extracting the two dozen or so picture cards and an accompanying instructions slip that were contained within. Dennis had no idea what he was looking at, distracted by his own internal voice which alternated between shouting 'inside out?' and 'Jack Spot?' with increasing volume and hysteria.

The promised leaflet of instructions proved impenetrable, whether read with care or recklessly, and while the cards seemed equally bewildering, these were more difficult to look away from. Each portrayed the same male face in an unbroken cigarette-smoke line that twisted and coiled back upon itself, occasionally wandering to limn a wing or the suggestion of a bestial countenance; form melting into vaporous form. There was no rational way to connect the images with horse racing, much less with Dennis's predicament. Mutely, he passed the cards to John, who took a pair of ugly National Health spectacles out of an inside pocket so he could examine the deck properly.

'Huh. Well, here's something I can help you with, at least. These are by Spare, the artist and magician, or that's what they say he is. When I first started work at the *Express*, there was this feller, Dennis Bardens, he was pals with him. I think I can remember Bardens telling me about these racing forecast cards – Spare did them, 1936 or thereabouts, and said they were "surrealist" to cash in on the big surrealist exhibition held that year. Can't stand the art world, what they tell me, so he sticks south of the river. Had a studio on Walworth Road, but that got bombed quite early in the war and he's been doing bad since then, by all accounts. Lives in a little basement on Wynne Road, over in Brixton. Austin Spare. Sounds like an interesting chap, although why Monolulu should see fit to land you with

Spare's screaming abdabs out of nowhere, that I couldn't say. Another drink?'

Another drink was a far better plan than anything that Dennis had so far come up with, and he gratefully accepted the reporter's offer with a nod. While John was at the bar, the condemned errand boy put the cards back in their manila envelope, in the torn-open white one, in the carrier bag down on the floor beside him. As he did this, Dennis noticed he was trying not to even touch the Hampole book, with Machen's *Cosy Room* used as a prophylactic barricade. He knew that this behaviour was just childish superstition, but then, inside out? Jack Spot? Having no rational way out of this ridiculous and terrifying situation, the irrational ways were all that he'd got left.

Presently, John emerged from the indoor pea-souper with a fresh pint in each hand, which meant that Dennis felt obliged to get a round in after that, and so on. It was a persistent hazard when one drank with journalists. The two men's conversation edged around Dennis's problem in an ever-widening circle, reaching no useful conclusions. Sounding already doubtful as the idea left his mouth, McAllister floated the notion of approaching the police, although that clearly wouldn't work. They couldn't keep him safe from Jack Spot, not forever, and they'd throw him out the nick if he so much as raised the subject of *A London Walk*. Besides, in January, this peacetime conscription thing had been brought in, eighteen months' National Service for all men above eighteen. Dennis was hoping that by living off the record up at Ada's he could give all that a miss, so the attention of the law was the last thing that he was short of. No, there had to be another way, although there wasn't.

After an immeasurable time in that establishment eschewed by daylight, John felt it was only right to put at least an hour or two in at the *Express* offices. He restated his offer of a place to stay, and said, 'You'll be alright,' but shook his head from side to side as he was saying it. Drifting away into the hoopla of surrounding smoke rings, he left Dennis nursing the remains of a fifth pint along with dwindling hopes that by this time tomorrow he might still be living and the right way out. Checking his mental processes to make sure that he wasn't too drunk to think clearly – without once considering that sober people didn't need to do this – he reviewed the unappealing menu of his options while he polished off his drink, those last few swigs that tasted more of spit than beer.

Dennis's first response to any of life's snags was always to do nothing and just see what happened, although in his current circumstances it meant sitting waiting for Jack Spot to find him, so that one was a non-starter. Getting the book back to Harrison was now impossible without the intervention of a spirit medium. Burn it or discard it and he'd have his innards on the outside, like the Wilson feller; an inverted glove puppet, but messier. And yet, giving the book to Spot, according to his landlady, would somehow make things even worse, although how was that possible? Involving the police was out, and through his pale-ale fog the only dim light visible was something that Ada had said: 'You can just stick it through his letterbox.' Dennis was reasonably sure that's what she'd said, although it might have been 'You can't just stick it through his letterbox', now that he thought about it. Still, he nearly reasoned, that meant that his letterbox plan had at least a fifty-fifty chance of paying off, far better odds than any of the other schemes he'd contemplated.

He'd head up to Soho, now that all the coppers would be gone, and post the Hampole volume back where it had come from, if by that Ada meant Flabby Harrison's now empty flat, and he was fifty per cent absolutely certain that she did. Feeling much better now he had a solid working strategy and was half-drunk, he knocked back his last quarter inch of watery dregs and stood up as decisively as he could manage. Picking up the haunted bag by its twine handles, Dennis made his way from premises unmeasured by the sun to the surprise of an already fallen night outside. Only when he was veering down the little alleyway off Fleet Street, where the Cheshire Cheese had stood for getting on four hundred years, did it occur to him that not

once in their lengthy chat had John McAllister described a single
part of Dennis's ordeal as tolerable.

Of course, the lookouts saw him before he was halfway up the
pitch-black crease of Berwick Street. The market had packed up
and gone save for invisible detritus in the squashy dark beneath
his feet, and with the absence of its noise and cram came an
intensity of hush, a more abandoned emptiness. Other than
half a dozen furtive clubs or knocking shops, the area's mostly
legitimate concerns were shut by six, leaving the district as a
labyrinthine shadow trap where streetlamps only reinforced the
blinkering gloom. Dennis ascended, bag in hand, into deserted
silence punctuated by his scuffs and stumbles. From the fizzing
apprehension in his stomach, he deduced that he was nowhere
near as drunk as he had hoped to be for this poorly considered
venture, just too drunk to have the faintest chance of managing
it properly. Above, the slate diagonals and listing chimney breasts
leaned in conspiratorially, their jet geometries against a starless
London sky. So far, so good, and he was thinking that his hopeless scheme might work out after all when the two men burst
from the sheltered door of E. J. Tate ~ Knitting Supplies, some
distance up the slope ahead of him, grey raincoats flapping noisy
in the breeze as though erupting from a pigeon loft.

One had a trilby that he held clamped to his head with one
hand as he ran. Beyond that they were hurtling shapes, monochrome patchworks racing purposefully down the night-blind
street towards him and his carrier bag, soles slapping hard against
the pavement's weed-split cheek with lightless shopfronts snapping back the echo.

'Oi! Fucking come here!' Voice like a furious dog, it frightened Dennis wide awake, and filled him with the bowel-freezing
conviction that he definitely wasn't going to fucking go there.
Turning on a sixpence, he threw himself back into the murk
he'd come from, desperate not to slip and meet his end over
a spoiling apricot. His pounding footfalls striving frantically to

match the downhill pull, he clattered into Soho's convoluted darkness with his thoughts in smithereens, poleaxed by shock.

A right turn near the bottom into Broadwick Street, all without conscious motive or volition, his pursuers still somewhere behind, but whether far or close he couldn't tell. Why on earth had he come here? It was the worst possible idea he could have had, returning by night to a crime scene, where there were now roaring killers at his heels and Dennis couldn't see where he was going. All his visual impressions were a squall of underexposed photos, upside down or overlapping as they flickered by: the rough-edged brickwork of a terrace end-house; metal street signs made unreadable by soot; four or five startled onlookers who shrank back into doorways, anxious not to get involved.

With gangster hoofbeats gaining, he propelled himself across the road and swerved into Ingestre Court, or Street, or Place – he couldn't read it – then a left turn, then a right, his dangling carrier swung out horizontally by centrifugal force as he took corners. Was the slab-and-rubber thunder of his faceless chasers louder at his back, and nearer? Brewer Street, possibly Bourchier Street, then names he didn't recognise, carious alley mouths that might lead to a literal dead end, all with his thumping heartbeat indistinguishable from the thudding boots of the men after him.

He didn't have the faintest notion where he was, nor any destination except out of this unbearable dilemma, so between the ale and the adrenaline, he was in an unprecedented state of being lost, both physically and psychologically. Tilting façades with unlit windows smeared past his peripheries and every breath was scalding in his gullet. Panting down a narrow entry, he could see what looked like a yard's wooden gate, either ajar or off its hinges, leaning open only a few steps in front of him. If he could nip in there before they saw him do it, they might run straight past, the way it worked in chases he'd seen at the pictures. Wild with panic, he pulled the gate open and was partway through it when he realised – wait, this wasn't right, he wasn't seeing this correctly, he was making some mistake – that it was wooden pallets propped against the passage wall, and not a gate at all, but then, how had he opened it? Unable to arrest his tumbling momentum, he plunged forward and then

*he is on his knees and puking in pellucid heaven, spattering the gutters made from gold, where scuttling to his vomit's thin meniscus on those auric cobbles, there are bottle caps with brewery insignias and spider legs of slivered cork, crimped edges glinting, tinkling as they lap the bile and beer ... immediately upright with revulsion, he sways, reeling in an overwhelming something ... all about are foreign structures, shapes ungraspable, powdered with luminescent dusk yet unmistakeably still Soho by their tilted kilter, by their signal atmosphere ... the air he's breathing feels too mighty for his lungs, which makes him sick again and now the beetle caps are crawling on his shoes ... he doesn't know what it all means but knows that he can't take it ...*

*this is almost Dean Street, if not for its scale, its shrilling undergrowth acoustic, its impossibilities ... filtered through twinkles, he sees urban landscape writhing at the brink of ravenous biology ... peony lampposts that have petals cast in wilted glass droop on gunmetal stems, and hanging cables squeak black rubber leaves ... eye-corner movement, rustlings in a turf of quivering litter, caterpillar Durex, not a thing that is not animate ... he tries a few steps but his legs are wobbling, and out of unsourced glimmer, there are crabs of broken crate whose eight limbs are articulated splinter; moths folded from nudie magazines with bosoms printed grey on water-damaged wings; a creep of fag-end maggots, heads burned black and soggy arses; anaconda drainpipes that detach from walls to slither clanking on the bullion slabs; chewing-gum molluscs inching to investigate his edibility and, understanding that it's really happening, belatedly he screams ...*

*the wingtip of a silver-paper dragonfly slices his forehead, drawing sudden blood, and gilded flagstones lever up in alligator jaws with smashed milk-bottle teeth ... a single-bar electric fire, shuffling and scraping, starts to wind its trailing flex around one of his ankles ... earwig Bakelite, tarantula suspender belts ... when through the crepuscule a locomotive force is rocketing towards him as he stands and shrieks and swipes screw-threaded hornets from his eyes ... a bloated human figure moving at tremendous speed so that he thinks his wool-shop ambush has pursued him here to this howling wherever ... it stops dead a few feet short of him in a great spray of thimble snail shells, newsprint topsoil, an advancing crate crab slammed to matches by the impact, shuddering into stationary focus as a much-inflated Maurice Calendar ...*

*nearly unrecognisable since Dennis saw him yesterday, the swollen trendsetter bulges against his pale fawn overcoat, even his flaking skin too tight for him ... soaking in perspiration, puffing with exertion, he looks unwell ... between breaths, he says, 'You're Knuckleyard? This is the worst way in you could have picked. Soho Entire's a vividistrict, you daft bugger. Come on,' and he kicks the one-bar heater so that it lets go and skitters whining over priceless pavement, swats a grainy pornographic butterfly, grabs Dennis by the hand without the carrier bag, and then they're off ...*

*sucked into pure velocity, Futurist streaks on umber, the two men career in teeming, thrashing half-light ... streaming breathless up a row that's more than Bateman Street ... a pack of rubbish bins with dented faces roll at them, easily hurdled ... doubloon crocodiles yawn open underfoot; the trick's to stamp down hard on the exchequer of their upper bite, where weak wire muscles cannot keep the mouth from closing ... putrid vegetable insects and doorways that flourish tongues ... down Frith Street Absolute, where inner-tubeworms bask in lurid Esso puddles ... the medusa nest of bicycle chain half up a sweat-beaded door flails at them, clicking, oiled and lethal ... sizzling along an Older Compton Street where inorganic foliage and fauna are less evident, Dennis pulled headlong in the slipstream of distended Maurice Calendar ... lights moving through grooved space ...*

*in the epitome of Greek Street are still fewer horrors, nor are knotted-stocking vines so prevalent ... strollers pass here and there, extravagantly clad amid scintillant dimness ... near the bottom is an old gas standard, thick iron-bolls at its base, where waiting by it is a ghost, translucent and bereft in threadbare clothes that you can see the desolation through ... Maurice hisses 'De Quincey' without explanation; without pausing in his cometary passage ... things whip by, almost too quick to see ... red rear reflectors burdening a gatepost bough like berries ... hubcap terrapins ... drains with incisors ... overhead, colloidal galaxies, hung in suspension ... all at once, Soho's behind them and they're stumbling to a standstill, there on an endless avenue, in that gigantic evening …*

*he can take in nothing save for fabulous enormity … the agoraphobic breadth of this new boulevard, its sky star-crowded and apparently decanting an ethereal twilight … figures that may not be people moving on the ostentatious paving … some at speed as coloured smudges, pulsing in saccades as if along pneumatic tubes of their own motion … passing back and forth upon the shining highway are unutterable transportations, sumptuous carriages that glide a foot or two above the wide road's lustre, cars with artificial leopard legs where wheels should be … surrounding architecture squirms from style to style with, on the further skyline, stupefying towers jab at the flocking nebulae above … and not three feet away stands the ballooning bulk of Maurice Calendar, bent nearly double as he gets his puff back, overstuffed hands propped against his too tight trouser knees …*

*talk about gone to seed … the one-time fashion innovator looks about to burst asunder, flesh so taut against the too small cuffs and collar that his skin cannot be differentiated from his shirt, as though the clothes are painted on … he raises his exhausted gaze to Dennis, but is still too winded to be capable of speech … patches of eczema on his pink cheeks, pudgy wrists, damp brow, where none were noticeable previously … crushed by miracles, caught in the spin of the unearthly, Dennis says, 'I'm – where are – this is –' before clamming up again, unable to pose questions big enough … and Maurice Calendar holds up one hand as if to indicate he needs a minute … then, after a lengthy pause, he finally replies, subsiding gasps employed as punctuation …*

*all sound, every syllable, bubbles away to liquid whispers in an aural distance: 'You're in the real London, on the Indices of Charing. You're not in Short London any more,' and he breaks off to breathe for a few seconds, sucking back each noisy lungful … an enormous jelly mould on casters trundles by and constellations without names jam-pack the firmament … 'It's London's theory, not its practice. Look, mate, I'm on me last legs here. I'm decadal, and if I don't get you back home sharpish, I'll be in me next stage and we'll both be goners. Where do you want taking?', and he stares hard as if Dennis should know what he's on about, or where they are, or anything …*

starting to shake as he goes into shock, Dennis gesticulates at golden tarmac, gastropodous chariots, buildings simultaneously rotting and regenerating, and he stammers, 'But – how can – it isn't –', at which Calendar looks miserable, groans wearily ... he's clearly going to have to educate this Knuckleyard before he can get on with his own urgent business ... he's not happy ... 'Listen, Ironfoot saw you up at Harrison's place yesterday. He guessed what you'd been lumbered with – old Hampole's book – and knew that it meant trouble. Jack Spot's after it, so Monolulu tells us. Thinks it's going to get him into this place. Me and Gog, Gog Blincoe, we said we'd do shifts, keeping an eye out for you in the briefs of Berwick Street. Both of us come from here, so breaking in and out isn't so much of a palaver as it is for shorties. Now, it's better if you're gone from the Great When before it does your bonce a mischief. This is not the place to drop you back, with Spotty's bruisers all over the hockey, so I'll ask you once more – where do you want taking?' ... understanding no more than a pinch of the foregoing, Dennis can but call to mind the reassuring thought of Tolerable John, who'd offered him a place to stay if all else failed ... after a prologue of 'I'm not – why does – that can't be –' and the like, he ends up saying 'Street Fleet' a few times, but luckily Maurice knows what he means ... looking relieved, he seizes Dennis by the elbow, mutters, 'Right you are,' and both of them stretch into speed vectors again ...

the zoom of everything ... Maurice drags Dennis, Dennis drags his carrier bag, their blurs reflecting briefly in the glister of the path beneath them ... on these so-called Indices of Charing, awe and terror are abroad, dressed as though for an evening out ... entities promenade, abstract flaneurs, each wearing its unique charisma like a stole ... a lady whose hair has been lacquered into an absurdly detailed galleon, having masts and sails and ropes and gun ports ... in celestial Leicester Square, theatres are replaced by giant mechanisms which recall the bright amusements of seaside arcades, realised as palaces ... Dennis's cheeks are rippling back towards his ears ... on both sides of the dazzling main road stand edifices that seem made from moving words and letters, each façade a page left fluttering in the rush of the two men, in their heart-stopping whiz ...

*they swerve left at the bottom, where the Eleanor Cross brushes over-populated heavens, then shoot off into a flaring vision of the Strand ... this whole experience is far too much; a fight between aggressively competing spectacles ... it all smells rich and sounds unearthly ... in the middle of the street, phantasmal traffic forks about a sculpted marble phallus of astonishing dimension that trails maypole ribbons from its tip ... mounted on the colossal glans, there is a cylinder of white and silver angled at the overhanging night, a telescope too large and complicated for a human eye to be applied, as though the vast erection had ejaculated new astronomy ... the pace they're going, discrete landmarks melt and merge with one another ... near the mouth of Surrey Street, a station-ary human figure, a young man clad in an old man's topcoat, stands with head tipped back and arms raised as if to embrace the instant, in a drench of emerald light that pours on him alone ... Maurice says, 'Arthur Machen,' but the name bowls past into their hectic wake before it has a chance to register ...*

*at once upon them, Fleet Street's various premises have been ingeniously folded out of newspaper, grave centuries of headlines as their masonry ... Calendar brakes and digs his heels in at the entrance to the greatly enlarged lane, but their resultant skid takes them to its far end ... brought to a halt at last in clouds of kicked-up gold dust, Dennis sneez-ing a king's ransom, rubbing fortunes from the corners of his eyes ...*

*punch-drunk and near collapse, he leans on Maurice, by this point as plump and yielding as a pillow ... each propping the other up, they stand amongst fluorescing flowers, some several times as tall as they are ... their location seems to be the verdant grounds of a glass ornament as big as a cathedral, one with lines that undulate rather than seek the upright ... Dennis is lost, every bit of him ... he doesn't have a clue what part of the metropolis this grand jewel and its garden represent ... his rotund rescuer, who now has blotches of unhealthy hue on coat and jowls alike, regards him solemnly ... even Maurice's voice is different; a congested nasal buzz that wasn't evident before ... 'This is the Fisbo opening in Furious Alsatia, off the Upper Scandals. It'll bring you out in Bride Lane. I can see you through it in one piece, but then I've really got to go, before I get so I can't even move' ... indeed, the style leader is looking worse with every passing moment, eyes beginning to cloud over*

*... distantly aware that they're discussing his release from this unbearable condition, Dennis fumbles in his carrier and retrieves A London Walk, brandishing it as he attempts to utter his misgivings and uncertainties ... 'This, though – can't I just – y'know, somewhere around here – if I left it –' ... Maurice shakes his peeling head ...*

*propelling Dennis down a grassy slope between the outsized stems, the stout sartorial pioneer places a gentle but insistent hand between the youngster's shoulder blades ... Calendar's fingers are, it seems, starting to fuse together ... 'No, chum, that's not something you can just leave anywhere. What you've got there, it's what they call a breach. You'll have to take it to the City Heads and let them sort it out. Just follow Monolulu's tip and you'll be— Oh. Hang on,' and Maurice brings them to a halt ... floating towards them through the falling starlight, winding between the smooth green trunks of a gargantuan bouquet, there comes a phosphorescent gauze that hovers at approximately head-height ... sinuous movement of a snake in water ... Dennis stands stock-still while it drifts nearer, crinkling and relaxing its white fabric as though sniffing at him like a dog ... after a thoughtful pause, it billows off into the stellar glimmer, and Maurice resumes both his unhelpful commentary and their downhill stroll ... 'Don't worry about that. It's one of the Arcana, and its title is Her Train. From what I gather, it's drawn to the smell of poetry' ... the insectival hum in Calendar's inflection is now more pronounced ... heart hammering against the cell bars of his ribcage, Dennis is convinced he's going to die; is perhaps dead already, blood congealing in a lightless Soho alleyway ... they're almost at the bottom now of their descent, and Maurice stops them in their faltering tracks ...*

*he directs Dennis's attention to a point beside the path where two of the huge blossoms have grown close together, only a few feet of swaying grass between them ... it may be the umbra of the flowering heads up high above, but in the gap that separates the yard-wide stalks there seems to hang a thicker darkness, a cessation of the starry fog ... Maurice still has one hand – appendage? flipper? – resting on the stripling's back, and as he leans in to confide, he has a funny smell ... his voice now fifty houseflies in a jam jar ... 'Look, I know it's rough the first time, when you haven't got the hang of the perichoresis yet, but you go and see Awstin, like the Ras Prince told you. He'll look after you. Now, nothing I'd like better than to stand around and natter' ... unobtrusively he's guiding Dennis closer to the patch of abdicated twilight, the black absence in the scintillation ... 'but I'll have to leave you here and get back to my Upper Beak Street lodgings in Soho Entire, or else there'll be a lot of mess. Perhaps I'll see you in a month or two's time, but I won't be me then. It's just how I am. Good luck with all this, Knuckleyard. Just watch out for the anamorphic spasms,' and with that, Maurice shoves Dennis forward ... taken by surprise, he trips face first into the dark framed by the monstrous shoots ... except they're not there any more, it's all – what's happening? – all gone, the scents and sounds abruptly gone, the whole place gone, he's falling, and the next thing that he knows*

he was on all fours, knees against hard London pavement in the middle of the night, and he burst into tears.

He was chock-full of words, names, pictures and sensations that he couldn't possibly begin to fathom; didn't even know what order the events had happened in, as with a half-remembered dream. He was in pieces, all the certainties of who and where he was gone down into a terrifying quicksand of incomprehension. The eighteen-year-old's attempts towards an adult personality that functioned in the world had come to bits like tissue paper, and so had the world itself. Nothing in existence was what he'd assumed it was, and Dennis grovelled weeping on a street he didn't recognise, carrier bag in one hand and the Reverend Thomas Hampole's double-damned book in the other.

Gradually, a little at a time, the city that he knew came back to him, dark where the other place was starlit, cold where it appeared to have no temperature at all. He heard the purr of motor traffic from not far away, and somewhere near were intermittent voices raised in drunken jollity, with none of these sounds spiralling into the aviary trills and echoes of his just-concluded elsewhere. Something had just happened for which he'd no words, no language except snot and crying. One with the shell-shocked metropolis around him, Dennis had been in the wars.

Posed like a dog amongst the senseless fragments of himself, he sniffed and snivelled, distantly aware of a reverberant and rhythmic tapping that seemed to be getting louder, drawing closer through the backstreet gloom. Pik-pok-pik-pok-pik, then a hesitation, then pik-pok-pik-pok-pik-pok and, finally, 'Where did you come from?'

Lifting a big head that felt too heavy for his neck, he tried to focus welling eyes – the left one difficult to open for some reason – on the source of the enquiring voice, female and unfamiliar, although in his present circumstances everything was unfamiliar. It was a young woman, unlit save for stray rays from a lamppost further up the street, which were nevertheless sufficient to set off the molten metal of her hair. He groaned and recognised the gorgeous streetwalker that he'd met, Jesus, was it only yesterday? He dimly understood that he must be in Bride Lane, evidently the girl's pitch, and now someone he'd hopelessly and briefly fancied was stood watching him while he sobbed like a little kid. He didn't feel like Winston Smith or Harry Lime. He didn't even feel like Dennis Knuckleyard. Abject and wretched, he gazed up at her through lenses made of quivering brine.

'N–nowhere. I ... I don't know. I don't know.'

Adjusting to the light, he saw that she was frowning now in puzzlement. She crouched down to his eye level and studied him more closely. Fleetingly, irrelevantly, he believed her upraised knees to be the loveliest he'd ever seen. She managed to maintain her calm, investigative tone, though he could tell that this was not without some effort.

'I walked down here not two minutes back, to stretch my legs, and there was nobody about. Now here you are. Have you been in a fight?'

He didn't know. Had he been in a fight? Had he received blows to the head that would explain all this? Why had she asked that question? Did he look as if he'd just been beaten up?

'It's just there's claret all over your mush. You've got a cut above your eyebrow.'

Dennis lifted one hand questioningly to his forehead, where the fingers came back wet and sticky. That, he thought, explained why he'd had trouble opening his eye: it was the red glue. But how had it happened? Picking mystified through the kicked-over jigsaw of his recent memories, he managed to say, 'No. No, not a fight. It was a sort of … silver paper, it just, it just flew at me. I didn't …', before realising what he sounded like and lapsing once more into racking sobs.

Judiciously, the girl stood up, perhaps attempting not to startle him with any sudden movements, straightening her skirt as she took a step back. He sensed that, in her estimation, he was shifting from pathetic to possibly dangerous, but there was nothing he could do to salvage things. His head was full of wildlife, foreign objects that he had nowhere to put. Making the situation worse, there were now other people in the nearby night – an old chap puffing down the street's far side, walking his dog, with a young couple giggling up the other way – and Dennis knew that him and the slowly withdrawing redhead must make quite a sight, or at least he must, on his knees and roaring; a big, shabby baby. He was bringing her the last sort of attention that someone in her profession wanted, and could hear increasing distance in her voice as she began to disengage.

'Yeah, well, long as you've not been set on. You should take more care, chum.'

Then it was pik-pok-pik-pok-pik-pok as she turned and walked back up the lane, presumably to once more take her place beside the lamp across the street from St Bride's churchyard. She was the sole human thing that he'd had contact with since Tolerable John had exited the Cheshire Cheese, and she was leaving him alone here with his mouth full of perichoresis, vividistricts, Fisbo openings and silver-paper dragonflies. More desperate not to be alone with his unutterable experience than he was to seem manly, Dennis called into the widening dark between them.

'Was it like net curtains?'

85

Pik-pok-pik … the girl stopped and turned back towards him. 'What did you just say?'

He himself barely knew, and much less why he'd said it. Probably it was because he'd started to associate the churchyard up the road with the glass sculpture from his fit, the contoured soap bubble that stood amongst floral immensities. In the strewn fragments of his hurricane-hit recollection, he was sure that it connected to something she'd said the previous day.

'The thing you said you'd seen. Was it net curtains, but all white and shining?'

For long seconds, silence reigned and then, unhurriedly, pik … pok … pik … pok … pik … pok. She stood there looking down, directly between Dennis and the uphill streetlamp, hands deep in her pockets, face unreadable in shadow, hair a copper halo.

'What's the book?'

Taken aback, he looked from her down to *A London Walk*, then quickly stuffed the grubby volume back into his carrier bag, exactly, he belatedly reflected, as a mad person would do.

'I, I, I, I can't tell you. I'm, I'm not allowed. It's better you don't know about it, to be honest. It, it, it's a lot of trouble.'

Once more, a protracted pause ensued while she considered this, surveying Dennis in his bloody, babbling wreckage and perhaps concluding that the book might indeed be a lot of trouble. Sighing in an admixture of resignation and annoyance, she crouched down again and skewered him with a gaze that brooked no argument.

'Listen to what I'm telling you. In my coat pocket, on a bunch of keys, there's one that isn't any use for opening doors, and that's because I've had it sharpened. If you ever get ideas – and, looking at you, I'll admit that isn't very likely – but, still, if you ever should, then you must understand I'm going to put your eye out. Am I making myself clear?'

He nodded vigorously, anxious to convince her he was in his right mind, but then spoiling the effect by telling her she was as clear as Christmas when he'd meant as clear as crystal. She stood up.

'And yes, it was net curtains, and they were all white and shin-ing. That's the reason why I'm doing this. It's not because you've got a winning smile or lovely personality: it's the net curtains.'

She extended a surprisingly small hand, empty of weapons, down towards him.

'Right, then. Pull yourself together. I'm Grace Shilling, and you're coming home with me.'

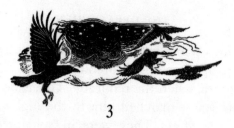

## 3

## *Catshit Manor*

In an otherwise deserted ladies' lav off Cannon Street, his irritated saviour insisted Dennis rinse off all the juice from what, as it turned out, had been a relatively minor cut, turning the water in the chipped handbasin pink like dentists' mouthwash. 'You're not going anywhere with blood all dripping off you. It draws sharks and coppers.' Patting himself dry, he looked up from a gory paper towel into the basin's mirror and, for a few seconds, found he couldn't properly identify with his own face, which briefly seemed a thing that he just happened to be wearing, eyes as blank as buttons.

When he was halfway presentable, they carried on towards the east across a punch-drunk city. Her hair shaped and shaken by the wind, the woman was a candle leading him along Threadneedle Street, its rearing bank masking profound anxieties behind an imperturbable façade, the same as everybody else. They wandered up the murky swim of Bishopsgate, still relatively populous despite the hour, and in amongst the lighted boozers and the home-bound market trade, she took him by his carrier-free arm. This was presumably to make them look more like a couple and thus less conspicuous, but it also allowed her to propel her rescued stray in the correct direction with a firm and even painful grip on Dennis's protuberant elbow. In the big dark overhead, he was surprised by how few stars there were, when normally he marvelled at how many.

Other than occasional sharp words from his short-tempered escort, they continued up the main road without conversation, of which Dennis was as yet incapable. He'd just begun to worry that they were approaching Shoreditch, where Ada had said he shouldn't venture, when the redhead – Grace, he thought she'd said her name was – marched him to the highway's other side and into Folgate Street. They were in Spitalfields, tall houses piling up the Leather Apron shadows to each side, cropping the panoramic night above them to constricted rectangles; making the lanes human canals, deep cuttings silted up by history. As it transpired, at Folgate Street's far end she'd got a ground-floor flat, which they were forced to enter by the means of panto-mime and Grace's mouthed instructions to avoid protesting floorboards in the hall. She didn't want the neighbours thinking she was bringing business home, even if Dennis didn't look like anyone's idea of business.

Her accommodation was three small rooms, but these smelled safe, and of her. They both removed their coats, and when she kicked her shoes off and lost some three inches in the process, Dennis felt still more ungainly by comparison. He perched on her settee, all knees and cranial bristle, while she made them each a cup of tea before she joined him there. Although his mug was cracked and ringed with tannin, he gulped down its over-sugared contents gratefully and, within minutes, it was like he'd had a blood transfusion. Vivid green eyes tracked his every movement.

'Have you got a name, or should I just keep thinking of you as "the liability"?'

He glanced at her resignedly before returning his attention to the tidelined teacup.

'Yeah, I'm, uh, I'm Dennis. Dennis Knuckleyard.'

He waited for the scorn and incredulity, but all she did was raise a pencilled eyebrow and say, 'Hm. Well, that's a useful name.' Taken aback by the word useful where he'd been expecting stupid, Dennis didn't think to ask her what she'd meant. The comment hadn't sounded sarky, and he thought that he might even count it as a sort of compliment. Grace took ten Craven 'A' from her slumped handbag, and the packet's mascot cat head, black on red, became immediately elegant in her white fingers. Lighting up, she plumed a writhing salamander of blue haze so exquisite it almost made him take up smoking on the spot, and narrowed her viridian gaze to an interrogator's lamp.

'So, Dennis Knuckleyard, what do you know about net curtains?'

Dennis ducked his head and rubbed the back of his neck absently, against the shaven grain. She looked so warm, had such a vitalising presence, and he genuinely didn't want her to end up the wrong way out. He told her what he could.

'It's like … I think I've got myself mixed up in something horrible by being told things, and I don't want to land you in the same boat. So if I miss bits out, it's not that I don't want to tell you; it's that I don't dare. Are you alright with that?' She pulled upon her cigarette and nodded. He went on. 'The only reason I'm involved in this, it's all to do with where I work, at Lowell's Books & Magazines just up the road in Shoreditch. Anyway, we had this book turn up …'

He trailed off, noticing that she already offered an expression of affronted disbelief before he'd told her anything at all unusual.

'Wait a minute. Lowell's Books, that's Coffin Ada Benson's place. You work for her? Someone told me she'd had six blokes buried alive in her backyard.'

Astonished and appalled, he gaped. Had everybody known of Ada's homicidal history except for him? He struggled for an adequate response, but all that he could manage was, 'What I heard, it was just the one,' realising once he'd said it that this wasn't much of a defence, for either him or his employer. Grace now had an element of wariness in her regard, but indicated that he should continue with his narrative. Clearing his throat, Dennis began again.

'We got this book in a job lot. It looked like rubbish, but it really put the wind up Ada. She said it was, well, not cursed exactly, but as good as. Said I'd got to get it back to where it came from before something awful happened, but I didn't, and it did: the chap I bought it off, I showed up at his place in Soho right when they were loading him on to the morgue truck. There were scuffers everywhere. Someone had done him in, and later I found out that it had been over the book. There were these criminals who'd heard about what it could do and wanted it themselves, like something from *Dick Barton*. This must sound as if I'm making it all up.'

She nodded, stubbing out her fag in half a bivalve that appeared to have washed up on the unsteady coffee table's wood veneer, an estuary memento.

'Yeah, it does, but then I've never known a story about Coffin Ada that was anywhere near plausible. So, when you say these crooks had heard what it could do, then what was that, exactly? What can this book do, apart from frightening Ada Benson?'

Dennis scrutinised her pale lavender wallpaper, held up with tacks where it was peeling, and tried hard to think of something he could safely tell her.

'Well, it … it comes from a place that's sort of special, and perhaps these people think the book is going to get them in there, like a ticket to the pictures. I don't know. All I know is, I've had a run in with it, and it's not for me. It's making me a nervous wreck, so that I'm all on edge and seeing things. You know what I was like in Bride Lane. I'm not like that all the time, I promise.'

She considered this. Pushing the sleeves of the grey jumper she'd had on beneath the raincoat to her elbows, she rose from the couch and fetched a teapot to top up their mugs before replying.

'I believe you. I should hope there's nobody who's like that all the time, but what's it got to do with my net curtains? When you said that you'd been seeing things …'

The idea of hallucinations offered him a way to speak of his experience that was nearly rational, and Dennis clutched it with both hands.

'That was one of the things I thought I saw, a length of gauze floating a few feet off the ground, shining like headlights. I was, you know, I was somewhere near the churchyard when it happened, so I thought it might be what you'd seen as well. It's stuff I'm not supposed to mention. I can only tell you that its name is "Her Train", but I don't know what that means. And it likes poetry, apparently, although I can't see how when it's a curtain. That's the lot. That's all I know about it.'

Grace leaned back on the settee to stare at the blank white ceiling while she thought this over. When eventually she tipped her burning copper head once more in Dennis's direction, she was wearing what appeared to be at least the run-up to a smile.

'I like the sound of that – "Her Train". So, that would be connected with Saint Bride, like it's a bridal train or something, yeah? That's poetry, in my book. Too poetic for someone called Knuckleyard to have invented, anyway. You're not having me on, I don't think. You seem fairly harmless, and that's the best hard-luck story that I've heard in donkey's years. What are you going to do, though, about all this mess you're in, this business that you can't tell anyone about? Is there somebody who could help you, where you live?'

He shook his head.

'She said I shouldn't go back while all this is going on. I live at Coffin Ada's.'

'Fucking hell.'

'I know. And as for what I'm going to do, I haven't got the foggiest. That book's the main thing. I'm supposed to take it back to somewhere in this other place, but now I've seen a bit of it, I don't know how that's possible. I've had some, well, some funny customers who've offered me advice, but nothing that I can make head nor tail of. I had that black chap, the tipster, Monolulu. He came up to me in Berwick Street, like he knew what was going on, and gave me something that turned out to be … here, you can see it if you like. I don't think it's forbidden.'

Dennis rummaged in his carrier bag, once more avoiding contact with the cloth-covered catastrophe that was the Hampole volume, and retrieved the envelope that held the racing forecast cards. His hostess took it from him, but did not immediately look at it, keeping her eyes on him instead. The frown was back, and what had looked like the beginnings of a smile quickly evaporated.

'Hang on. You're telling me that the most famous black bloke in the country gave you this, out of the blue, and that he somehow knows about this trouble that you're in? I've got to say, you're not making it any easier believing all this, are you? I mean, seriously, Prince Monolulu?'

He shrugged helplessly, and spread his hands.

'It's just what happened. I was … I was in a different life when I woke up this morning, then it all fell in on top of me. I've had a really funny day.' It was the best he could come up with.

Grace regarded him for a few moments, undecided, then turned to the item resting in her lap. She took the small manila envelope out of the larger white one and pouted incredulously at the words SURREALIST RACING FORECAST CARDS before removing and examining the cards themselves. She flipped one over, then another, and the distrust trickled gradually from her face as if suspicion were a liquid. While she studied the array of images, squinting and leaning close to trace their smouldering contours, Grace's features lapsed into a childlike wonderment that caused Dennis to once more ask himself how old he thought she was. Older than him, judging by her voice, her bearing and her manner, but not too much older. Perhaps twenty-one or twenty-two? Eventually, she tore her gaze free from the pasteboard oracles and looked back up at him.

'I've not seen anybody draw like this before. The way he does a line, it's like he's winding wool, like he's gone off into a trance and taken everybody with him. What's his name?'

She sounded as if she knew something about art, and Dennis felt pleased with himself that, on this one occasion, he could make out he knew something, too.

'It's this chap Spare, who lives across in Brixton. My mate John, he made me think I should perhaps go over there and see if he can help me. Someone … someone else I met suggested the same thing. I wasn't sure if he was joking or not, but John told me – Austin, that's the artist's first name, Austin Spare – that people say he's a magician.'

Brushing flames of hair out of her eyes, a gesture that he could have watched all day, Grace took a last look at the cards before replacing them in their two envelopes and handing them to Dennis, who returned them to his carrier-cum-albatross. She lit another cigarette and then responded.

'A magician. Well, I dare say I've heard stranger things, although they're mostly things I've heard from you this evening. He's a smashing artist, though, there's no gainsaying it. Alright. You'll probably turn out to be a bloody nuisance, but at least you're interesting. If you've nowhere else to go, you can stop here until you've sorted yourself out. I shouldn't mind it, either, if you took your mate's advice and went to see this Spare chap down in Brixton. Even if he wasn't any help to you, I'd like to find out more about him. You do that tomorrow and I'll look upon it as your contribution to the rent.'

Accepting her conditions without hesitation, Dennis babbled his relief and gratitude, while she reminded him about the sharpened key. They both relaxed a little after that, with Grace putting a match to a malodorous paraffin stove, much alleviating the October chill. She asked if he'd had anything to eat, then took him through into her tiny kitchen where she made them both a cheese and onion omelette with some bread and butter, chatting tersely as she served it up in two enamel dishes. Wolfing it down ravenously, mouth too full to talk, he learned that she'd been an evacuee, one of the kids packed off to somewhere outside London during the hostilities. There were still thousands of them, four years after the war finished, that had not been reunited with their homes and families. Sometimes this would be because their old homes were no longer standing, or because their parents had been either killed or were too hard up to accept their children back.

Grace was in the first category. Placed with a couple up in rural Derbyshire and suffering the unwanted attentions of the husband, she'd absconded back to a gutted metropolis during the war's concluding weeks, only to find that Mum and Dad and house had all been taken from her by a buzz bomb. For a time, she'd slept rough – public lavatories, blitzed churches, an abandoned car – surviving on what she could pinch from shops or washing lines. Dennis supposed she would have been sixteen or seventeen when this was going on. Inevitably, Grace had learned from observation what the best employment option was for girls without resources and, reluctantly, had cut her life to suit the cloth. By her account, she'd done alright: she'd managed to get by without a ponce or a protector, which was hardly easy but was how a lot of women on the game preferred to handle things. Not a majority, by any means, but a fair few. She'd stopped at fleabag lodging houses until there was cash put by to rent her Spitalfields accommodation, and now here she was. She thought that one day she might like to be an actress, or a dancer. Having by this point devoured his omelette, Dennis interjected that he one day hoped to be a secret agent, and Grace told him to grow up.

Before she went to bed, she fetched him a plaid blanket so he could sleep doubled up on her settee, instructing Dennis to augment it with his raincoat if he got too cold after she turned the paraffin stove off. She had a duplicate front door key for the next day in case he got back from Brixton before she was home, and told him there was a communal bathroom on the upstairs landing, but that, rather than alert her neighbours, he'd be better pissing in the kitchen sink. Leaving a shaded table lamp to see by, she informed him, quite unnecessarily in his opinion, that she slept with her upsetting keyring underneath her pillow, and, with that, she wished him a good night.

He was too full of unfamiliar voltage to consider sleeping straight away, and couldn't close his eyes without commencing footage of a rush down avenues impossible, dragged in the wake of an expanding Maurice Calendar. Wishing he had something to read that at the very least might bore him into an unconscious state, he suddenly recalled the Machen book that Ada had suggested he peruse, *The Cosy Room*, currently nestling in his carrier bag beside *A London Walk*. Thinking that he could do with a stout pair of tongs, he gingerly removed the Rich & Cowan first edition from its brown paper container and flicked to the story that his landlady had recommended, the ambiguously titled 'N'.

At first, he struggled with what he perceived as stuffiness in the tale's presentation, although by the time he'd read a page or two, the burnish of its language and its atmospherics had seduced him. It appeared to be about a group of genial if quarrelsome old friends, who'd met to reminisce upon the vanished London of their youth over a glass or two of steaming punch. By turn avuncular and argumentative, they bickered over the supposed existence of a paradisiacal area in Stoke Newington called Canon's Park, a rumoured place without the least shred of supporting evidence.

It was a yarn told in five parts, and Dennis only reached the third of these before his skin began to crawl. A short way down its opening page there was the following: ' ... he chanced to light on a shabby brown book on his untidy shelves ... It was called *A London Walk: Meditations in the Streets of the Metropolis*. The author was the Reverend Thomas Hampole, and the book was dated 1853.' Shooting a nervous glance towards his string-handled receptacle, Dennis read further. The remainder of that third instalment was a lengthy passage quoted from the Reverend Hampole's tome, in which the amiable clergyman put forward an unorthodox philosophy. Hampole maintained that a more absolute reality endured behind the flimsy scenery of the material world, made out of nothing save 'Heavenly Chaos', with the reverend providing a supporting anecdote that seemingly referred to the Stoke Newington location recently debated by the story's bibulous and tetchy colleagues.

Grace's lamplit living room acquired a pall of gathering unease, and shadows that he wasn't used to. Now regretting his poor choice of bedtime literature, he persevered through the remaining sections of the narrative to its finale. Though increasingly unnerved, Dennis discovered he could still appreciate the cautious and oblique way in which Machen edged around his

startling subject matter – his conception of the human realm
as a mere safety curtain, a dilapidated rag, threadbare in places,
that was pulled across a more substantial world. 'N''s penulti-
mate episode had one of the punch-quaffing comrades spend
an evening in a tavern known as the King of Jamaica, where
the working men he drank with offered further confirmation
of the liminal Stoke Newington address. This led to a concluding chapter where the querulous companions were once more
assembled, with one of the comrades, Arnold, now convinced
by his experience that the elusive Eden of Stoke Newington
existed, while his fellows seemed unshaken in their scepticism.
And then Dennis reached the story's closing lines, where Arnold
succinctly summed up his comprehension of events: 'I believe
that there is a perichoresis, an interpenetration. It is possible,
indeed, that we three are now sitting among desolate rocks, by
bitter streams ... And with what companions?'

Dennis closed *The Cosy Room* and dropped it back into the
carrier without looking, not wanting to even see the Hampole
book by this point. He took off his jacket, tiptoeing into the
claustrophobic kitchen where he urinated quietly into the sink,
then ran the tap for a few seconds until he felt less uncivilised.
Arranging blanket, coat and jacket on the truncated settee,
he took his shoes off and then slipped beneath the makeshift
bedding, folding his long body into an uncomfortable Z-posture
on the too short couch. The word 'perichoresis' from the tale's
conclusion was embedded in his skittering thoughts where it
resounded disconcertingly, partly because he didn't know its
meaning, partly because he was sure that Maurice Calendar
had used it. As exhaustion wrapped its heavy arms around him,
Dennis reached out to click off the table lamp and told himself
he hadn't understood the Machen story, while remaining fearful
that he had. Eventually, he slept.

The unexpected sun slapped him awake into a room he didn't
know and an immediate spill of non-specific dread. Prising apart

sleep-lacquered lids, he noticed first a single filament of red-gold hair shed on the nearer arm of the settee, prompting a memory of Grace – Grace Shilling, had she said? – and where he was. His gaze next lighted on the carrier bag, which explained and identified the dread.

Uncramping himself, he sat up, deducing from the timbre of the silence that he was the only person in the ground-floor flat and possibly in the whole house. He'd evidently slept for longer than he meant to, and his wary rescuer had no doubt already gone out to get on with her day. She must have dressed and breakfasted while making a considerable effort not to wake the drooling stranger on her couch, which Dennis found both touching and embarrassing. When he was relatively confident that none of Grace's neighbours were at home, he crept upstairs and found the bathroom that she'd mentioned, treating himself to a brisk cold-water wash and brush-up before darting furtively back to the rooms below. Lacking her presence, these seemed without use or meaning, like deserted stage sets when the characters and dialogue were somewhere else. Putting his jacket, shoes and coat on, Dennis tidied up as best he could, which is to say he left his blanket neatly folded at one end of the settee, and once more ran the tap in Grace's kitchen sink, just to be sure. Hefting his carrier bag and pocketing the house key he'd been trusted with, he walked out into Folgate Street and Wednesday.

Spitalfields hunched scarred brick shoulders, unimpressed by the surprise deluge of sunlight, and corralled the district's ingrained blackness into narrow, overshadowed lanes where dark could loiter until nightfall. Dennis winced and squinted his way down Commercial Street, past the uproarious market and the church with tongues of soot licking its corpse-white flanks, to find himself a cheerfully dishevelled café that appeared too recent to have fried an egg for Jack the Ripper. Here he gloried in a robust sausage sandwich – slabs of fresh bread, soft and baked to flaking umber at the edges, soaking up the hot grease of the bangers – washed down with a cup of tea he knocked back scalding hot, for the astringency. Asking the undernourished waitress for a second cup that he could linger over, he gazed worriedly into its cloudy depths and tried to think about his situation, quickly realising that both the thinking and the situation were impossible. He had a mob of gangsters after him, and he was either stumbling into something supernatural or he was going mad. He was about to go south of the river, all the way to Brixton, seeking a magician who'd been recommended by a famously eccentric racing tipster. Everything about his life and circumstances was, it seemed to him, unbearably precarious.

When he was halfway through the beverage, Dennis was struck by something that he recognised, despite the rarity of the phenomenon, to be a sensible idea: if he was heading into danger, he should have someone with a degree of influence who understood about his problems and could maybe intervene if things went haywire. Tolerable John had said already that he didn't want to be involved, but there was Clive, Clive Amery, in many ways Dennis's hero, brimming with capability, connected to the legal system, and thus perfect as a second or a safety net. No sooner had the name occurred to him than a bright shaft of hope broke through his cloudbank of anxieties, bringing a sense of reassurance, albeit tentatively, that he'd not allowed himself to feel in days. He finished his tea hurriedly, and knew somehow that this decision would make an enormous difference to the way that his predicament played out. Buoyed by a sudden optimism, he paid up and exited the café after asking for a pocket-dragging weight of copper pennies with his change.

He rattled back along Commercial Street to the fire-blackened church, and squeezed into a phone box that stood to one side of its intimidating portico. Inside, the oblong stack of stale air had a modern, plastic smell that was betrayed by undertones of toilet, and the huge directory was slumped and dog-eared like a decomposing tree stump. Turning the thin pages, Dennis searched his recollection for the law firm where Clive worked, looking for Dolden, Green, Dorland & Lockart before he remembered this had been another company; one that he'd simply noticed in Clive's notepad. Finally, his intermittently astute unconscious

mind supplied the name Jessop & Wilks, whose number he found
easily after his long and pointless Dolden dead end. Dialling, he
experienced an obscure satisfaction in the rapid clicking as the
dial rotated back to zero after every digit.

When somebody picked up the receiver at the other end, a
beeping was commenced that carried on until sufficient sweaty
pennies had been crammed into the dented slot. A woman's voice
announced the company name in an enquiring tone, and Dennis
asked her if Sir Dennis Compton-Knuckleyard could have a
word with Mr Amery. When Clive answered the phone on his
extension line some moments later, he already sounded cheerfully amused by this uncalled-for interruption to his working day.

'Lord Oxydol! Well, what an unexpected pleasure to receive a
call from you. Do say that it's about my knighthood.'

Dennis laughed. He wasn't used to telephones, and always
marvelled at the closeness they permitted with somebody who
was miles away; more so than with someone in the same room,
where there was not that sense of intimations whispered, crackling, into his ear.

'Yeah, well, I asked my mate, the Duke of Persil, but he said it
wouldn't wash. Look, Clive, I'm sorry about calling you at work.
It's just, I've got myself mixed up in something that's a bit peculiar, and I wanted you to know about it in case anything should
happen. So that you could, you know, keep an eye out for me.
I'm not living up at Ada's any more, so I'm more or less on my
own, now.'

'My dear boy, you know I always like to keep an eye out for
you working-class types. That's why I've still got my watch and
cufflinks. What exactly are you on about?'

Out through the smeared panes of the phone box, Dennis
watched a red-faced tramp with chimney-brush hair weaving
through the weeds and bird-soiled slabs of the adjacent churchyard, trying to escape the unaccustomed dazzle. He told Clive
what he was on about, though not exactly

'I can't tell you everything, but there's this secret part of
London hardly anybody knows is there. I've had a gang of villains

after me, who want an introduction to this place, and ... Oh. Hang on.'

The pips were sounding, so he forced more coins into the slot before resuming.

'What I've done, I've blundered into something that's important, and I'm trying to blunder my way out again. I'm just about to go across to Brixton, where I'm told there's this chap who could help me. Wynne Road's where he lives. You'll laugh, but it's one of the books that I had in my Oxydol box that's kicked all this off. I've got to get it back to where it came from, in this, well, this different part of London that I said about. I know this all sounds crackers, but if I can meet up with you soon, I'll tell you the whole story then. I just need somebody who's got their head screwed on, to talk it over with. I might be through the worst of it by Friday, so I could call into Bond's again when you were on your lunch break, if that sounds alright?'

'Dennis, it sounds absolutely bloody fascinating, mate. I always knew that you had hidden depths, and now here you are on the run from criminals and telling me about some terribly exclusive part of London, curtained off from public scrutiny. Right up my street! Much as I hate to say this to a scruffy Bolshevik such as yourself, I'm quite impressed, young Knuckleyard. Make that very impressed. You've got an enviable capacity for getting yourself into interesting trouble, and I'm going to be all ears on Friday. Shall we say just after one o'clock?'

Relieved, Dennis had time to babble his agreement, gratitude and rushed farewells before the pips sounded again and he replaced the plastic barbell in its cradle. As he shouldered open the phone box's heavy door to step once more into the morning shout of Spitalfields, he realised that he felt OK, despite the bruisers, books and bedlam visions. The brief chat with Clive had put him into a much better frame of mind. It wasn't so much that the call had made him any safer – Clive's involvement wasn't going to stop somebody shooting Dennis in an alleyway – but more that Clive had been impressed by what was going on. That meant a lot. Dennis didn't impress people very often, and especially not people he looked up to. The young barrister's admiring tone made Dennis's ordeal seem more like an adventure; an outlandish string of anecdotes he could show off to Clive when they met up, the day after tomorrow. Greatly reinvigorated, he strode through the dirty sunlit bustle of Commercial Street, heading for Aldgate and Tower Bridge, seeking the wet wound of the Thames.

The sun went in as Dennis reached the iron river's further side, reminding him and everybody else that it was still October, and that any sheen of optimism could be suddenly withdrawn by no more than a whim of meteorology. He hoofed it all the way to Elephant and Castle – a corruption of Infanta de Castile, if he remembered right – then got the bus down Kennington Park Road and into Brixton.

Some distance along the Brixton Road he thought he spotted Wynne Road running off from the main artery, out through the streaky porthole that he'd rubbed in the bus window's condensation with his coat sleeve. Snatching up his carrier bag, he hurried from his seat to the rear platform, but the juddering vehicle did not present an opportunity for Dennis to alight until it slowed for its next stop, at least a quarter-mile past his intended destination. He walked back up the dejected thoroughfare to where he might have seen the turning, gathering his first impressions of the famously dilapidated district as he went. With grimy buildings clinging to existence beside pulverised expanses that had given up the struggle, it looked pretty much the same to him as every other part of London; no worse and no better. He supposed that bombs were, unsurprisingly, great levellers.

Nor did the Brixton faces he encountered seem more destitute or more dispirited than those found in the streets of Shoreditch. Flowing past him on the cracked grey pavement were the same aggrieved young husbands who'd been demobbed into dustmen, the same stout old widows who'd lost family in two world wars and wore their burst blood vessels like a cheaper rouge;

the mouths all creased by poverty, the eyes all bloody-minded in their fierce determination to get through it. Looking at the almost monochrome parade about him, it occurred to Dennis that the English coped with deprivation by reworking misery into a ragged-arse mythology. They shared a fag with Gracie Fields on Mother Kelly's doorstep or they dossed with Flanagan and Allen underneath the arches. They all lived in songs, in radio catchphrases, in skits from the few films they'd seen, and there they found a sentimental heroism that might keep them warm through this long economic winter. With an application of ferocious will, they turned their itchy coats to ermine.

The one novelty he sighted, something that he'd never seen in Shoreditch, was a pair of coloured chaps stood talking by a bombsite just past Stockwell Road, most probably a couple of the ones who had come over from Jamaica on that boat, three or four months ago. He felt a bit let down, childishly disappointed by their failure to be exotic. Obviously, he hadn't been expecting the cartoon theatrics of a Monolulu, but he'd thought his first West Indians would be more – he didn't know – more tropical or something in their dress and their demeanour, throwing back their heads to laugh and wearing bright fruit-salad tunics. Instead, the two men were clad in what was practically Great Britain's national costume: white shirts under poorly fitting black suits from a second-hand shop; shoes last worn by somebody's dead uncle. Their discourse was urgent, and they both, if anything, looked cold and worried. Nobody was laughing.

Wynne Road, just a little further up, turned out to be a sorry corridor of terrace houses that was at least mercifully brief if going door to door proved necessary. Luckily, it didn't: Dennis asked a passing matron with a shopping basket full of tripe and trotters if she'd heard about an artist living somewhere in the street, at which she gave a throaty laugh of recognition.

'Oh, you're looking for old Spare, then, are yer? 'e's with Millie Pain at number five. You want to watch out he don't turn you into summat nasty with 'is voodoo and what have yer. 'e's a proper warlock – or what's left o' one, at any rate. Don't tell 'im as I said that.'

Evidently cheered by their exchange, the offal-bearing woman was still bubbling with phlegmy chuckles as she went on with her outing, leaving Dennis to find number five amongst the battered residences listing there beneath a blank white sky.

Despite stiff competition, it was easily the most defeated-looking dwelling in the terrace, with slates missing from its roof and a residual dampness in the lower courses of its brickwork. The ill-fitting door and window frames suggested ongoing subsidence, while the paving slabs outside were partially concealed by pigeon shit in constellated starbursts and, as well, by three dishevelled cats. They paced, and mewed in alternating tones of pleading and complaint, emaciated strays with matted tails or tattered ears. Dennis was forced to lean across these scabby sentinels in order to knock on the door, and when a tall and pallid woman answered, the malnourished trio flowed into the house around her ankles, only giving way to a quartet of other felines who were coming through the portal in the opposite direction. One of these escapees, a grotesquely wrinkled grey thing with sour lemon eyes, was possibly the ugliest living creature that he'd ever seen. Seemingly unconcerned by the flea-bitten tide about her slippered feet, the lanky female stared at Dennis slightly too long before saying, 'Yes?'

She seemed to be in her late fifties, her eyes big and watery, her chin small and receding, although probably a pretty enough woman in her day. She wore what looked like a long picnic frock from an entirely different era, with a much-darned navy cardigan on top of it and a loose noose of several beaded necklaces descending to her waist. There was a rumour of pink lipstick circling the mouth and absolute indifference in the glistening oyster eyes. Intimidated, Dennis swallowed hard.

'Sorry to bother you. I'm looking for an artist chap called Austin Spare. I wondered if—'

She shook her grey bob almost imperceptibly, her features still immobile.

'I'm afraid that Mr Spare isn't receiving any visitors at present.'

Seeing that she was about to close the poorly hanging door, he blurted desperately that the reclusive artist had been recommended to him by Prince Monolulu, at whose name the woman's slightly hyperthyroid eyes rolled heavenward. She exhaled down her nose and made a tutting noise. Returning a by-now-resigned gaze to her gawky caller, she said, 'Please wait here' in an annoyed tone, before drifting off over the hallway's worn-out carpeting towards the house's rear. Reaching the passage's far end, she turned a corner and was out of sight – albeit still jarringly audible – as she shouted to someone, in a different voice to the polite delivery she'd used with Dennis.

'Awstin? Awstin, there's a feller here to see yer.'

The response was gravelly and muffled. It was hard to tell where it was coming from.

'Well, tell 'im I'm not 'ere.'

'He says that Monolulu sent him.'

An extended pause.

'Ah, fuck. I s'pose you better send 'im down, then. Bloody Monolulu.'

Stepping once more into view, the woman glided back along the shadow-crowded passage, drooping hoops of necklace rattling in the half-light. 'Mr Spare says that he'll entertain you in his studio. It's up the hallway's other end, then downstairs on your right.' She nodded her clearly unwanted guest inside and then, while he was briefly turned away to pull the front door shut behind him, seemingly evaporated with a fading clink and clatter into the surrounding murk. Alone in empty silence, Dennis made his way up the benighted channel, nostrils flinching at the heavy and dispiriting perfume of damp. This wasn't the accommodation where he'd pictured a magician living, or an artist, or, well, anybody really. At the hall's furthest extremity, from a cramped alcove to the right, what seemed to be a cellar door hung halfway open on to brick-and-mortar steps,

descending into seeping artificial brightness. Having no alter-
native, he climbed down apprehensively into the underworld,
uncertain of his footing, on the chipped stairs or in any other
sense.

Reaching the bottom, shoulders zebra-striped by powdered
whitewash from the stairway walls, he was stopped in his
tracks by the impossible minuteness of the subterranean realm
that waited for him: barely six-foot square, it was a cube of
compressed energy and cold air, buried at the claustrophobic
centre of the world. A tiny cellar window in the far wall had
been boarded up, placing the burden of illumination on a sixty-
watt bulb, dangling and bare, that drizzled only a thin sediment
of light. The failing radiance, browning like old fruit or heir-
loom photographs, settled in sepia dust upon the room's two
chairs, both piled with newspapers; upon a roughed-up chest
with all its drawers jammed open by protruding tins and imple-
ments; upon the squirming undergrowth of imagery propped
up against the sides of the enclosure, glowering from canvas, card
or radio circuit board; upon a nude stone floor that swam with
cats; upon the spindly easel where the man was standing.

With his back towards the cellar steps, the artist was positioned
only inches from the tacked-up paper portrait he was worrying with a pastel crayon, perhaps leaning in to see his picture
adequately in the useless light, or else without the floor space
to step back. He wore an indoor raincoat, old shoes that were
separating slowly into their component parts, his hair exploding out in grey parabolas of smoke as if from a direct hit by a
V-bomb. Neither sturdy nor yet tall – possibly five-nine or five-
ten – he was a figure built from dust who nonetheless filled the
small room to bursting with the thrumming pylon of his presence, this before he turned and spoke.

'And 'oo are you, when you're at 'ome?'

The voice was granular and crunchy, like a walk through
cinders, and the face was unforgettable: cheeks hollowed
by rear molars fallen out, rain-coloured skin where he'd not
shaven, mouth a crumpled and mistrustful pen stroke and then,

underneath a knotted forehead, the twin outlets of a white-hot furnace. A depleted body, dressed in a raincoat, old tweed jacket, jumper, shirt, vest, all its clothes at once, and held up only by magnesium-flare eyes. Caught in these unexpected headlights, Dennis's mouth closed and opened three or four times before he remembered words.

'I'm Dennis. Dennis Knuckleyard.'

The vagrant illustrator frowned, then slowly shook his puff-ball head and issued an amused noise like a draining basin. All around, from the peripheries of vision, imbecilic satyrs writhed against constraining pencil lines and seemed to share the mirth of their progenitor.

'Huh huh huh. More like Knacker's-yard. Come on in, if you're comin', and sit down before I sprain me neck. You 'ave that seat what's up the end, without the cat on.'

Making a concerted effort not to wake the sprawling tabby in the other pew, Dennis attempted to comply, but was uncertain what to do about the newsprint heaps that both chairs had in lieu of cushions. There was no room for them on the floor, and in the end he followed the cat's lead to sit with an autumnal crackle, perched atop a creasing pillow made of *Tit-Bits* and *Reveille*. Meanwhile, Austin Spare ignored his new arrival and continued to smudge highlight down one raddled cheek of the old lady whose delineation had been interrupted. After some few minutes, when he had presumably achieved or else abandoned the effect that he was after, the reputed sorcerer tossed his brief stub of Naples Yellow into the prolapsing chest of drawers, turning from the unsteady easel to more thoroughly inspect his visitor.

'So, Monolulu sent yer, is that right? And what's that 'eathen bugger saddled me with now? From lookin' at yer, you're not 'ere to 'ave yer picture painted. No offence, like.'

Having failed to understand that Spare was noting his unsuitability for portraiture, Dennis assured the splattered revenant that no offence was taken, and proceeded to explain as best he could about his plight, which was to say not very well at all.

He'd got as far as Hampole's book and Flabby Harrison before the artist said, 'Oh, dear,' and scooped the semi-conscious cat unceremoniously on to the floor, so he could sit down on the stacked newspapers in the chair next to his new acquaintance. From below a hanging-garden brow, phosphorous lanterns swung in Dennis's direction.

'I know what this is in aid of. You've tripped over the Great When, is that the long and short of it? You've 'ad a scrap with the Theoria.'

Through dim air weighted with the smell of cats and turpentine, under the gaze of viscous travesties, Dennis conveyed incomprehension via the medium of a protracted, noisy fidgeting.

'I don't know what that is.'

The fleapit visionary bobbed a cloven chin.

'What, the Theoria? Well, it's a posh word, that. Ecclesiastical. The divine essence of a thing, as near as I can make out, like with Plato and 'is world of ideal forms. It don't much matter what you call it. You've been in the other London, ain't yer?' Dennis nodded miserably, a small boy owning up to trespass on forbidden wasteland. Unsurprised, Spare grimaced and went on. 'Yeah. Yeah, I thought as much. And 'ow old are yer? Seventeen, eighteen? That's no age to get mixed up in all this palaver, is it? Sixteen, I was, when I got a gander at the Beauty o' Riots, wadin' through a punch-up outside Newgate. I don't think I've been right since.'

Distracted by the ambient filigree of breasts and melting animals cavorting at the corners of his eyes, Dennis tried hard to follow what was being said to him.

'But, I mean, "Beauty of Riots", what's that? And all this other London place, how can it even be there? I've got no idea what's happening. It's like everything's gone crackers since the war.'

The painter reached one hand down and allowed the displaced cat to grind her forehead on his varicoloured fingers. He looked pensive, lips pushed out and smouldering brow knitted, all his features crammed in a compressed band halfway up his face.

'Well, I'm not disagreein' with yer, but the other London, that was crackers long before the war. Crackers before the Romans, that was. It's a Symbolist substratum, as yer might say, what our London's standin' on. The ol' Beauty o' Riots, she's what they call one of its Arcana, one o' the big symbols what 'ang out in that neck o' the woods. Y'see, that world, it's realer than the one what we're in. Our world's just a shadow next to that, up on the wall o' Plato's cave. If this London is what they call the Smoke, then that place is the Fire, you follow me? This 'ere is echo, and that there is music.'

Suddenly, as if he'd thought of something, the lead-pencil conjuror abandoned the ingratiating feline and sat upright, tilting his fog-shrouded cranium back away from Dennis, wanting to observe his sitter from a few more inches' distance. The incendiary eyes were narrowed to a tighter beam as Spare considered the unravelled young man's likely narrative.

''ang on – you say this 'arrison bloke, 'e 'ad 'is digs up in Berwick Street? You didn't … nah. You didn't end up in Soho Entire for your first visit, did yer? All banana-skin tarantulas and wooden barrows with 'ands on their 'andles? You poor bleeder. 'ow did you get out o' there without a postbox 'avin' all yer fingers?'

Although still scared witless by its subject matter, Dennis was surprised to find himself enjoying the extraordinary basement conversation. Talking to somebody who took all this business in their stride, as if it were just something that occasionally happened in the normal run of things, was an incredible relief, and one he hadn't known how much he'd needed. He ventured a rueful smile and gestured to the healing cut above his eye.

'I got this off a silver-paper dragonfly, but I expect it could have been a good sight worse. No, what it was, I had a stroke of luck. This chap I've seen about, Maurice, he charged in, fast as anything, and pulled me out before the pavement alligators swallowed me.'

A heavy wagon passed along Wynne Road outside, so that the cellar rumbled in a sympathetic drum roll. Spare let out a bark of laughter.

'Maurice Calendar? What's that flash 'arry doin' outdoors this late in the decade? I'd 'ave thought 'e'd 'ave 'imself cocooned away by now. Nah, 'e's alright, is Maurice. Easy to get on with, don't yer think, for sayin' that 'e's from the other London? Born and raised there, Maurice was. 'Im and 'is market-trader mate, ol' log face, Blincoe, they're a couple o' the ones who spend a lot o' time in this world, nippin' back an' forth between the two like yo-yos. I should think as all the mob up that way would 'ave been keepin' an eye out for yer – Blincoe, Maurice, Monolulu, Ironfoot. They'd 'ave got wind o' yer 'ampole book the minute it washed up in Soho, penny to a quid. Let's 'ave a butcher's at it, then, this bit o' tat what's causin' all the uproar.'

Idly supposing 'Ironfoot' to be the disproportionate man with the built-up shoe he'd seen in Berwick Street, Dennis reached nervously into his carrier bag and noticed that his hand was shaking as he passed *A London Walk* to the engaging subterranean.

'Sorry. It still frightens me a bit, to tell the truth. Maurice said that I'd got to get it to some people that he called the City Heads.'

Riffling through the badly weathered volume with a scowl of disapproval, Spare looked up at Dennis momentarily before returning to his vexed inspection of the Reverend Hampole's *Meditations in the Streets of the Metropolis*.

'Well, they're not people, or not any more they're not, but looking at this bag o' tricks, I'd say Maurice is spot on. Supernatural glimpses 'ere and there, that's not a problem, but an artefact like this, it's evidence. Bring the 'ole lot down, this could. It's a breach, an indiscretion as you might say, and the 'eads will want it takin' back. It's not a good idea to keep 'em waitin', but I can't go anywhere today because there's people what I'm meetin' up with, later on. You come by earlyish tomorrer and I'll see what I can do. And in the meantime, I'll 'ang on to this, if that's no skin off your nose.' Spare waggled the Hampole book. 'It'll be safe with me, but I don't know as you'd be safe with it. When one o' these things is about, all sorts can 'appen.'

Dennis, very much aware that 'all sorts' was a category that included 'inside out', could only nod his acquiescence and his gratitude that somebody would willingly take the infernal object off his hands. He knew that this would still require a second visit to the place he couldn't bear to think about, but reasoned that this time it wouldn't be as bad. He'd have Spare with him, it would be during the hours of daylight, and this time he'd be prepared for the experience, he was confident. Starting to feel a bit uncomfortable at being eyed by all the slithering chimeras that decorated the unearthly illustrator's studio-cum-coffin, Dennis wondered if he should confirm their rendezvous for Thursday morning and then take his leave. The artist, though, did not seem in a tearing hurry to be rid of him.

''ere, I just 'ad a thought. You said as this thing 'ad escaped out of an Arthur Machen story, if I 'eard yer right.' He once more held the book up in one hand, before consigning it with a dismissive toss to the untidy pile of amputees and hieroglyphics teetering beside his chair. 'Well, in that case, these people what I'm meetin' later, you might want to come along. It's these two dabblers, Ken Grant and his missus, Steffi. Ken, he knew ol' Crowley, who dropped off the twig a year or two back, and I reckon that they're 'opin' I'll be a replacement Beast. No thanks, mate. Not my cup o' tea. Still, they've got cash, they're interested in me drawings, and that Steffi, she's a little smasher, so that's why I knock about with 'em. Thing is, they don't 'alf know a lot o' people what they're keen to introduce me to, and one they said they'd bring along tonight is Johnny Gawsworth. 'e's a proper lush, but 'e was Machen's publisher and 'is biographer. We said we'd get together at the Elephant and Castle, sevenish, so come along if you've a mind. It might be you could learn a thing or two.'

While not entirely certain that he wanted to learn anything about the works of Arthur Machen, the youth thought it would be rude not to accept Spare's invitation when the man was going so far out of his way to be helpful. And besides, the Elephant and Castle was on his route back to Grace's flat in Spitalfields. It wouldn't hurt to pop in for a drink with Austin and his magic mates before he carried on home, would it? Mumbling that it sounded great if Spare was sure he wouldn't be intruding, Dennis found his gaze drawn to one of the cryptic, ink-limned forms that lined the sunken studio, realising too late that it was an intricately wrinkled and misshapen penis of absurd proportions. In fact, now his eye was in, he noticed genitalia crawling everywhere about the chilly premises like bearded molluscs, and could feel the colour rising to his cheeks unbidden. Fortunately, his host appeared too pleased by the prospect of a forthcoming night out to notice.

'It might be a laugh, you never know. Come on up top, and we can have a nose about to find a bit o' nosh before we go. It's always best to line yer belly 'fore you 'ave a drink.'

The painter was already up and heading for the cellar steps, with all the basement's cats immediately on the alert, a furry torrent flowing up the twilit flight before him. Picking up his noticeably lighter carrier, Dennis checked to make sure that the Reverend Hampole's book was still where Spare had chucked it – and not rustling after him across the studio's marvel-cluttered floor – before he followed his new colleague and the feline exodus up the brick stairway. Making polite conversation as they stumped back to street level, Dennis offered up a casual enquiry.

'You've got rooms upstairs here, then?'

Almost at the top step, the fog-haired figure stopped and turned to peer back down at Dennis, furrowing a wart-jewelled brow in puzzlement.

'What d'yer mean? That's my room we're just come from. Studio, livin' room, and if I put the two chairs facin' one another, where I kip as well. It's not a palace, granted, but when Millie offered me it after Jerry blew me last 'ouse down, I moved in sharpish. Beggars can't be choosers.'

Now they were both up in the occluded hallway where the cats were waiting for them, circling and mewing, hard to make out against carpeting as mangy and discoloured as themselves. Dennis was speechless, struggling to assimilate the fact that somebody of such ability lived, worked and slept in a dank oubliette hardly as big as Coffin Ada's flowerbed. No wonder that the man looked ill save for the vigour in his wildfire eyes; a more than healthy soul incarcerated in a more than ailing flesh. Preceding Dennis down the hall towards the nearest of its doors, the mildewed genius was still muttering about the dematerialisation of his previous digs.

"'itler, that was, 'oo bombed that, gettin' 'is own back 'cause I wouldn't do 'is portrait. Paint that fascist arse'ole? I should cocoa! It was that same air raid buggered up me drawin' arm, what meant that for a few years I was leadin' with me left, before I managed with me right again. 'ere, tell yer what, come through into the kitchen. I made a few bob from dirty pictures last week, so I shelled out for a bag o' coal, and Millie said as we should 'ave a fire goin' later on.'

The house's kitchen, small and poorly stocked, was none-theless much cheerier and more spacious than its underground accommodation, with the promised coal fire spitting from an inset hearth and chequered tiling underfoot, rather than crumpled monsters. Told to sit beside the kitchen table while his many-coated host hunted for something edible, Dennis was still attempting to take in the down-at-heel enchanter's previous statement. Hitler's portrait? Dirty pictures? He became suspicious that his new acquaintance might have simply made these details up, then wondered why he was contesting things which were at least remotely possible after their talk about a place that wasn't; straining at a gnat. He busied himself with a copy of last week's *Reveille* that he found there on the tabletop – an article reconstituting meat from the Whitechapel murders sixty years ago – while Spare discovered, on the stove, a half-full saucepan of bubble and squeak, which he proceeded to warm up.

This welcome mess of remnant cabbage, spud, boiled bacon, who knew what, turned out to be a meal intended just for Dennis, with the illustrator's only nourishment being the last few mouthfuls in a pint bottle of milk retrieved from a corroded meat safe by the back door. Wolfing down his banquet of leftovers, Dennis asked himself how anyone could stay alive in such conditions, let alone still fill a canvas, or a room, with their unearthly energy and coarse refinement?

When the pair of them were finishing their various repasts, there came a funny incident that it was hard to pick the bones out of: simply to fill the silence that descended once he was no longer chewing, Dennis gestured to the weekly pseudo-newspaper with its reheated Ripper speculations on the open centrefold. Remarking that he was himself at present lodged in Spitalfields, he asked Spare if the artist harboured any thoughts concerning the still-popular historic homicides. Austin replied by crumpling the middle pages of the rag into a ball that he bowled underhand into the roaring fireplace, meanwhile raising a cautionary finger to his lips and fixing the eighteen-year-old with his incendiary sockets. Stranger still, he then said something that seemed wholly unconnected with the recently incinerated article, though everything about Spare's bearing and delivery conveyed the exact opposite.

'And lissen, same thing goes for this lot that we're meetin' up with later – not a dicky bird about the different London. Gawsworth and the Grants, they've never 'eard of it, and best we keep it that way. Machen knew, apparently, and so did Crowley and old angel britches, Dion Fortune. Perhaps Mathers and a couple o' the others, but beyond that it's a secret between us poor sods who only know about it 'cause we 'ave to. On the matter o' the Great When, we keep shtum, alright? There are some rotten ways to perish in this world, but blabbin' about that place is amongst the very worst of 'em, in my experience. So not another word until tomorrer.'

Was the antique carnival of Jack the Ripper, then, somehow related to the other London? After the alleged magician's admonitions, Dennis wasn't going to ask. They discussed other subjects, and the cellar dweller, with his mushroom pallor, swilled Dennis's plate and fork off underneath the cold tap, then called goodbye to his landlady before the two men went out into risen mist and already descended dark. As they walked to the Elephant and Castle, both the pub and district named for it, Spare chatted amiably about Brixton, hands deep in his pockets, near invisible against the curdling night save for an intermittent headlight splash of egg-yolk yellow.

'Brixton's gone downhill since I first come 'ere. Used to be that if you 'appened on a woman leanin' out a window and you took her from behind, she'd 'ave at least looked round to find out 'oo it was. The area still 'ad a bit o' class back then, I'm tellin' yer. All airs and graces.'

By the time they reached the famous hostelry, the other parties were already there, nervously seated in a corner of the lounge bar and conspicuously better dressed than the assembled regulars of the establishment, which wasn't jam-packed, being the midweek, but was still boisterous. A darts match was in progress, weighted metal hummingbirds thudding their beaks into the pitted board, and at the pub's Joanna a deadpan cadaver tinkled his way through the 'Harry Lime Theme', the tune winding in amongst the chuckling bar crowd with its poisoner's cakewalk. Several of the rubicund and beefy patrons called hellos to 'Awstin' and seemed pleased to see him, none more than the trio of interlopers backed into their anxious corner.

The Grants looked like a presentable young couple, both with dark coiffures, the husband's hair having a liquorice glister and the wife's descending in an inky tumble to her shoulders. They gazed marvelstruck at Spare as if he were a griffin, albeit one who'd fallen on hard times. The other fellow, Gawsworth, wearing stained tweed inappropriate for both that century and that end of town, was already invertebrate with booze and looked to have been poured like mustard into an oak chair, from where his legs had overflowed on to the varnished floorboards. Spare, if anything more undernourished-looking in the lounge's stronger light, introduced Dennis as 'a student what I'm 'elpin' with perspective' – a nice way of putting it – and Kenneth Grant insisted on providing both the artist and his suddenly inducted understudy with a pint of stout. They talked across the crowded table, with a loose net of blue cigarette smoke trembling above them, knotting itself briefly into one of Spare's grotesques before unravelling into another.

Ken and Steffi, as they styled themselves, quickly monopolised the wan delineator with a gush of occult queries, while the 'Harry Lime Theme' shaded into 'Don't Bring Lulu'. Hadn't Spare once worked with Crowley on the latter's periodical, *The Equinox*? What had been his impression of the late Great Beast? When the reply was 'an Italian ponce 'oo's out o' work', the conversation shifted to the duo's reminiscences of those last years at Netherwood, the boarding house in Hastings, where Ken recollected being present for a reconciliation with Christian magician Dion Fortune, herself recently deceased. 'They got on rather well, as I recall, but now they're gone, the occult landscape's looking somewhat empty. One could even say that you are its last mountain, Austin. I remember Crowley once said ...' It became apparent that the table was divided between those lucky enough to have once known Aleister Crowley and those lucky enough not to have done, these being Dennis and John Gawsworth who, disqualified, fell into their own outcast conversation.

Gawsworth was immensely likeable, perhaps in his late thirties or his early forties, with an earnest face that wore a neat beard and a permanent expression of wary surprise, that of a burglar by unexpected torchlight. Crumpling forward in his chair to make himself heard over cheers or groans resulting from the darts game, Arthur Machen's self-appointed Sancho Panza voiced conspiratorial asides in the perplexed tones of a country gent marooned on the harsh streets of an abominable city.

'They're right, of course. These last few years have been jolly unkind to occult types. Dropping like flies: old Crowley, Fortune, Harry Price, the lot of 'em. Damned shame and all that, but when Arthur Machen passed away the Christmas before last, the magic-wallahs seemed to have forgotten him as thoroughly as the reviewers.'

Here the literary squire shook his large head despondently and took another gulp of gin, one elbow resting in the table's film of spillage where the Guinness toucans smirked from sodden beer mats. Dennis asked if Machen, then, had been connected to the world of magic, at which Gawsworth gruffed his affirmation.

'Crikey, I should say! He joined the Golden Dawn, you know, in the mauve nineties, when you had a lot of writers doing that, Algernon Blackwood, Sax Rohmer and so on. But with Machen – I don't know. I think losing his first wife, Amy, had a lot to do with it. He told me he was inconsolable, the poor chap, wracked with sorrow and in a precarious mental state. So much so that he seemed to be accosted by the characters of his own fictions, or that's what he said, and that his nightly strolls were through a London which had been replaced by an entirely different city. It was after this experience that he became a member of the Golden Dawn. Hoping to find out what had happened to him, I suppose, although I don't think that he had much luck. He wasn't with the order very long, at any rate. He thought Kabbalah was intriguing, but he found the rest of it – the dressing-up and secret names and all that – to be self-important twaddle. Always spoke his mind, did Machen.'

At the bar, somebody in a cloth cap made a questionable comment to a skinny barmaid and was violently acquainted with the outside pavement by a bull-sized landlord. Trying to look scholarly, Dennis regarded Gawsworth with a quizzical expression.

'So, this different city Machen thought he saw, it made a big impression on him, then?'

Gawsworth, even through his gin haze, was emphatic.

'Oh, my word, yes. The idea that there might be a higher world concealed behind our own was central to his work, right to the end, but London seemed to be the only place that he could see it from. On his first visit here, he had what I suppose you'd call a vision, standing awestruck in the Strand and witnessing what he described as London's sacred essence; its "Theoria", as Machen put it. He could be a bugger for obscure religious terminology, if he was in the mood. Then, after Amy Hogg died, he had further glimpses, as I've said. I used to think that he was speaking metaphorically, about the different world available to someone of poetic insight, but these days I'm not so sure. Sometimes I harbour the unsettling suspicion he was being literal, talking about somewhere that – to him, at least – existed physically. I'd say those revelations were the most profound experiences that he ever had.'

Across the table, Steffi Grant was sounding vexed as she reviewed the difficulties of succession raised by Crowley's passing, while her husband nodded thoughtfully and Spare examined his black fingernails. Increasingly absorbed in what Gawsworth was saying, Dennis steered their discourse to the matter that was foremost in his mind.

'It's funny, I was reading one of Machen's stories just last night, about another London hidden behind this one. For a title, it had just the letter "N". I don't know if you've heard of it …'

From his nostalgic melancholy, Gawsworth lit up like an alcoholic Christmas tree whose cheeks were coloured bulbs.

'Heard of it? My dear boy, I was the one who got it published! There were all these tales that nobody had seen outside the ghost-story anthologies of lovely Cynthia Asquith, and I thought they should be gathered up in a collection. Machen didn't like the idea, and tried hard to talk me out of it. Said all the stories were substandard and not worth the bother, which was tommyrot, but then he often found my runaway enthusiasms irritating, I suspect. Finally, he insisted on including a new story, so that the collection should, at least in his eyes, have some proper merit. That was "N". To my mind, it's one of his greatest pieces and, as it turned out, one of his last important works.'

Pensively, Dennis sipped his stout and, wearing a moustache of foam, asked Gawsworth why the story was called 'N', fearing the answer might be something glaringly apparent to a more attentive reader than himself. But the biographer could only spread his hands and widen his already wide eyes, pushing out his bottom lip into a pout of glum bewilderment.

'Haven't the foggiest. I asked him the same thing myself, when he made his submission. I'd suggested that perhaps it stood for

North, because it's all about North London, but he only looked at me and smiled – rather annoyingly, I thought. Wouldn't confirm it or deny it. All I could get out of him was one of his conundrums. He patted me on the knee, and said, "Here we commence the missing second half of London's alphabet." Make what you will of that.

'One of the finest writers that this country's ever seen, but heaven knows, the man could be a trial. Tricky Welsh mind, you see, forever coming up with things that will deliberately mislead his audience. "N" is a marvellous example – first, he softens up the reader with unlikely facts, such as the difficulty there is in locating the precise part of Stoke Newington where Edgar Allan Poe was schooled, for instance. Then, once he's established an air of authentic reportage, he introduces elements that he's invented but which sound just as convincing, like the book that he describes and quotes bits from, *A London Walk*. Devilishly clever, don't you reckon, as a literary device?'

Dennis became aware that from the table's far side, Austin Spare was shooting him a warning glance while seemingly engrossed in what the Grants were on about, reminding him that there were things not open to discussion here. Thus chastened, Dennis feigned surprise, proceeding cautiously.

'Huh. Well, I fell for it, hook, line and sinker. I thought it must be a real book that I hadn't heard of. So, you're saying Machen made it up?'

Gawsworth smiled, smug with his insider knowledge and oblivious to Dennis's. Even the cardboard toucans seemed amused while drowning under their pale-ale meniscus.

'Absolutely. Made the book up, made the author up – the Reverend Hampole, was it? – made it all up for an earlier novel, *The Green Round*, and then referred to it again in "N". Each of the works concerns a grander London than the one which we perceive, so I suppose having the same imaginary book in both tales makes a sort of cockeyed sense. Where did you come across the story, incidentally? I hope it wasn't an abridged appearance in some tatty magazine.'

Across the room, the darts match was called off by mutual consent before somebody lost an eye. The ambient smother of brown-blue tobacco smoke was heavier now, as was the adjectival swearing: ruddies had pupated into bloodies as the night wore on, before eventually hatching in their adult form as fuckings. Dennis reached one hand into the carrier bag beside his pub stool, pulling out the copy of *The Cosy Room*, and also Spare's horse-racing oracle that he'd snatched up by accident, still in its tipster's envelope. Gawsworth was overjoyed, as though one met with a beloved child after a lengthy separation. At Dennis's invitation, he took the collection in his hands, turning it this way and then that, admiring the wallpaper understatement of the green-and-white wraps, lifting it to his roseate nose and breathing in its stale bouquet.

'Well, I'll be blowed! And isn't it a magnificent creature, although I say so myself? You know, I've not seen one of these in years. That's made my day, that has. I don't suppose you'd like it signed, at all? I mean, I know that I was merely the compiler, not the author, but, still, if you wanted, I'd be only too pleased to affix my scribble to it.'

While the volume technically belonged to Ada, Dennis didn't see how the compiler's signature could harm its saleability. He grinned and nodded his plucked-chicken head, assuring Machen's Boswell that the scribble would be a tremendous honour. Beaming like a child, although a drunken one, Gawsworth produced a lovingly mistreated fountain pen from his breast pocket and proceeded to inscribe *The Cosy Room*, in bright blue ink and a clear hand that barely trembled. This activity attracted the attention of the table's other half, and Spare's jocular comment was near shouted to be made out over the nearby piano, then meandering from 'Hush, Here Comes a Buzz Bomb' on to 'I Live in Trafalgar Square', without a noticeable change of key.

'Stone me, I didn't know we'd got the autograph hounds in tonight. 'ere, Dennis, wossat other thing, in the white envelope? Looks like it's one o' Monolulu's tips what 'e 'ands out.'

Dennis admitted that it was, and sheepishly confessed that it contained Spare's own Surrealist Racing Forecast Cards. Amid considerable mirth, the artist requisitioned Gawsworth's pen and volubly insisted that he too should sign his work for their young visitor. "'oo shall I make it out to? Should I just put Dennis Knacker's-yard, or what?' Struck by an impulse that was either altruistic or self-serving, Dennis asked if the manila packet with the cards in could be dedicated to Grace Shilling. 'She's the woman that I'm staying with at present, and she thought your art was smashing.' Underneath the printed title on the inner envelope, Spare carefully penned, 'For Grace Shilling, with regards, from tuppenny-'apenny Austin Osman Spare'. Everyone laughed, Dennis replaced the two signed items in his carrier and, having apparently exhausted a restricted repertoire, the waxen pianist once more commenced the 'Harry Lime Theme'.

Finishing his stout, confirming his next-day appointment at Wynne Road and shaking everybody's hand, Dennis picked up his bag and exited the Elephant and Castle before etiquette demanded that he get a round in and stand everyone a drink. Being the conscientious type, this didn't make him feel particularly good, but, then, since he was relatively broke, it didn't press upon his conscience any further than the second or third lamppost.

The overcast hour it took to reach Spitalfields – across Tower Bridge, as an immense weight of black water crashed invisible below – had not one star, the sky emptied of promise rim to rim. He walked up through the Minories to Aldgate while the city nursed its wounds and made sounds in its sleep around him, muttered distant brawls or coughed backfiring cars. Cutting along Whitechapel High Street to the arse-end of Commercial Street, the east wind blew a chandelier chain of police-car bells from somewhere by the river at his back, and he allowed himself to think that he was making progress with his lunatic dilemma. He was going to get through this in one piece, and with luck that piece would be the right way out. With Spare's assistance, by this time tomorrow night he'd have returned the nondescript and terrifying book to where it came from, as his former landlady had stipulated, and might be a few steps closer to regaining something like a normal life. All of his problems had boiled up like silverfish out of *A London Walk*, and he felt certain that they'd melt away once he was rid of it. His feet beginning to complain, he passed the closed café where he'd scoffed down his breakfast, and resolved to be more positive about his situation.

Being pulled by Maurice Calendar through the impossibility of the different London, he supposed, had been exciting, although not so much as it was frightening. Meeting with Austin Spare and his associates seemed full of mystery and enchantment, but the sheerest upside to Dennis's present circumstances was Grace Shilling, by a mile. He was inordinately chuffed with himself in instructing Spare to sign the racing forecast cards for her. It wasn't that he thought the gift would make her fall into his embrace or her bed: if it just stopped her from reminding him about her sharpened key so frequently, then he'd be more than happy. All he really wanted was to get back to her flat and see how that face looked if it was pleased with him.

He passed the Spitalfields church, squatting in the night with dunce-cap steeple and a stony porthole for its mouth, a giant clown screaming only silence over the surrounding yards, over the history-stained Ten Bells, bulging with light and voices on Fournier Street's far side. A little further on, he crossed the road and turned left into Folgate Street, rehearsing as he went his presentation of Spare's autograph to Grace. Should it be nonchalant, or did it need a build-up? For the first time in his barely started life, he was returning home to someone female who was not his mum or Coffin Ada, and he found that he was looking forward to it with only the slightest twinge of apprehension.

When he reached what he was sure was the right number, he retrieved the borrowed house key from his pocket and let himself in as quietly as he could, attempting to avoid those floorboards in the downstairs hall that Grace had pointed out as noisy troublemakers. He could tell from the thin crease of light beneath her room's door that she was at home, but thought it best to knock politely before entering. After a longer pause than he'd expected, Grace said to come in, in a flat tone suggesting she was unenthusiastic about their reunion, but then she didn't know about the racing forecast cards.

He was two steps inside before he worked out that things had gone badly wrong. Grace sat bolt upright on the rickety settee, completely still and white with dread. They weren't alone. There was a fellow who resembled a more threatening Glenn Miller standing by the unlit stove, and, Dennis realised belatedly, another bloke behind him, just inside the door. A third perched on the sofa beside Grace, an oversized man with a crafty smile, a prominent mole on one cheek, and eyes that looked as if they found amusement in appalling things.

'Look what the cat's dragged in,' said Jack Spot.

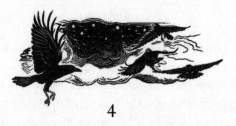

# 4

## Of Popes and Pot-Pourri

By the seashell ashtray on the coffee table was a straight-edge razor, open in a V at ten to two, anticipating trouble come quarter to three.

If they'd had time to talk things over, Grace and Dennis would have probably agreed that they were equally to blame for their shared nightmare. Dennis, for his part, hadn't informed Grace that the murderous criminal seeking the Hampole book was Jack Spot, nor that Spot already had Dennis's name. Conversely, Grace hadn't made clear to Dennis that when she'd said his tough-sounding moniker was 'useful', she'd meant as pretended pimp that she could use to menace rowdy or non-paying customers: 'You do know that I'm one of Dennis Knuckleyard's girls, don't you?' She'd employed the strategy already twice that day, which evidently had been once too many.

They sat side by side on a couch as precarious as their situation, eyes fixed dead ahead, not looking at each other. Both were terrified and struggling to keep it from their faces, gazing levelly above the folded blade and ashtray at the figure sitting just across the table from them, on a chair retrieved from Grace's kitchen. Two impassive thugs stood silent, one to either hand – Glenn Miller on the left, an olive-skinned chap on the right – a pair of brackets that contained the seated man's coiled-spring malevolence as an aside.

The widely publicised king of the underworld, in nicely tailored umber suit and blue silk tie, was peering down into the carrier bag that Dennis had just handed to him. Under a retreating hairline, Spot's brow creased with inauspicious puzzlement. Dapper and dangerous, like a grenade sporting a pocket handkerchief, at last the tall, well-fed man lifted his enquiring gaze to the young couple who sat facing him over the razor-laden table. When he spoke, the barely restrained East End snarl was that of an enraged dog struggling with elocution lessons.

'Where's my fackin' book, then?'

The balloon of fear inflating inside Dennis for the previous five minutes was now bigger than Dennis himself, containing him and Grace within its paralysing stillness, in its swell of apprehension that awaited an inevitable, catastrophic pop. Desperate attempts to strategise had proven useless, all his thoughts a blizzard, and nonsensically distracted by the leftmost goon's remarkable resemblance to a disappeared bandleader. In the crushing knowledge that he could find himself dead or earless at a moment's notice, Dennis could only rely on instincts that he knew to be notoriously unreliable. These were all at that moment strenuously advising him, whatever else he did, not to attempt a cover story. His one half a chance, as far as he could see from inside his anxiety-inflatable, was to be as straightforward and as truthful as his circumstance allowed. He cleared his throat, still uncut.

'Mr Comer ...' Unbelievably, Dennis's memory had retrieved Spot's proper name from one of the newspaper articles about the man, and done so just when it was needed. 'Mr Comer, I am much too scared to tell you any lies. I wish to God that you'd found Harrison the night before I saw him, and not the night after, because then it would be you was lumbered with the bastard thing, not me. That book ... it isn't what you think it is.'

This wasn't going well. Spot's stare, formerly merely quizzical, was now refrigerated. He spoke through a worryingly frozen smile, while that left-hand enforcer looked more like Glenn Miller by the instant.

'Oh, yeah? And what do I think it is?'

Dennis discovered he was blinking frantically, aware that his next words might leave his cheeks in shreds. Beside him on the listing sofa, Grace was breathing slowly, through her nose.

'If I'm right, you think it's a passport to a ... well, another part of London, one that most people don't know is there. And yeah, having the book means that there's bound to be some dealings with, you know, the other place, but it's not like a passport. It's ... I don't know. It's more like a warrant or a summons. It's more like a sentence.'

Seeming now more interested, the racketeer narrowed his calculating eyes.

''ow's that, then?'

Playing on a wireless in Dennis's head was Miller's 'In the Mood', although he really wasn't. Ears full of imaginary clarinets, he pressed on with his summary for the defence and/or last words.

'It's a long stretch of obligation where there's no rewards; there's only penalties. I was told that if you don't get objects like *A London Walk* back where they came from, you could end up ... have you ever heard of somebody called Teddy Wilson, from out Lewisham way? Got found in a state I can't even imagine, all for trying to throw away a book just like the one you're after.'

Spot, at this point, shared a concerned frown with his stout, olive-skinned accomplice before turning back to Dennis.

'Mr Kankus 'ere, some time back, 'e informed me of a chap 'e'd 'eard about, south of the river, what 'ad turned up in a, shall we say, unusual condition. That this Wilson, was it, who was all the wrong ... ?'

'The wrong way out? Yeah, that was him.' He felt Grace stiffen on the couch beside him, and could hardly blame her. Like Jack Spot, the inside-out book dealer was another detail of his story that he'd not seen fit to share. It hadn't seemed the proper time, although he had to grudgingly admit that right now was a great deal worse. Spot thrust his lower lip out thoughtfully as he considered Dennis's foregoing argument. He drummed the digits of one hand against the table's worn veneer, a small intaglio ring on his little finger adding a metallic tick to the percussion. After a few moments, the celebrity crook ceased this tense accompaniment and exhaled heavily, as though he'd come to an unsatisfactory conclusion. With an air of deep regret, he picked the razor up and opened it, regarding Grace and Dennis with eyes that were oddly fatherly and deeply disappointed.

'Well, all what you've said is very useful, and I shall be takin' it into account, believe me. Just the same, I can't 'elp noticing that you've avoided the main thrust of my enquiry, which, if I recall, was, "Where's my fackin' book?"'

Dennis was now as stiff as Grace, the pair of them become the wooden couple in a painted weather-house, blanched as if lit by lightning. When Spot had produced the mother-of-pearl-handled item earlier, both had observed the tailor-made, tubular, inside jacket pocket he'd retrieved it from, this carefully kept evil: evidently something of a speciality. Bolt upright with the electricity of panic, Dennis tried to think of something non-disfiguring to say, all the time wondering if when Spot cut his face in half, the taller of the two enforcers would shout, 'Pennsylvania, six-five-thousand!' Mouth almost too dry to speak, let alone blither, he had no choice but to stick with honesty as his best policy.

'In Brixton. There's this chap there I was told could help me get the book back to this, well, this other district. He said that he'd take me there tomorrow morning, and that I should leave it overnight with him for my own safety.'

Jack Spot rubbed an idle forefinger beside his nose, and glanced up, smiling, at the brace of heavies before looking back at Dennis with the brief smile now evaporated.

'From what I can see, it looks like 'e was wrong about that last bit, weren't 'e? Now, why don't you cheer us up by tellin' me this facker's name and where he lives?'

Because, well, then there'd be no reason not to murder him and Grace, the way these men had murdered Flabby Harrison? Because it would bring havoc down upon a gifted individual that Dennis rather liked? Because it would be cowardly? All of these answers bubbled on the teenager's chewed lips, and all of them were less than adequate. Waiting for inspiration, he stalled unconvincingly.

'You don't want him. He's just an old bloke in a basement with a load of cats, painting his pictures, mumbling about magic. He's a bit touched, to be honest. I should leave him out of it. Oh, God, no, don't ...'

These last syllables were occasioned by the mob boss leaning forward and bringing the repurposed shaving accessory towards Dennis's eyes, which were tight shut for several seconds before he eventually realised that his executioner had paused. He opened them to Spot's face only inches from his own, features contorted by a struggle between rage and trepidation, the titular blemish on his left cheek quivering like a volcanic island in a sea of deepening pink.

''old on. 'old on a fackin' minute. You say Brixton, and you say as 'e paints pictures. It's not wossername, that black magician in the papers, is it? Spare. It better not be fackin' Spare, or ...'

Dennis nodded mutely, braced for the forthcoming slash, but Spot slammed down the razor with an anguished growl and said, 'Aow, fack! Fack my old rags! Fack! Fack!', and more in this same tenor, for what seemed like an unbearably long while. The brute lieutenants looked as startled and disturbed by their commanding officer's tirade as his intended victims, everyone stock-still and staring as a sharply dressed Mills bomb of angry malice trembled, at the threshold of explosion, in a Spitalfields flat too small to contain it. In the end, Glenn Miller intervened with a profound East End inflection that greatly reduced the otherwise remarkable resemblance.

'Jack, don't 'ave a tizzy. This ain't nothing we can't 'andle. We can be in Brixton 'fore the boozers shut, get this Spare geezer to cough up yer book, and it'll all be good as gold.'

Not visibly placated by this well-intentioned summary, the gangland potentate scotched back his kitchen chair and, rising to his feet, confronted his unduly optimistic underling.

'No, Sonny. No, we fackin' can't. I've 'eard about this bloke, an' 'e's a fackin' warlock. 'e does magic, and not fackin' card tricks, either. I've 'ad all the bad luck I can manage, thank you very fackin' much, an' I'm not goin' near 'im.'

At this, the more fleshy and darkly complexioned henchman, Mr Kankus, tried to introduce a gravel-throated voice of reason to the increasingly noisy interchange.

'All that's a load o' pony, Jack, you know it is. You let me 'ave a word with 'im, 'e'll 'and it over, toot sweet. I don't give a monkey's whether I get cursed or not.'

Spot wheeled to fix his hireling with a furious stare, his voice the warning hiss of steam from an eruptive boiler. 'Solly, you're not listenin'. This cunt can make it rain. Can make it rain shit, if 'e likes. There's no worse place in the 'ole fackin' country for my fackin' book to end up.' Something seemed to strike the racetrack overlord at this point. He scowled into space, and then turned his unfortunate attentions back to Dennis. 'If that's where it is, o' course. 'ow do I know you're not pullin' my pisser with this fackin' rigmarole and tryin' to put the wind up me, droppin' that bleeder's name to put me off me stroke? 'oo says as fackin' Spare knows you from Adam?'

Trying hard not to make any sudden movements, Dennis gestured nervously towards the carrier bag that stood forgotten by the mobster's feet.

'I–In the bag. There's these cards that he'd done. I had him sign the packet for the lady here.'

As he was saying this, he nodded his head sideways, and in doing so glimpsed the aghast expression that briefly contorted Grace's lips and eyelids, although whether this was a reaction to the signed gift or to being called a lady was not easily determined. Spot, meanwhile, stooped to retrieve the nested envelopes from their brown-paper reliquary. Extracting the manila inner packet from its pallid outer counterpart, he glowered in uncomprehending fury at the printed legend, then at the handwritten dedication writ beneath it, then at Dennis.

'What's this, then? Surrealist fackin' Racing Forecast Cards? Is this cunt makin' money out o' racin' in a way what I'm not? Because if 'e is, 'e must be fackin' magic.' Dennis found he couldn't offer any pertinent reply to this, and so Spot transferred his unwelcome scrutiny to Grace. 'And you're Grace Shilling, then? Well, that's competitively priced, I must say.'

Grace calmly returned the gangster's enraged stare, the same way she returned his disrespectful comment. 'Yeah. I used to be Grace Tanner, but I'm doing better these days.'

Which elicited a throaty laugh from Solly Kankus, and permitted the intrusion of brief conversational normality into the otherwise hair-trigger atmosphere. Taking advantage of this opportunity to further her stab at de-escalation, Grace pressed on in the same deadpan tone, gazing unblinkingly into Spot's fuming fuse-wire eyes.

'Look, if I'm honest, I'm finding all this quite nerve-wracking for some reason. Is anybody bothered if I have a fag?'

The Whitechapel Napoleon's colour deepened thunderously, his ire a wave of hot force rushing at the seated woman through his floodgate countenance only to break, confused, against her impassivity. Spot's face retired from demonism into a disgruntled puzzlement.

'Yeah, actually, that's not a bad idea. I could do with one meself. Why don't you flash the ash, and keep yer gob shut?'

Pouting her resentment at this commandeering of her tightly rationed Craven 'A', Grace plucked the pack of ten from a black handbag perched between her ankles and, after she'd pointedly withdrawn her own first, offered them around. Everyone except Dennis took one, and the three gangland intruders bowed their underlit visages reverently over the same match flame as they sparked up, like appalling magi at the manger. Some of the room's tension was released in gathering smog beneath its plastered ceiling, or as grey precipitate accumulating in the seashell ashtray, on the table next to the still-open razor. Sitting back down, Spot regarded Grace and Dennis pensively.

'Look, just supposin' all that what you said was on the level, far as I can tell, that still leaves me – well, us – with an enormous fackin' problem. See, I need to 'ave a word with someone from this … other neighbourhood, let's say. This is a matter o' some personal importance, right? So if you're sayin' it's not gunna 'appen, then what good are you to me? Why shouldn't I just top the pair of yer, and write off this 'ole fackin' magic-book lark as a load of shit?'

Having already come to the conclusion that this fucking magic-book lark was far worse than just a load of shit, Dennis could only concede that the question was a fair one, and well put. For lack of an immediate answer, he fell back upon improvisation as he struggled to contrive a plan, or possibly the plan for a rough outline of the first draft of a plan.

'There … look, there might be something I can do to get you what you want. I don't know, not for certain, but there might be.' Dennis let his gaze dart up to, first, Glenn Miller, then across to Mr Kankus, then back down to Spot. 'Perhaps if we could talk more openly about this other place … ?'

Spot worked his tongue around the inside of his cheek, bulging the mole disruptively as he considered. At length, he fixed Dennis with a warning stare, the gist of which was unmistakeable.

'Fair dos. I can see that there might be sense in your suggestion, young man.' He glanced up at his associates, offering a perfunctory nod. 'Alright, then. Solly, Sonny, take this brass outside while me and Master Knuckleyard 'ave our discussion. Sit 'er in the motor, ten or twenty minutes, and no funny business, not until I've got a clearer 'andle on this fackin' can o' worms.'

The brass, or brass nail, rhymes with tail, was obviously Grace, while Dennis himself was, most probably, the fucking can of worms. He definitely felt the part, his stomach a container of cold, writhing things that formerly had been intestines. Standing at the mumbled invitation of Spot's double-act subordinates, Grace carefully enunciated, 'Fucking nerve,' as she was led out of her own hard-won accommodation. Unexpectedly, she looked back on the threshold and gave Dennis a tight, anxious smile that seemed to say, 'I know that your stupidity is bound to doom us both, but good luck anyway.' It was a look that didn't set the bar too high, for which he was extremely grateful. Then the door clicked shut and Dennis was alone with London's overdressed and vicious fixer. Jack/John/Jacob Spot/Comacho/Comer/Colmore flashed a chummy grin, intended to put the eighteen-year-old at his unease and visibly succeeding.

'Well?' he said. 'Come on, let's fackin' 'ear it. We en't got all day.'

Dennis drew in a deep breath while he still had the capacity to manage such a thing.

'The two fellers outside, they were the ones in wait for me up Berwick Street on Tuesday, last night. Am I right?'

Spot nodded, unimpressed. 'You are. Sonny the Yank, Solly the Turk, but then they're not the 'ardest couple to identify, I wouldn't think. Although they are notoriously fackin' difficult to get away from if they're after yer, so 'ow did a long streak of piss like you manage to pull it off? They said they saw you scarper down some little fackin' alley and then you were gone. Where were yer?'

Once more, Dennis hoped the truth would set him free.

'I was in the wrong London, in the part of it that corresponds with Soho. It was horrible. I'd fallen in by accident, and it was all alive and trying to eat me. There were busted crates grown into wooden spiders running at me, there were dustbins with their lids clapping like jaws and metal snakes made out of drainpipe. Look, I'm nowhere near as smart as you are, Mr Comer, but I'm not some dimwit who'd be telling you a half-baked yarn like that, not when you've got a razor on the table, if it wasn't what I saw. The other London is a fucking madhouse that's not meant for normal living people. Just remembering it makes me want to spew, and I'm supposed to go back there with Spare at ten o'clock tomorrow morning, or I end up inside out like the book-dealer chap, or something just as bad. To be quite honest, if it weren't for Grace, Miss Shilling – she just took me in and hasn't heard all this – then I might well be better off if you did me tonight and put me out of my misery.'

Spot's expression, set in sweaty alabaster, was unreadable but wasn't one of open disbelief. He looked as if he might be trying, unsuccessfully, to picture crate arachnids.

'Yeah, and I may very well still do that, if you don't give me a reason not to. What would 'appen if I did, ay? What would 'appen if you didn't turn up at your black magician's billet in the mornin', because you and your Miss Half-a-crown were bobbin' with the rubber johnnies down at Wapping stairs?'

This painted quite a picture. Dennis swallowed unattractively.

'I don't know. I suppose that Spare would have to take the Hampole book back to the City Heads without me, and then that would be the last that anyone would see of it.'

The East End kingpin made a grimace of dissatisfaction.

'And what's that, then? What's the City Heads when they're at 'ome?'

Unable to recall a time of ever being in his depth, Dennis was nonetheless aware that he was getting out of it. He carried on, not quite regardless. 'I'm not sure, but it sounds as if they're the ones who run the other London, like they're some sort of committee, or—' He broke off. Something had occurred to him, although he wasn't sure how he should put it. 'Mr Comer, can I ask you something? I don't understand why, after all the stuff that I've been telling you – the drainpipe snakes and hungry dustbins – why you've not cut me already. Is there something that you've seen or heard that tells you I'm not lying? Sorry. Perhaps I shouldn't ask.'

Spot stubbed his cigarette out in the seashell and deliberated. He subjected Dennis to a long, appraising stare before replying.

'Breathe a word o' this, and it'll be yer last. Last word, last breath. You understand me?' Dennis nodded and the tyrant of the turf went on. 'It was in 1936, Battle o' Cable Street. You might 'ave 'eard of it. Sir Oswald fackin' Mosley and his fackin' Blackshirts, all dressed up and yiddified – that's terrified o' Jews shoutin' the odds, where I grew up. Well, I'm not 'avin' that, goes

without saying. I was only in me twenties back then, but I went
down to the dust-up with a load of other narked-off Jew boys,
my lads, and we gave them fascist cunts what for, them and the
coppers what was guardin' 'em. That's 'ow I got me name, see?
Because I was always on the fackin' spot when there was trouble.'

Dennis had heard otherwise, but felt that this was not the
time to offer any contradictions, or to glance at the distinctive
mole that had more probably provided Comer's nickname. Spot
went on.

'Well, anyway, we charged straight through the police body-
guards, tryin' to get to Mosley and 'is fancy mates. I'd got a
sofa leg I'd filled with lead, and I was cavin' in the cunt next to
Sir Oswald when the coppers all piled in on me at once. Put
me in fackin' 'ospital, but just when I was passin' out, I looked
towards the fightin' what was goin' on all round us, and I saw
the queerest thing: there was this fackin' woman, twenty foot tall
if she was an inch. Redhead, like your Miss Ten-bob-note. She
'ad 'er tits out, and she was just stridin' through the mob, nice as
you like, and everybody looked the other fackin' way as if they
couldn't see 'er! Twenty fackin' foot tall, on my life! You might
say that was where I first got wind that there was something
fackin' funny goin' on in London, and the bits and bobs I've
'eard across the years since then 'ave only made it funnier. So,
you tell me about your fruit-crate spiders, I'm not gunna bat a
fackin' eyelid, am I?'

Once again, the crime king's argument was unimpeachable.
Chancing his arm, Dennis here made an interjection that he
thought could perhaps be of relevance.

'The woman that you saw, I think she might be something
that's called the "Beauty of Riots". Spare mentioned her to me.
He said he'd seen her once, when he was a young lad.'

Spot chewed this over with a contemplative frown.

'Beauty o' Riots, ay? Yeah. Yeah, that sounds like 'er.' Spot
gave Dennis a look that seemed so out of character it took
the younger man a moment to identify it as both troubled and
annoyed. 'This magic stuff's a fackin' circus, ennit? Fackin' giants

and blokes turned inside out. Gives me the fackin' willies, tell yer that for nothin'. It's not fackin' proper, is it?'

Suddenly, Spot seemed to be in need of reassurance. Dennis shook his head in sympathy.

'No. No, it's not. From what I've seen of it, it's bedlam. It's a right chamber of horrors. Look, I know that this is not my business, but if you've seen what the other London's like and you don't fancy it, then why are you so set on getting in there? You said that you had to talk to somebody from that neck of the woods …'

This earned another thoughtful pause while the chief crook considered his alternatives. At last, appearing to have come to a decision, he leaned forward with his elbows on the table and fixed Dennis with a noticeably blink-free gaze.

'Son, I don't know as I can trust yer, but I do know I can kill yer. So, we'll let that be our understandin', shall we? Now, you asked me what I wanted from this fackin' goblins' picnic, so I'll tell yer: I want peace o' mind. I wanna know for certain that some schemin' cunt's not gunna knock me off before I'm fackin' forty. See, all my life, I've worked 'ard for what I've got. It used to be it was the I-ties runnin' all the racetracks, Harryboy Sabini and the like. Then fackin' Kimber an' 'is Brummy Boys, they squeezed out the Sabinis, and so me and Billy 'ill, we come along and done the same to them. Kimber cooperates with us now, right as ninepence.'

Spot performed a curious rotation of his head, cartilage crackling audibly, then tightened his blue silk tie by a noose notch.

'O' course, what with Billy spendin' so much time away in nick, the upkeep o' the operation largely falls on me. I like to think that I've expanded it into a very profitable business. Trouble is, earnin' that kind o' reputation means I've 'ad to put me own name forward, in the papers an' all that. And now that Billy's out o' prison, I can tell 'e thinks I'm puffin' meself up an' tryin' to take over. I mean, thanks to me, we're doin' better than we've ever done, but trouble's brewin', I can feel it in me water. See, while Billy was inside this last time, I made what I will admit were one or two mistakes. The London airport balls-up last year, for a kick-off – we thought we'd got the security guards doped up, but we 'adn't, and they turned out to be dressed-up coppers. Nothin' tyin' it to me, but every facker knows I was behind it. Most important, Billy knows, an' 'e don't like it.'

Up beyond the flaking grey of Grace's ceiling, someone bumped and stumbled on the upstairs landing, probably one of the house's other tenants on a visit to the loo. Spot sniffed dismissively and fiddled with his cufflinks, ill at ease as he approached his story's crux.

'My situation en't as comfortable as what I'd like, and I could do with some assistance gettin' out o' shtuck. From odds and ends what I've picked up about this other place across the years, I gather nothin' 'appens 'ere what en't first been decided there. This other London, that's the organ grinder, an' our London's just the fackin' monkey, as I understand it. And from what I'm told, all o' the city's various endeavours 'ave their figure'eads what run things from this fairyland o' theirs, and that includes its criminal endeavours. What I've 'eard, there's, like, a god of villains in this different London, an' I reckon that's the chap I need to 'ave a word with … or, if I can't do that, that somebody needs to parlay with on my behalf. Can you see the way my mind's goin' 'ere?'

With mingled hope and worry, Dennis thought he could.

'D-Do you mean these City Heads that I'm supposed to meet tomorrow? Well, I don't know who they are, exactly, and I've not heard anything about this god-of-crime bloke, but, yeah, perhaps I could put your case to them, perhaps arrange a meeting, if that got me and Grace off the hook.'

They were both leaning in towards each other now, and Dennis noticed that with their long lashes, the arch-felon's eyes had something feminine about them, almost pretty despite being full of ugly things. Spot shook his head and sighed.

'No. I'm afraid "perhaps" won't be enough. That won't get anybody off the 'ook. See, what I'm thinkin' is, you need a strong incentive if this lark tomorrow's gunna turn out 'ow I want. This is the way it's gunna go: you and your bird can stop 'ere overnight, with one of my lads outside, watchin' front and back. First thing tomorrow, we come round and somebody runs you to Brixton, while the tart stays 'ere with us, all day if necessary. If you turn up 'ere tomorrow night with somethin' I don't wanna 'ear, we'll do the pair of yer. If you run off, we'll finish 'er, then come and look for you – and we will find you. Let's be very fackin' clear on that. Conversely, if on your return you have good news for me, then all of us can reach an 'appy fackin' endin', can't we? So, then, 'ave we settled on a gentleman's agreement?'

Spot held out one palm expectantly and creased his face into the rictus grin of a triumphant salesman. Dennis stared appalled at the extended digits, pink and neatly manicured.

'But … I've not got the first idea of how the other London works. I've only been there once. You know that I can't promise to keep my part of the bargain.'

Both the hand and smile remained in place.

'That's true. But I can promise to keep my part, which is what you should be focussed on.'

And so it was that when the heavies ushered Grace back into her own living room some moments later, Dennis Knuckleyard and Jack Spot were both shaking on their private deal, and Knuckleyard alone was simply shaking. The straight razor, folded shut, was restored to its snug interior jacket pocket. Grace seemed unperturbed by her gangster-accompanied interval, and there appeared to be a difference in the manner with which the two henchmen treated her, the way Solly the Turk gestured politely to the sofa's empty half while indicating that Grace should sit down. Both men, however, were unwaveringly hostile when they looked at Dennis.

Now convivial, Spot reiterated the arrangements for that night and the next day, before announcing that Sonny the Yank could drive him back to Hyde Park Mansions and his girlfriend Rita in Cabbell Street, while Solly the Turk took the first watch outside. As the three men were leaving, the darkly complexioned thug popped his head back around the door and spoke to Grace.

'When I'm back 'ere tomorrow mornin', sweetheart, I'll bring you that pack o' Craven "A" I promised yer. Sorry about the threats an' that. You 'ave a good night.'

Grace allowed the man a little smile of gratitude that was half wince, and with a final hangman's glare at Dennis, he was gone. Both Dennis and his inconvenienced hostess found that they were shivering, and so Grace lit the paraffin stove and they goggled in mute horror at each other, albeit relatively temperately. Later, Grace would thank him for the autographed Surrealist Racing Forecast Cards and they'd confer before she went off to her bedroom and left Dennis to his largely sleepless sofa, but there in the wake of Spot's departure they were speechless, tongue-tied with the upsets of the day. They both knew that they had a lot to talk about, not least their individual contributions to the ongoing predicament, but neither one knew where to start. At last, Grace broke the silence by referring to the issue that was hanging heavy on both of their minds.

'Didn't that bloke look like Glenn Miller?'


On the Thursday morning they were up and dressed by eight, which was when Jack Spot and his men came back, with every-one except the criminal entrepreneur appearing rough and far from rested. Solly Kankus, who was not remotely Turkish and was in fact Jack Spot's cousin, was made Grace's minder for the day while Spot himself popped in and out on bits of other busi-ness. Dennis had seen Kankus surreptitiously slip Grace a packet of ten Craven 'A' on his arrival, and concluded there were prob-ably worse killers she could be held hostage by. As for his own ordeal, it was decided that Sonny the Yank – now carrying a black cane that looked worryingly like a swordstick – would drive Dennis to his rendezvous with Spare in Brixton. This trip south, borne on a tide of writhing blue exhaust beneath gunmetal heavens, entailed very little in the way of conversation. Dennis learned that Sonny was no more a Yank than Solly was a Turk; that his real name was Bernard Schack; and, yes, it was a swordstick. They'd just pulled in opposite the entrance to Wynne Road when Sonny made this last point clear, as his extremely anxious passenger was climbing from the car: 'That little Grace girl, she's worth ten o' you. You let her down, you don't turn up this evenin' with whatever it is Spotty wants, and I solemnly swear that I will run you through from arse to gullet. Now get out.' When Dennis hunched across the Brixton Road towards his fated destination, he could feel Glenn Miller's eyes, in cold facsimile, boring into his spine. Grace, it appeared, had made something of an impression.

All in grey, the crumpled terrace wallowed in a luxury of bleakness as he made his way towards Spare's doorstep, once more carpeted in cats, although possibly different ones to yesterday's. Answering Dennis's half-hearted knock, the tall landlady with the faded-wallpaper demeanour didn't bother speaking to him, nodding instead to the cellar entrance at the far end of the hallway with a rattle of her beads in lieu of words. Halfway through his mumbled apologies, she disappeared with nothing but the ghost of her cheap scent to say she'd ever been there. Fearing that no good would come of this, fearing that him and Grace would be no more by nightfall, he went down the bare brick steps into the artist's permanent electric gloaming.

The impossibly small basement cubicle seemed somehow different to the way it had the day before, and Dennis realised with a start that Spare – halfway across the room and bending over with his back turned – had been tidying up, or at least moving mountains of exquisite refuse into new positions. Previously unseen areas of wall were visible, exposing distressed plaster and some childlike chalk lines, a skewed rectangle perhaps left over from some rough-and-ready geometric calculation, no doubt formerly concealed behind a dune of leering fauns. Spare, shifting a stack of unravelling devils closer to the chest of drawers, looked round with a disarming grin as he heard Dennis's hesitant tread behind him. There were only four cats, but it seemed like more.

'Ah, Mr Knuckleyard! Good mornin' to yer. I'm still gettin' ready, an' I'm not long out o' bed. Got a bit plastered with the Grants an' Gawsworth after you went 'ome last night. Stone me, that Johnny Gawsworth, he can't 'alf put 'em away. Asked us all back to 'is place when they called last orders, so that 'e could serve us coffee with M. P. Shiel's ashes in it. Fuck that for a game o' soldiers. I told 'im that coffee made me fart since my experiences in the First World War, then staggered to me rest. What about you? What kind of night did you 'ave?'

Which was, obviously, quite a saga. Spare was someone else that Dennis hadn't told about Jack Spot, and although Spare smiled when he heard about the mobster's dread of him, the windswept moorland of his features clouded over at the mention of Spot's deal, with Grace's life and safety as a bargaining chip. Surrounded as he was by copulating horrors, the magician's lip curled in distaste.

'Well, that's unfortunate. Makes things a touch more complicated, but we'll 'ave to see what we can do. 'ere, tell yer what, open that cupboard door for us so I can put these last few odds and sods away, then we can get on with our business.'

Eager to comply, Dennis's hand had closed around the cupboard's bulbous doorknob before he remembered it had been a looping chalk scrawl halfway up the wobbly rectangle, and that Spare's cell was much too small to have space for a cupboard, but by then

*the loosely scribbled door is opening away from him on to a sun-speared sunken garden, and there's summer in his lungs, orchestral thunder in his thudding heart, the soft force of Spare's hand against Dennis's back, encouraging him out into the sound and light of a translated morning ...*

*he stands shaking in a ringed drystone enclosure, set a good ten feet into the earth with soil-and-wood stairs climbing to the surface, nameless flowers erupting from their interstices ... overhead, the sky's a pouring dazzle ... the South London oracle steps out into the submerged yard, closing a portal that from this side seems a stoutly timbered affair after*

*him, and looking like a different man ... his layers of shabby clothing
are the same, and likewise his lined face, but where the pumice smoulder of the painter's hair had been is now a blinding phosphorous, a
film frame trapped in the projector's gate and melting into empty glare
... something apologetic in the artist's tone ... 'I didn't mean to take
you for a mug. It's just the crossin's easier if you're not thinking of it
consciously, blunderin' through a door that's not really a door. Bit like
me sigils what I do: it only works when it's not on yer mind' ... Spare
walks towards the rough-hewn steps and runs one hand back through
his white mane of St Elmo's fire, self-consciously ... Dennis is just now
noticing malformed miniature faces, a grotesque precipitation in the weird
delineator's wake ... 'Sorry about me barnet, as well. It's just 'ow I look
when I come 'ere. And take no notice o' these ugly mushes followin' me
everywhere. They're atavistic personalities I'm sheddin'. Anyway, come
on. The sooner we get started then the sooner we'll be finished' ...
solemnly they mount the steps towards the opening, with Spare ahead
and Dennis batting at the imbecile visages showering from the strange
old man's ball-lightning hair ...*

*ground-level Brixton all around is an engulfing swirl of giant paint
in constant flux between distressed brick terraces and garden-suburb
fields; between stark monochrome and too ripe technicolour; between
disagreeing centuries in furious debate ... the skull of sky enclosing
everything rains light in the straight downpour of a wrestling match, or
Greek theatre ... Dennis isn't vomiting, but still feels far from steady
at the creep from turf to tarmac underfoot ... he can't take it all in,
doesn't have room, and Spare's already wading off impatiently into the
sometimes filth and sometimes flowers, leaking a contrail of insufferable
countenances ... 'It's Tower Bridge we're 'eaded for, or Bran's Span,
what they call it 'ere. Then up to where the 'eads are – an' I've got yer
poxy book tucked in me pocket, by the by. After we're done there, I'll be
turnin' back, but I've sent word to Monolulu, so with any luck 'e'll meet
us and take you the rest o' the way 'ome. Now, buck up, an' try not to
step on any fairies or inchoate forms' ... they're trampling roughly north
along what might be an exaggerated Brixton Road, where the bucolic
hedgerows blossom into Atlantean chip shops, into gibberish-scrawled
shutters and unfathomable enterprises before shrivelling back to grass*

*and bushes weighted with gargantuan strawberries ... behind them, they leave flickering Deco palladiums, crystal windmills scattering paint-box smudges and the cast-off selves of the disgruntled mystic ...*

*near as bilious as on his first excursion, Dennis staggers where Spare strides, both men waist-deep in wriggling history, climbing towards Camberwell Immaculate through slip and shimmer from horizon to horizon ... there are figures blurring into momentary focus everywhere about: a grey child railing from a soapbox; an untended pram that holds a year-old baby with a painted lightning bolt across its puzzled features ... and a great tornado of a creature that storms down the centre of the road through squirming symbol, liquid time, descending on the Burn of Brixton while the artist and the errand boy head past it in the opposite direction ... Spare inclines his blinding locks towards the spectacle ... 'That's one o' yer Arcana, that is. That's the Inferred Saracen' ...*

*approximately eight feet high, it flaps and wraps and ravels in a ribbon squall of incompatible couture, whip strips of zippered leather overlayering vivid fabrics, baggy denim, orchid skirts and threadbare second-hand suits in a constant flail ... in shape and gait it is now he, now she, flowing in gender seamless from one moment to the next, from undulant to angular, from drunken slouch to dance to riotous scatter ... intermittently exposed, the being's skin shifts through the spectra between palest tan and ink-black that is almost blue ... likewise its hair, erupting into spheric shrubbery, unpeeling into swaying ropes of tangle and receding to a fine suede in which cryptic runes are somehow etched, or else concealed by pork-pie hat, by knitted yellow-green-red, by full covering with veil and the brief, slanting insolence of a beret ... six arms it has, that reprise the continual swim and gesture of a Hindu god, and at its many hands a slippery montage of coloured bottles, paperbacks, gramophone records, knives, guns, Bibles, roll-up cigarettes, nice handbags, oversized American hamburgers ... as its self-transforming flutter hurries down the stunning avenue towards the district's heart, it wears an envelope of wildly various song and music, fragments tuning in and out like random fiddling with the wireless dial ... the apparition dwindles on the brilliant thoroughfare, moving away from them, and Dennis glances in bewilderment to Spare for explanation ...*

*features lit unearthly by his halo mane, the cunning-man of Wynne Road stabs a jutting chin at the increasingly remote southbound phenomenon* ... *'It looks and sounds like that because it's made from bits o' past an' bits o' future, tossed up like an 'istory salad. Been 'ere in the 'igher Town as long as anybody can remember, but these days you see a lot of it 'ere in the Burn o' Brixton or across in Nottin' 'ill Sublime, where yer've got the West Indians comin' in. I've tried to draw it, but it's near enough impossible to get the movement, all them bandages o' different years forever windin' round it'* ... *none the wiser, Dennis asks if the impressive being is perhaps the essence of black people, but Spare shakes his head, dislodging a brief rain of dandruff Calibans, and says, 'Nah. It's the Inferred Saracen, the essence o' what white people imagine about black people'* ... *and they continue with their spectral promenade, and the great distance that they tread slips effortlessly by in a smudged torrent of backyards and miracles as they retrace their passage of the previous evening, up through Taller Walworth and the skirts of Blazing Lambeth, pulsing in the endless noon* ...

*the Elephant and Castle is replaced by a tremendous sphinx, high as St Paul's and hewn from limestone, with its body a war pachyderm that wears a castellated howdah on its back, and has a carven face resembling Eleanor of Castile, the Infanta, as symbology hedges its bets* ... *the monumental woman-headed tusker seems more stable, more continuous than the surrounding structures that are rotted and regenerated with each passing second* ... *Dennis is slapped speechless by streets that are all and only language, leaving any small talk to his incandescent escort* ... *'Not to state the bleedin' obvious, but this is where Blake got 'is Golgonooza from; 'is fourfold city what's forever fallin' down an' buildin' itself up again, along with everything that's in it. Tell the truth, it's where I get me goats that turn to tits and candle wax, all the inchoate forms I warned you not to step on earlier. All of us artists, poets and ne'er-do-wells 'ave done alright from the Great When, an' if it sometimes needs a favour in return, best not to 'ang about. That's why I'm with yer now – I mean, you seem a nice enough young feller, but I know it's what the 'eads would want, so it's my obligation, if you like. And Monolulu's, if the fiddlin' bugger bothers to turn up'* ...

amongst the temporary rural turf furring the pavements underfoot, Spare indicates one of the aforementioned clusters of material substance in transition, the inchoate forms ... pallid and glistening in the grass, at first it's a discarded portion of cooked chicken, but the savoury muscle unpeels and reties itself upon the poking bone ... crisp skin in petals, lifting from the meat that bifurcates and splits into its new configuration, and at last a woman, naked and four inches high, shakes grease from her uncurling wings before she flitters dazedly away amongst stems that are shrinking down to kerb and cobble ... at which Dennis asks, 'Was, was, was that a fairy?' and the flare-haired illustrator nods another dozen tiny lechers, brutes and cretins into momentary being ... 'If you like. Fairies an' goblins an' all that, they boil up naturally out of the pseudo-matter 'ere, the legendary mulch. Three or four 'undred years ago, if people talked about this place, they'd name it as the Land of Cockaigne, or they'd call it Fairyland. Mind you, for sayin' that, you don't get many fairies round 'ere lately. It's a different century, where all the undecided shapes resolve themselves into stuff what's more Freudian and modern. Anyway, can't stand round natterin' all day, not if we're gunna get you to the Bonce Tribunal' ... scared to ask what that might be, Dennis falls into line behind his paint-stained Sherpa and they soldier on into a shuffled urban history beneath the sky's torrential shine ...

approaching the black, steaming palace of an overstated railway station, they behold a great and vicious spike of glass that sizzles up as if to slash the stratosphere, but then subsides to flat horizon in the blink of a dilating eye ... on an exalted Borough High Street, with the hidden river tumbling not far ahead, Spare of a sudden grabs his young charge by a scrawny arm and drags him into the Epiphany of Stoney Street ... 'Oh, fuck. Get up against the wall, an' sharpish. It's an anamorphic spasm' ... hurrying to comply, Dennis remembers Maurice Calendar using the same expression in a cautionary context, but is even so entirely unprepared for the disorient of the experience ... he doesn't understand what he is seeing ... there's a visual ripple shuddering across the landscape, from the Over-Borough racing east to Perfect Bermondsey, a travelling distortion moving through the ground, the atmosphere, and everything it passes is stretched instantly enormous before swift contraction once the lensing shiver has moved on ... buildings balloon, entities

*elongate, swelling and dwindling in the seismic fisheye pulse ... traffics
of chariot or palanquin rubber upwards into skinny strings, then just as
quickly snap back to a manageable size, continuing their journeys as if
nothing had occurred; as if what had just happened was quite normal
... indeed, Dennis would assume the bulging visuals to be a disorder of
his eyes alone if not for the anxiety in Spare's ...*

*after a taut, unmeasurable interval, the optic pressure front reduces to
a distant migraine-jangle over Rotherhithe Unfolded, far off to the east
of this incessant everything, at which the destitute enchanter raggedly
exhales ... 'A bit too close for comfort, that was. Anamorphic spasms,
they're a weather pattern, 'ere where all the shapes are shiftin' an' there's
nothin' stable. You won't see 'em more than once in a blue moon, but
when you do, steer clear of 'em' ... the artist turns and stalks off up
the relatively narrow lane of trees, no, cottages, no, slithering silver filigree, and Dennis trots behind him babbling questions in a literal and
figurative effort to keep up ... 'But why does everybody say they're
dangerous? The things and people they affect go back to normal straight
away with no harm done, it looks like' ... plainly irritated, Spare glares
back across his shoulder through the drizzle of depraved personas ...
'Yeah, well, that's because the things and people they affect are made
out of ideas, where it don't matter if you stretch 'em out a bit. If they
were made o' beef an' bone an' bits o' gristle like what you an' me are,
it'd be a different story, mark my words. No, it's a good effect, an' I can
use it in me pictures, but I've seen what 'appens if you don't get out the
way in time. You ask Jack Neave if yer run into 'im. Now, shut yer yap
an' follow me up here. I'll show you summat dangerous, if that's what
yer after' ...*

*at its top, their paradisiacal defile runs into the Despairs of Clink
Street, where is something terrible ... a heaviness descends, a gravity
that slows their pace towards the warp of wharf and warehouse bordering a still-unsighted river ... to their left extends a street-long absence,
a wide area of demolition that, almost alone amid these metamorphic
terraces, seems not to be continually renewed ... it looks as if a great,
grim structure loomed here once, a single towering and tottering wall still
standing at the site's northernmost end, with, halfway up, the empty
brickwork tangle marking the remains of an ornate rose window ... it*

*belatedly occurs to Dennis that this must be where the prison stood that gave its name to prisons everywhere … the crumbling window overlooks now an enormous cavity, where the deep cellar regions of the famous penitentiary have been scooped out, its bowels exposed to the relentless, always midday sky … his tutor's grubby hand, firm on Dennis's shoulder, shoves him gently closer to the pit's edge … 'Since we're passin', I thought you should see this. Go on, 'ave a butcher's. It's a big 'ole what they're in, so they can't 'urt yer' …*

*in the thirty-foot-deep yawn of the gaol's excavated innards is a nightmare hatchery, with creatures that are neither insect nor umbrella spidering fastidiously on the penal rubble, clambering across each others' intricately grooved and slotted backs, some several dozen of them, ratcheting and clicking … standing at the chasm's broken edge, Knuckleyard moves his head from side to side in terrified denial … on examination they have only five legs, more articulated starfish than arachnid, with a glistening jet membrane stretched between … clattering, rearing, seeking purchase on the rough sides of their subterranean pen but falling back into the melee, upturned, kicking, ghastly and majestic as piano skeletons … glitter of lenses in a briefly exposed stomach … with each failed escape they modify themselves, they fold unwanted body parts away into their casing's many apertures, Swiss Army organisms, sliding shut or opening from one configuration to another, and all their extremities have fists of needle, hook and frightful knife … a gaping beetle nest of dreadful engines …*

*now the hand between Dennis's shoulders hauls him back from the appalling precipice, almost paternally, and in his ear, the basement hierophant's gruff mutterings resume … 'They're called the Popes o' Blades. Been 'ere for donkey's years, but nobody's any the wiser about what they are. Best guess is they're precursors to these homicidal maniacs we 'ear so much about at present, 'eath and 'aigh and that lot, things what kill just for the pleasure of it. It's a fuckin' awful sight what stays with yer forever, and you must be wonderin' why I showed it to yer in the first place' … still in shock and staring blankly, Dennis only nods as he is led through stupefying alleyways in the direction of the bridge, while Spare explains … 'I wanted you to know 'ow seriously you 'ave to take this place, an' what the consequences are if anythin' goes* 'aywire: a big enough upset in this London would mean lights out for the other one; for ours. Even this place's minor problems bring about catastrophes where we come from. Remember yesterday, when you were in our kitchen, and I flung that article from the Reveille on the fire? Well, this is why: one o' the Popes got out in 1888, an' what was worse, it managed to break through into Short London before anybody realised it was gone. Most probably, it got in by one o' the Liberties – they were these areas o' London what were allowed different tradin' regulations – since they're just about the oldest of the back doors leadin' into the Great When. My guess is, it used the entrance near the Liberty of Norton Folgate, up in Spitalfields where your young lady 'as 'er digs. All o' that autumn it were on the loose and killin' women, an' it took a couple o' this place's heavyweights to bring it back 'ere. Sixty year ago, that was, and still mentioned in the Reveille, so be warned. Anything what leads back to this place, we don't talk about it' ...

they have by now reached the fever dream of London Bridge, and Dennis isn't sure he can go on ... his previous visit to this churning province, mostly taken up by vomiting and screaming, had been no more than ten minutes in duration, whereas this delirious ordeal seems never-ending and the pressure of merely existing at such levels of intensity is near unbearable ... the artist's casual reference to Grace Shilling, sitting up there now in Folgate Street with Jack Spot's men, betting her life on Dennis's return ... it wakes a pang of panic in him still, but, viewed from these asylum pastures, doesn't feel as real or as immediate, where there is nothing save the more-than-real, and many eras have immediacy ... the pair traverse the bridge's boiling continuity, convulsing between Roman wood and Norman elm, twelfth-century stone, supports dissolving from nineteen great arches down to five, to three, as the span reaches out across the cold, surging eternity of an immortal Thames ... the edges of the structure are a foment of mills, churches, houses, bubbling up to seven listing storeys before simmering back down ... a phantom tide of transports and pedestrians moves at the brink of visibility around them, Danes and peasant insurrections, funeral processions for dead kings with torch-bearers five hundred strong, metallic millipedes and two-floor buses in anachronistic commute ...

*then the river crossing is behind them, and with the abruptness of a journey in a dream, they're on the pall of Ratcliffe Highway, in a fizz of ghostly whores and sailors, making their approach to Shadwell Melancholy ... the despairing clank and cry of pirates drowning in their chains at Wapping Old Stairs drift inland from off the timeless waterway, sounds twisting and contorting in this latitude's peculiar acoustic ... turning left into a flattered Cannon Street Road, it occurs to Dennis that he's yet to see the golden pavements of his previous outing, reasoning that such may be confined to the four-folded city's central districts and not to be squandered on its outskirts ... he reluctantly concedes that these are the first near-coherent thoughts that he has managed since he turned that drawing of a doorknob in the Brixton artist's cellar ... overcome by the enormity of his experience, he's convinced that there are things he's missing, things that he's not seeing properly ... a problem with his vision that has troubled him throughout this current venture, a grey, blurring movement on his ocular periphery that's not there when he looks at it directly ... he's about to mention this to his more knowledgeable chaperone when the magician lifts one palm and calls a halt, the cease of movement shaking loose a further scurf of faces from Spare's arc-light hair ... 'We're 'ere' ...*

*a little way up from the Ratcliffe Highway's salty notoriety, just short of the perpetually recurring Blackshirt brawl in Cable Street, they've stopped outside somewhere that looks the way a public house would if it had been canonised, its spoor of hops worn like a halo ... a snub-cornered chapel of intoxication that, as with the Elephant and Castle or the gutted Clink, appears immune to the continuous transmutation which afflicts its neighbours ... on its signage, where the swinging board is decorated with yet more symbolic ambiguity – a youthful French prince in a golden coronet whose body is that of a porpoise – is the legend 'Crown & Dolphin' ... seeming vexed, Spare frowns along the road in both directions, murmurs, 'Still no sign o' bleedin' Monolulu, then,' and turns to address Dennis, fishing in his jacket pocket for the bad-luck Hampole volume as he does so ... 'I expect 'e'll turn up in 'is own good time, so we might just as well get on with what we're 'ere to do. This place might look like it's a boozer, but it's more a parliament. It's where the City 'eads assemble, and where 'opefully they'll take this shillin' shocker off yer without further incident. C'mon, let's go through to the front room so that we can get this business over with'* ...

*the weighted brass and glass of the establishment's main entrance pushes open on to a brief passage where the lilies on the wallpaper are moving, withering or blooming independently, and then it's through a latched door and into the haunted mumble of the Crown & Dolphin's spacious bar ... the City Heads have been arranged in a rough circle at the room's perimeter ... each is contained in a glass bell jar with a generous amount of pot-pourri to conceal any odours, all of them alive and talking, none of them still wedded to a body ... long diagonals of dust and light lean in through chinks in the drawn velvet curtains to define a glimmering indoor twilight, heavy with the redolence of flaking petals and the susurrus of ancient conversation ... there are possibly thirty or forty of the gossiping decapitations, by Dennis's paralysed and flinching estimate ... he numbly follows Spare across the room's dull claret carpeting, through a convenient gap between the bottled craniums and thus into the ringed tribunal's centre ... the glazed hubbub dies away, and scores of eyes that should have long since dried to sockets turn in puzzlement to Knuckleyard and the itinerant magician ...*

*moulting more redundant personalities, Spare brandishes aloft the battered first edition of A London Walk and takes the floor ... 'Gentlemen, ladies, my apologies for interruptin' your discussion. I am Zos, an adept from Short Brixton, 'ere to 'elp this mortal boy in the return of a breached artefact to your safekeepin'. It's the 'ampole book, what Arthur Machen took a gander at when 'e first come 'ere. It's already done a bit o' damage although, luckily, so far it's nowhere near as dreadful as that balls-up with the Soames collection, Fungoids. 'ow do all these bastard things keep gettin' out? No disrespect intended'* ... *the enchanter faces a specific cluster of the watchful trophies while he's speaking, although Dennis is as yet incapable of telling one jugged remnant from the next, all of them shabby and ungroomed, all of them pallid save a couple that would seem to have been dipped in tar ... from the receptacle that Spare appears be addressing, one of the chopped eminences clears its ragged throat ... male and in middle age, the black hair hangs in lank and greasy locks about his meaty features, jewelled with warts on cheek and brow line, there behind the thumb-smudged glass, and Dennis realises with a lurch that it's Oliver Cromwell …*

*clearly nowhere near its rumoured resting place in Red Lion Square, the relic nut of the dead, dug-up and dismembered Lord Protector looks both angry and embarrassed, shifting with a rustle of unease amid its nest of desiccated flowers … 'Sir, we are as much perplexed by these escapes as you yourself. It might be that they are the work of parties seeking the disruption of our higher town to serve their personal imperatives, but whether Barebones, rogue Arcana or some further faction, we cannot be certain. Be assured, the matter shall reach resolution swiftly and with great severity' … the muffled voice is grudging and officious, bristling with ill-concealed impatience, and the cold eyes of the regicide are swivelled now to Dennis … 'Thank you for your timeliness and your discretion in returning this unfortunate bedevilment to us. My name is Oliver Williams-called-Cromwell. Who are you?' … Dennis finds his hands are shaking, palms suddenly wet with perspiration as he answers to the severed head of England's most successful and most ruthless revolutionary … 'I'm Den, Den, Dennis Knuckleyard. I'm sorry. I'm not used to this' … the captive capitals shuffle themselves around as far as they are able in their scented grit and prickle, eyes meeting conspiratorially, any remaining eyebrows lifted … finally, after conferring with his white- and red-haired neighbours in the jars to either side of him, what's left of Cromwell raises once more its slate gaze to Dennis … 'Knuckleyard. That is a clan we have not heard about before this day. The appellation seems to us outrageous, but is in some way not unfamiliar. Friend Swedenborg, what are your own thoughts on the matter of this young whelp's disconcerting name?' …*

*the white-haired revenant in the adjacent vessel is an older man whose skin is ironed-smooth tissue paper, beard coiled like a sleeping cat in the crushed lavender, his piping voice almost inaudible from underneath the glinting dome … 'He is, I think, familiar to our future, for are we not angels who know naught of time? That being so, the choice of his admission is not ours to make, and is already in a sense resolved. Whether this fore-remembered Knuckleyard should bring us benefit, misfortune or the pair in tandem, we can but sit in our lucent bulbs and let his comedy or otherwise play as it must' … after a moment's* contemplation, the malignant egg that is now all of Cromwell rocks and totters slightly, nodding in so far as it is capable of doing so ... a ripple of agreement seems to run through the encircling crania, transmitted in a language of squints, blinks, pursed lips and non-committal grunts ... a woman with protuberant eyes, possibly Anne Boleyn, develops hiccups ...

with this article on the agenda settled to their satisfaction, the council of overdressed skulls gradually resume their previous apiary drone of muted conversation, buzzing softly from their separate glass hives ... hugely discouraged, Dennis harbours the impression that the Lewis Carroll audience has been concluded, but then Spare steps forward, his armada-beacon haircut spilling cameo deformities ... "old on a minute. Beggin' your illustrious pardon, I'm not done. This young whelp, as yer call 'im, 'e's put 'imself an' 'is loved ones in 'arm's way on your account. Right now, there's a Short London gangster, Jack Spot, got 'is girlfriend 'ostage, threatenin' to execute the pair of 'em if Dennis can't arrange a meetin' between Spot an' the Great When's epitome o' criminal endeavour, 'oo I'm guessin' is still 'arry Lud. There's one bloke dead already because you lot can't keep yer man-eatin' books shut in their kennels. Never mind takin' the piss at 'is daft name, just get the 'opeless little bugger out of 'is predicament, an' keep the peace in both our 'ouses, ay?' ...

at this impertinence, the gathered delegates furrow their many brows, save for the few coated with hardened tar, who cannot ... trying to shake his head but only wobbling, the tyrant puritan is adamant in his refusal ... 'No. A common cutpurse, while in life, shall not be granted entrance to our holy purlieus' ... in the bottle-hushed commotion, the red-headed specimen residing next to Cromwell lifts his reedy tones above the whispering uproar ... 'At your sufferance, I am John, who is Williams also, falsely called the murderer of Ratcliffe, and so emblem to injustice and her sanctimonious sister. In matters of criminality, mine is the senior authority. I move that Master Lud be granted licence to step out into the transient domain, there to conduct this exchange without trespass' ... following a brief and mostly mouthed debate, the fragranced horrors reach some manner of consensus and the Cromwell remnant is obliged to grudgingly make his concessions ... 'Very well. If Master Lud *should prove agreeable, we shall permit this interchange. Do you propose a site and an occasion?' ... after first conferring with the human suppli- cants, the flame-haired scapegoat suggests Arnold Circus in Shoreditch – where there apparently exists an aperture between the Londons – offering the next day's midnight as a schedule for the dialogue, to which the architect of interregnum sourly agrees ... 'Then we are done. Please leave the damnable book on the floor where you are standing, that our servitors may presently secure it. I bid you good day' ... dismissed, the two men drift in apprehensive silence past the ever-wilting, ever-bloom- ing lilies in the hallway, back on to the sparkling résumé of Cannon Street Road, with a contrite Ras Prince Monolulu anxiously awaiting their emergence ...*

*marvellous in his erupting ostrich plumes and garment of embroi- dered charms, the trackside dandy is an English dream of Africa who seems less out of place here than he had in earthly Berwick Street ... 'Ah! Mr Spare and our young sprinter of this Tuesday last! Forgive me for the sluggishness of my arrival, but my morning has been spent escaping the deceitful rogues who claim they are my creditors. Confound them and their so-called promissory notes! How went your natter with the sainted loafs of bread? Did you return their piece of dog-eared juju without injury?' ... Spare nods, and mugging atavisms burst against the bogus prince's robe of moons and shamrocks ... 'I suppose it went alright, seein' as neither of us are wearin' our bladders on the outside like a pair of underpants. There's complications, though. Jack Spot's after a chat with 'arry Lud, and 'e'll top matey 'ere an' 'is young lady if it en't forthcomin'. You tell Ironfoot when yer see 'im that the 'eads 'ave granted us a meetin' for tomorrer midnight, up by the ol' rookeries in Arnold Circus. 'e'll know what to do' ... the tipster and the conjuror consult while Cannon Street Road's soul foams up prismatic everywhere about ... once more at Dennis's eye corner is dust-coloured movement, although when he looks there's nothing there ... scratching his head, displacing scabs of obsolete identity, Spare looks uneasy, eager to depart ... 'I don't like bein' 'ereabouts for too long at a stretch, in case I get the 'eebie-jeebies. Monolulu, 'e'll accompany yer from 'ere, an' I'll nip back over the Centuries o' Thames to me black 'ole o' Brixton. 'ope it all works out, young Knuckleduster. Look us up, if you should get 'ome in one piece'* ... *and with his literal headlight and his comet tail of sloughed monstrosities, he strolls away downhill towards the Ratcliffe slaughters and the river's billion-gallon rush of moment ...*

*bleeding colours into the surrounding jamboree, Prince Monolulu smiles encouragingly and claps Dennis on the shoulder ...* 'Let us hurry, sah, the quicker to be done with all this harum-scarum. Mr Spare is right to say that too much travel here will lead us only to the booby hatch, and we must rush to our appointment in Stoke Newington Miraculous' ... *as stately and involved with gambling as a riverboat, the talismans of his apparel billowing like banners, he steams off into the scrambled myth and chronicle with Dennis bobbing in his wake, caught up in the man's hurtling energy ...*

*they charge through fantasies of Whitechapel and Spitalfields, where the tall church is now a latticework of interlocking ivory daggers, brown stains on their cutting edges, and where, in a lower world than this, Grace Shilling loiters in unlovely company and waits for Dennis to get home ... there are displayed albinos, crocodiles paraded in the effluent Nile of a gutter and still, in his side sight, balls of optic fluff that are dispelled by the most fleeting direct glance ... Dennis is dogging Monolulu's footsteps through a tangle of constrained Elizabethan passageways, peopled by intermittent serfs and flickering centurions, ducking low wooden beams that grow out of thin air to bridge these narrow, tilting streets he doesn't know, and now he asks his symbol-decorated escort where they are ... the Epsom witch doctor pauses amid a temporary flock of herded geese, and looks back over one embellished shoulder at the gawping adolescent ...* 'Why, we are in the Persist of Cripplegate, a very famous part of dear old London, flattened by the fucking bastard Germans, and I will make no apology for my improper language. A young gent of tender years such as yourself will very likely not remember such a place' ... *they move on through the huddled lanes that vacillate between cobbles and mud, the geese dissolving into a black carthorse who snorts steam, and Dennis yelps excitedly on realising his location ...* 'I've been into Cripplegate, when I was little and me mum took me there shopping once or twice. I was out in the Blitz the night they bombed it, nine years old I must have been, and sheltering in Glasshouse Yard just up the way when all of the incendiaries were coming down. God, I'd forgotten that. And *when the air raid finished, I saw something, in the fire and smoke, just for a second. It was like an archway, but I think it had, like, little rooms with windows piled on top of it'* ... *the turf diviner beams and lifts a piebald hand to indicate the soaring structure rising from the flagstones, duckboards, tarmac path ahead of them* ... *'Then you were privileged, my friend. You saw the Cripplegate itself. I would lay odds that your glimpse was brought on by Germany's despicable bombardment, which made cracks in both the entwined cities, oh, my word, yes! Although I recall that Glasshouse Yard was one of London's Liberties, places unusually susceptible to jiggery and pokery. That may have been what did the trick'* ...

*incapable of speech, Dennis trails after his gregarious guide, sleepwalking under the arched portal that he'd long ago dismissed as shell shock, the old Roman gate demolished to permit a widened road, two hundred years before he'd been conceived* ... *he foggily recalls the horror-stricken figure reeling in the firelit aperture, but manages to steer that thought away before he has a chance to inwardly encounter the name Shakespeare* ... *he's got too much on his plate already, and the grey blots are still there, elusive at the margins of his vision* ... *they continue through the self-dismantling territories, making their way north beyond the Sleep of Bunhill where Blake, Bunyan and Defoe sit perched on headstones in fluorescent conference, on into Shoreditch Remarkable, the Hoxton Stumbles, Crackling Hackney and the Stamp of Shacklewell* ... *mile after mile of curdling and clarifying splendour, terrors of hybrid significance in all their Sunday finery, a monsoon of distractions notwithstanding the ongoing difficulties with his eyesight* ...

*these last are resolved, unpleasantly, on the Apotheosis of Albion Road, as Knuckleyard and Monolulu reach the fraying borders of Stoke Newington Miraculous* ... *here are a myriad of flowers of unfamiliar hue, constant between the insubstantial architecture and the stuttering manifestation of its populace – entrepreneur Svengalis, slavers, abolitionists and lost Pre-Raphaelites – surfacing and submerging in the trickle of its time stream* ... *noticing once more the optic fluke that hovers at the fringe of his perception, Dennis turns and looks at it directly in the expectation that it will evaporate but, horrifyingly, this time it doesn't* ... *seated on a fist of rock that juts from the uncanny flora is the memorably* hideous cat that he'd last seen yesterday morning, pouring out through Austin Spare's front door when the magician's landlady had opened it ... a suede of gristle-grey so fine upon the pelt that it looks naked, every crease and fold of its repulsive skin exposed to view ... without the camouflage of fur, the felid's epidermis is too thin to fully mask the queasy mechanisms of its jaw and the attendant muscles, lending it a peeled look ... nothing but contempt in its piss-yellow eyes ...

catching sight of the sickening creature just a second later, Monolulu becomes motionless so instantaneously that he might have turned to chinaware ... what most unsettles Dennis is the startled recognition and stark fear suddenly gripping his hereto fore unflappable companion ... 'Please, sah, do not move. We are in danger for our lives' ... the cat licks one unappetising paw and says, 'Oh, you're in worse danger than that, and standing still's not going to help. If things have reached the point where you're talking with me, then, frankly, nothing's going to help' ... the voice, upsettingly, is male and human, but with yowling twists of pitch at unexpected intervals ... the stomach-turning sphinx stands up and stretches before hopping from its granite pedestal down to the violet grass, uncomfortably close to the two men's rooted feet ... it paces in a slow, deliberate circle that compels the victims to perform a shuffling rotation at its centre, turning like a frightened cake stand lest it get behind them ... in its padding orbit, the cat's jaundiced gaze does not shift from them for an instant, with the barely covered bone whip of its thin tail switching irritably back and forth ...

unable to restrain himself, Dennis asks Monolulu what their perse-cutor is, in a hoarse whisper that the beast inevitably hears ... stopping abruptly in its tracks, it cocks its anatomical depiction of a head and icily regards the pair ... again the voice, unsettling and detuned ... 'They call me Charming Peter' ... finding himself in a conversation with a cat and no idea how to proceed, his normally loud colleague staying wisely silent, Dennis tremulously asks, 'And why, why, why is that?', to which the cat replies, 'Because they have to' ... with no warning, it steps forward until it is standing at the youngster's flinching toecaps, tilting back its head to nail him with a sodium-lamp stare ... 'Listen to what I'm saying. I can harm you in ways that you didn't know existed. I pulled Teddy Wilson inside out as easily as if he'd been a washday sock, and *he wasn't a fraction of the problem you'll turn out to be. You're going to be the worst mistake those putrid noggins ever made, perhaps the one that brings this city down around their perfumed ears. Listen to what I'm saying. If I could, I'd disembowel you now before you've ruined everything, but that's not how it works. Just know that when the day arrives, it will be me who's coming for you'* ... *at this point, with great reluctance, Monolulu feels compelled to put his oar in* ... 'Charming *Peter, I implore you, sah. This young chap cannot be the obstacle that you suppose. Please do not form an untoward impression of the boy because of his naivety'* ... *the cat subjects him to a nearly fleshless smile* ... 'Oh, don't you worry about this walking disaster. You've got troubles *of your own. Your death, when it occurs, will be the doing of black magic. But I mustn't keep you. You have lots to think about'* ... *and then, with a last withering inspection of the cowering Knuckleyard, it's gone into the drifts of unknown flower* ...

*despite the animal's repeated admonitions, Dennis had stopped listening when Charming Peter had claimed authorship in the demise of Teddy Wilson, and can only stand there trembling, nothing in his head but deafening fire alarms of panic* ... *by his side, the vivid racing fore-caster is pale as cigarette ash, winded by the hairless monster's forecast and for once devoid of spiel* ... *the cat has evidently got his tongue* ... *with neither man willing or able to remark on what just happened and a knot of doom nested in both their bellies, they continue in near silence through the sumptuous gardens of Stoke Newington Miraculous, flaring with wraiths of flesh and brickwork* ... *suffragettes and burning pillar boxes, unimaginable entertainments and a stadium chant that echoes in the higher world's unearthly soundscape, ringing from the future* ... 'Harry Roberts is our friend, he kills coppers' ...

*finally, their trek concludes at an Edenic park, where the unprecedented blossoms are contained by bastions of fabulous design* ... *still barely able to converse, Prince Monolulu indicates a rearing wall of windows at the meadow's furthest end* ... *one of the apertures up on its highest floor is standing open and seems shabbier than the rest, an ordinary builder's ladder soiled with whitewash propped incongruously beneath it, out of place in these transcendent reaches* ... *at the ladder's foot, his sobered guide conveys with an extended palm that Dennis should be first to climb the spattered, splintery rungs … stupid with dread and glory he ascends, almost completely unaware of what he's doing, still preoccupied by that unutterable cat … he can hear Monolulu, heavy on the treads behind him, as he nears the gaping fenestration, paintwork peeling on its weathered frame … he can't see anything past the chipped ledge, with whatever interior exists beyond become a square of solid blackness in its contrast to the drenching light outside … still trying to recall the worst of Charming Peter's horrid monologue, he's unprepared for the thick, powerful arms that thrust from out the inky dark to grab his gabardine lapels … he's struggling in empty space, and then,*

before he knew it, he was grovelling and wheezing on the stained linoleum of a cabbage-scented hovel, the untidy junk of a material world piled everywhere upon its busted furniture. This time he didn't puke or weep, but both his mind and stomach were performing somersaults, wrenched by the shock of his transition. Dennis became haltingly aware that there were voices in the dingy room with him, and groggily he levered himself upright to see who it was.

The gnarled and bulky market trader that he'd clocked in Berwick Street the other day hulked to his left, and to his right there was the oddly built man with the dragging orthopaedic shoe. Between them, being helped over the ledge into the gloom of the apartment, a clearly exhausted Monolulu cursed and swore, 'Never again! That is the last time, or I am a Dutchman. The last time!' Out through the window, framing the pretended prince, were the pavilions and the unimaginable blossoms of a dissident reality, a madman's heaven tinted by a broader rainbow.

This time, Dennis fainted.

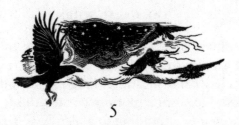

5

*Woodenhead*

When the world returned to Dennis, it was not immediately recognisable. Horse-blanket curtains had been
pulled across the problematic window at the room's end, shutting out the alien sunshine and replacing it with an unshaded
lightbulb, dangling from its twist of flex. The cluttered living
space, to Dennis, appeared unaccountably and wholly wrong,
from floor to furnishings to the three men who were apparently
in the apartment with him: nothing changed or shifted, everything stayed resolutely as it was from one slow minute to the
next. The murmur of the other parties' discourse did not shrill
or bubble up into a fanfare of imaginary instruments, remaining
at a register that now seemed flat and two-dimensional. The
normal was for a few moments foreign, as with the attempt to
walk on solid ground after a spell at sea.

He found himself sprawled on what felt like an inadequately
sprung settee, his body limp as someone made from wool.
Nearby, sat hunched on a low stool, the disproportioned chan-
cer with the iron boot was speaking as he held out an exotic
object made of liquid, bone and rising vapour, which Dennis at
last identified as a hot drink.

'Here, get this down yer – a nice drop o' Rosie with three
sugars. That'll sort you out.'

Taking the proffered cup in nerveless woollen fingers,
Dennis sipped, surprised as the warm sweetness seeped into his
system and the habit of material being gradually came back to
him. Details of his environment unhurriedly swam into focus

as he reassembled what existed, jigsaw piece by jigsaw piece. He noticed the unsteady ladder that he'd lately mounted, evidently pulled back in and resting on its side against the skirting board. Up in one gloomy corner, the imposing fruit-and-veg purveyor sat attending to a plainly agitated Monolulu, who was fretting over his foretold demise, to be occasioned by black magic. 'Sah, I'd sooner be back marching for my meals with the Salvation Army than go near that slinking fiend again! It pisses poison everywhere, and looks like it's been skinned! I wish with all my heart it could be boiled to glue!' The market vendor's guttural commiserations were too softly spoken to be audible, though this did not decrease his overpowering presence: even from his couch on the far side of the untidy quarters, Dennis could see muscles standing out like tree roots on the big man's neck and forearms. Blincoe, that was the chap's name. Gog Blincoe.

Closer to him, crouching on a few inches of footstool, the character with the built-up shoe had his attention on the couple in the corner, listening to Monolulu's tirade of complaint and Blincoe's gravelly reassurances, eyes sad and sympathetic beneath overgrown black brows. Without the customary hat to cover it, the fellow's hair was long and lank down to his collar, but, on top, was hardly there at all. He wore his heavy coat indoors against the late October chill, and at his wrinkled throat, a purple silk cravat bunched in its ornate silver fastening. He turned his somehow noble head to Dennis and smiled wearily, nodding towards the still-indignant tipster.

'Charmin' Peter, ay? Sounds like you 'ad a run-in with that scabby little fleabag, from what Monolulu 'ere's been tellin' us while you were spark-out. I'm Jack, by the way. Jack Neave, but people call me Ironfoot. Lovely to meet yer.'

The worn-leather voice was soft, warm and accommodating, and, to Dennis as he surfaced from his swoon, seemed an aural equivalent to the revivifying tea he was already halfway through. At Charming Peter's name, though, he made an attempt to sit bolt upright, managing an unimpressive forty-five degrees before subsiding back on to the sofa's lumpy cushioning. The man with mismatched legs gazed at him questioningly, while Dennis tried to recall what words were for.

'What, what, what's Charming Peter? What's he for? What, what, what does he do?'

Neave turned the corners of his mouth down and then tipped his head from one side to the other, indecisively. His mannerisms and his intonations seemed to have been probably acquired from marketplaces, fairgrounds or the draughty ends of seaside piers, Dennis decided.

'Well, if I'm succinct about it, 'e's a mouthy little cunt. 'e's, like, a frightener, and an enforcer, what's called a performer in the criminal fraternity. That's not to say, however, that 'e can't do you a mischief – in all likelihood, a fatal mischief – if you piss 'im off. Officially, he's answerable to the City 'eads, but if there's something or somebody that 'e thinks needs doin', they don't ask too many questions. They're a mixed bag, are the 'eads. Ol' Swedenborg and ginger nut, John Williams, they're alright, but Cromwell and 'is mates you need to keep yer eye on. I mean, they're not goin' anywhere, but all the same. A lot of 'em are just as crafty now as when they were on shoulders.'

Dennis's partial recuperation had been spotted by the duo on the chamber's other side, who now pulled up their spindly chairs to the settee, both of them towering over Ironfoot Jack, squatting beside the couch's nearer end. Down at its foot, Prince Monolulu remonstrated volubly, the blustering outrage doing nothing to disguise the fact that he'd been shocked to his flamboyant core.

'Thank heavens that you are recovered from our grave ordeal. I feared the mangy brute's insinuations may have speared your vitals, as they have my own.'

Seated on Monolulu's left, Gog Blincoe lifted up a spade-sized hand with pale hairs curled like shavings on its back, to still the forecaster's offended ire.

'The London Cat will do as it will do, and cannot have a part in our discussions. To my mind, more pressing is the matter of

Jack Spot and the young woman. That is business that we must put right, and do it sooner rather than too late.'

With a protruding jaw and his small eyes like knotholes, the street vendor's face was contoured something like that of a wild boar or a head from Easter Island. The deliberation evident in Blincoe's every word or gesture had an aura of such gravity that Dennis once more tried to lever himself upright to show his respect, this time with more success. His head still swimming, he sat on the sofa's edge and, prompted by the trader's mention, thought with sudden paralysing clarity of Grace and the appalling trouble they were in. Dazedly gaping at the men around him, he attempted to convey such useful information as he could, stumbling on words and dribbling his syllables.

'Grace – the young woman – Spot's got her in Spitalfields. He said, he said that if I didn't get him the arrangement that he wanted, he was going to top the pair of us. He said ...'

Once more Gog Blincoe raised a weighty palm, the loops and whorls of which were not restricted to its fingertips, and with a curving lifeline so deep that it looked as if a saw had slipped. His voice had the low, splintering creak of ships' holds in the night.

'We have been told about your situation, Mr Knuckleyard. Along with our absent acquaintance, Mr Calendar, we have been watching out for you since the bad book turned up in Berwick Street. And now, if we hear right, the Heads of the Great When have been petitioned.'

Ironfoot Jack had straightened up from his uncomfortable footstool, repositioning himself on the couch next to Dennis now a space was vacant. Lighting an unfinished dog-end that he'd taken from behind one ear, his interjection was a thing of billowing blue-grey.

'Our Abyssinian royalty 'ere tells us 'ow Awstin swung a deal with Cromwell and the rest, allowin' 'arry Lud into the short world so that 'im and Spot can 'ave their chit-chat.'

Monolulu sucked on his front teeth dismissively and nodded.

'What my one-and-a-half-legged friend says is, for once, entirely accurate. Their villainous discussion will take place in

Arnold Circus at the witching hour tomorrow, by which time I hope to be somewhere else altogether. I can no longer afford to interfere in magical affairs, now I've been rudely told that they will be the death of me. I think that it is time for me to cut my losses.'

Blincoe's shrug was like that of an oak in strong wind.

'Be that as it may, our earliest priority must be the woman who is being held a prisoner. Despite what the City Heads have said, we have no guarantee that Mr Spot shall not betray his bargain, and so do away with Mr Knuckleyard and the young woman, once he has the thing he wanted. My proposal is that I might walk with our young colleague here to Spitalfields where he has his appointment later, there to have a word with Mr Spot myself. It may be that I can convince him to observe the correct protocols, and in this way spare these two innocents further misfortune.'

With a grunt of effort, Jack Neave rose from the settee and limped across the lino to retrieve an ashtray from the table near the thickly curtained window, keeping up the conversation as he went. Watching him walk, morbidly fascinated by his barrelling gait, Dennis observed that the man's pumping elbows, probably employed to keep his balance, looked instead like the twin pistons powering his compact engine as he hauled his gammy leg back to the couch and resumed his position.

'Good idea. I don't imagine that a puffed-up little 'ard case like Jack Spot will want to muck about once you've explained things to 'im. As for all the Arnold Circus folderol tomorrer night, leave that wi' me. While you're off down in Spitalfields, I can get most o' that set up from this place without goin' too far out me way.'

Still putting himself back together from the mental rubble he'd been left in, Dennis started to pick up on bits and pieces of the back-and-forth that he did not yet fully understand.

'S-So where's this place, then? I'm guessing that we're in Stoke Newington, but, but the window that you covered up, that opens on the other London, doesn't it? How is that possible? I mean, this room looks like it's been here a long time. Why haven't people found it?'

Monolulu and the junior partner of M. Blincoe & Son dead-panned at each other before turning to regard their stockier associate, as if agreeing Neave should be the one to furnish Dennis with an answer. The old bohemian stubbed out his cigarette and sighed.

'It's where I'm livin' at the moment, in my ongoin' attempts to solve the Problem of Existence. It's a little 'ideaway 'ere in Stoke Newington I 'eard about a year or two ago. The bloke what owned it couldn't let it out for love nor money, on account of everybody sayin' it was 'aunted – now, the view out through the window 'ere ain't like that all the time, but then you'd only 'ave to see it once for it to make a supernatural impression, wouldn't yer? So, anyway, I snapped it up for next to nothin'. As for why nobody's found it, well, they 'ave, only they didn't know what they were lookin' at, most of 'em. Only one who did, as far as I can see, was Arthur Machen. This, unless I'm very much mistaken, is the 'ouse 'e wrote about in "N".'

Dennis's mouth was hanging open like a storm drain. With the realisation that the place where he was sitting was the one he'd read of in *The Cosy Room* at Grace's flat, the full enormity of what he was involved in hit him like a train. Even the bibulous protagonists of Machen's tale never laid eyes on this location, but saw it described in Thomas Hampole's mythical *A London Walk*, the non-existent tome which, for the past week, had been ruining Dennis's life. It was as if the world he'd thought to be a solid was instead a layered thing, made up of slippery fables all competing to be real, books within books. He'd fallen through the fragile paper page into a different narrative, where circumstance was without limitation, as were the unfathomable jeopardies. He'd clumsily tripped out of fact and on to the precarious sliding floor of fiction, where nothing was safe. Unable to make any progress with this daunting thought, he opted to deploy another question.

'And, if I can ask, who's Harry Lud, this chap that Jack Spot's meeting up with?'

Monolulu snorted in derision.

'Oh, hardly a chap, I can assure you! He is altogether of a different cut!'

Sitting beside the tipster on a chair that looked too flimsy to support his weight, Gog Blincoe shook his great totem-pole head. Long and lugubrious, his flat face seemed incapable of animation.

'Mr Lud is reckoned one of the Arcana, which are, so to speak, the foremost signifiers of the Higher Town, and so must be approached with caution. In the case of Mr Lud, who is no less than the quintessence of all crime, that caution must be doubled. I doubt any good shall come to Mr Spot from this audition, but that is not our concern, so long as no harm comes to anything this side of the divide. Now, lest my ears deceive me, I have just heard the Stoke Newington church clock striking for three. We had best be about our business in delivering this young woman from her captors.'

With similar protests from his joints and the boards under the linoleum, the tradesman stood, compelling the three other men to stand too, if they wanted to remain in earshot. Blincoe was still dressed as though for market, in a lengthy apron of rough hessian, his shirtsleeves rolled back and exposing his enormous lower arms, with thick blond springs of hair erupted from their backs as though fresh from the lathe. The right arm sported what appeared to be a pale and old tattoo, a simple heart containing the word 'Mum' that, through an accident of the long-faded ink, looked almost chiselled or engraved. Jack Neave, with something motherly in his attentiveness, bustled and clanked about the murky room as he made ready to show Dennis and the giant fruiterer out to the street.

'Come on with me, you two. And if 'is 'ighness 'ere can wait till I get back, I'll treat 'im to a tot o' rum while 'e pours out 'is troubles.'

Monolulu sniffed.

'It will take more than alcohol to ward off the dark sorcery that I am promised ... which is not, of course, to say that I refuse your offer. My best wishes to you, Dennis Knuckleyard. I hope that you and Mr Blincoe are most valorous in the rescue of this poor, unlucky girl. White man for pluck!'

Leaving the turf predictor with his ostrich feathers sagging and unkempt in the low-wattage half-light, Ironfoot Jack led Gog and Dennis through a dreamlike labyrinth of unlit landings, stairs and passageways until they reached the stout front door, which Jack unbolted.

'Good luck with that spotty little berk. You be at Arnold Circus by eleven, Friday night, so me and Gog can put yer straight before the eminences turn up for their chinwag. I don't know if we can count on Monolulu bein' there. 'e's in a funny mood, after your brush with Charmin' fuckin' Peter. Very quiet, for one thing, did yer notice? Or at least, not deafenin'. It's a bad sign. Anyway, you get on down to Spitalfields before it rains. See yer tomorrer.'

The door, final as a coffin lid but with brass letterbox and knocker, closed on Neave's comradely grin and they found themselves in the backstreets of Stoke Newington, a lengthy hike in front of them and black clouds massed like an armada overhead. Squinting towards the iron sky, Gog rubbed his hands together as if trying to start a fire, then tipped his finely wrinkled features down to favour Dennis with a sober, businesslike expression. 'Right then. Let us two be off.'


They'd walked most of the Kingsland Road's long drop in silence before the first heavy spots fell, Blincoe seemingly comfortable with keeping mum if there was nothing useful to be said. Gripping the raincoat's collar tight around his scrawny neck, Dennis glanced up in envy at the taller man who seemed oblivious to the sudden cloudburst, spattering droplets sluiced from his impassive face down seams and creases that functioned as guttering. Around the point where Kingsland Road turned with a retail flourish into Shoreditch High Street, their eventual destination nearing, Dennis felt compelled to make sure that his taciturn accomplice was prepared for confrontation.

'Will you be alright with this? I mean, Spot and his heavies have got weapons. Razors, knives. Guns, probably. It's just, I don't want you walking in there without ...'

Although the al fresco salesman's lined visage seemed too immobile to permit a smile, the log-slide rumble emanating from his chest was very like a chuckle.

'It does seem to me that all of us – saving for those limbless through injury – are bearing arms, and I believe my own to be sufficient. But what of yourself? Are you better recovered from your meeting with the London Cat than our friend Monolulu?'

They were not far from the junction with Commercial Street, walking against the rain, and Dennis shrugged his sodden shoulders in reply.

'I don't know. I suppose so, although I'm not sure how much of this I'm really taking in. I feel a bit numb, to be honest. What about Prince Monolulu, though? It sounded as if he was swearing off the other London, for fear of that, well, you know. The cat thing.'

Gravely, Blincoe shook his head, showering Dennis with the run-off.

'That is as may be, though to avoid the Great When shall avail him naught. Much like myself and my currently inconvenienced fellow Mr Calendar, the London Cat – that I refuse to call by any other name – is one of those that look enough like something from this realm to pass for normal, and may so go back and forth between the two domains. For Mr Monolulu not to venture on the Higher Town means little, when it may as readily come visit him.'

Attempting not to think about his own exchange with Charming Peter, Dennis wiped the water from his dripping eyebrows with one hand and steered the conversation on another tack.

'Yeah. Austin, Mr Spare, he said that you and Maurice Calendar came from the other place originally. I'm surprised you can be bothered with this world at all, considering it's pissing down like this half of the time. Back at the flat up in Stoke Newington, you were the one who kept insisting that the first thing was to get Miss Shilling out of harm's way, when you've never met her. I'm dead grateful that you did, but can't help wondering what makes you so concerned. I mean, I wouldn't want to handle this without you, but I can't see why you're making it your problem.'

Blincoe swivelled his eyes sideways under barely used lids and regarded Dennis pensively for a few moments, before turning his arresting countenance back to the deluge and responding.

'Am I right in thinking Mr Spare showed you the Popes of Clink Street?'

Dennis nodded warily, unsure where this was headed.

'Might it likewise be the case that he informed you of the terrible calamity that took place in the late Victoria's reign, when one of those baleful contraptions managed to discharge itself from its confinement, so that emissaries of the Great When were required for its recapture?'

They were then crossing the busy road, eliciting vexed horn blasts from a massive green Pickford's removal van that roared out of Great Eastern Street, which the stallholder did not suffer to acknowledge. Dennis once more answered Blincoe's quiz in the affirmative.

'He said the other place had sent a couple of its heavyweights to this world, so that they could catch the thing and take it back to where it came from.'

Blincoe grunted as the put-out Pickford's wagon growled off down Commercial Street.

'Aye, that were me and Mother made responsible for that grim undertaking. Popes of Blades are not without resource, and it had been evading notice by configuring itself as something broken or discarded, heaped up in the corner of a premises without remark. At last we came upon it in a yard off Heneage Street, and I allowed my mum to beat the creature to submission because being herself feminine, she had the greater hatred for it. We returned it, somewhat crippled, to its prison hole where it was swiftly killed and disassembled by its cousins. Many said that we had done a noble thing in its retrieval, although we ourselves thought otherwise.

'Here is my point: whatever we'd achieved, we'd not achieved it quick enough. More than a three-month it had taken us to find that wretched mechanism, and in that time, some five women, young ones by my reckoning, were cut to bits by the sour fruit of our ineptitude. This will explain my zeal that no more bystanders should come to mischief as a result of my unwieldy sluggishness.'

Dennis was still absorbing the foregoing anecdote, unsure if it was about what he thought it was about, and came close to colliding with the cabbage peddler when his huge companion stopped abruptly in their weighty tracks. Through windswept sheets of drizzle, Blincoe took in his surroundings before venting a despondent sigh.

'Now that I think of it, I have not been about these parts since that November night, some sixty years since. I see now that, though I never meant to, I have been avoiding it, along with all the memories that are its residents. I still recall my mother calling that malign device a little bugger when she stamped its thorax in, and I remember also the thick clicking sounds that it made in reply, much like the chain of a malicious bicycle might do. This is a sorry place, I think.'

It was only when Dennis followed the titanic merchant's nearly wistful gaze that he too, with a chime of cardiac panic, realised where they were. The metal black and white sign bolted high up on the wall of the row opposite, its letters accented with rust or pigeon shit, said 'Folgate Street'. They had arrived, and Dennis was surprised to feel his knees go weak. Blincoe, appearing not to notice, pointed to the nondescript terrace of shops across the pittering road from where they stood.

'It was up there it had got in, we reckoned, through what used to be the Liberty of Norton Folgate. All the Liberties are gateways. Why, just past that barber's is a panel that bears an advertisement for liver pills, but, in a low light and a hurry, might be taken for a door. You know how such things work by now, I trust, which is to say that they work best by happenstance.'

He once more ground his roughly textured palms together, absent-mindedly, and peered through the persisting shower at the wet front doors of Folgate Street.

'It is my understanding that the woman we have come here to assist has her address upon this very lane. Since I can see no profit in delaying matters, shall we be about our business?'

Though delaying matters had always been Dennis's preferred approach, he found he had no argument to counter Gog's more direct attitude. Reluctantly, and with his stomach knotting into animal balloons, he led his vast confederate across the rain-lashed street to Grace's doorstep.

He still had his borrowed key, and so the two of them went in the front and down the squeaking hall to what he hoped was the right flat, where he knocked timidly and heard a man's voice tell him to come in. Swallowing nervously, he turned the worn Bakelite handle.

His reception looked like a publicity still from a horror film, with everybody motionless, and the assembled cast – Jack Spot, Solly the Turk and Grace herself – staring wide-eyed at Dennis as he made his fumbling entrance. Or rather, as he rapidly accepted, staring at what was behind him.

Spot and Solly Kankus jumped immediately to their feet, both of them startled and the former clearly angry, eyes like an affronted scrapyard dog.

''oo the fack's this? I never said you could bring anybody with yer! If you've fackin' ...'

Pointedly closing the door behind him, the imposing vendor of fresh produce stepped around the stammering Dennis and held up a worryingly big placating hand.

'I am Gog Blincoe, and I come here as a spokesman of the different city, to discuss the terms of our engagement with you.

Meaning you no disrespect, there are first things which I must ascertain before we may commence our haggle.'

Without offering the incredulous Spot even a glance, plainly indifferent to the criminal's response, Gog lumbered past him and the equally astounded Kankus to where Grace had been sitting throughout all this, perched mutely on the edge of her collapsible settee. Crouching upon his mammoth haunches, the experienced market man gazed searchingly into the motionless girl's apprehensive eyes. With their two heads in such proximity, the great disparity in scale between them was so marked that they might have belonged to different species. Dennis noticed that Grace trembled almost imperceptibly as Blincoe spoke to her, his voice the patient rumble of a cart on cobbles.

'Mistress Shilling, I am glad to find you in fair health, and have but one interrogation for you: have you, in the time of your captivity, been handled roughly or else harmed in any way? If it is so, then tell me, and I shall kill both these scoundrels on the instant, sparing all of us further involvement with this irksome difficulty.'

Spot and Kankus stared at the squatting colossus with respective speechless outrage and mounting alarm, then exchanged a bewildered glance with one another before looking back to the apparently untroubled Blincoe. Grace, for her part, had not dared to take her eyes from those of the solicitous and gentlemanly Soho ogre for a second. When she answered him, it was in tones much younger than the twenty-something years that Dennis had supposed for her, as though the presence of this fairy-story monster had reduced the tough streetwalker to an awestruck child.

'No. Don't do that. Nobody's been hurt so far, and I'd like it if it carried on like that.'

Jack Spot was bordering upon the apoplectic, his mole quivering.

'You'll fackin' what? Kill us, is that what you just fackin' said? Do you know who I am?'

Taking his time, the ponderous leviathan rose from his crouch, straightening to what must, in Dennis's estimation, have been getting on for seven feet, taller than the not-insubstantial Spot or Dennis by a hand or two, and with the gravity of both men put together. Blincoe turned and scrutinised the gangster with unblinking eyes that held not the least measure of concern.

'Yes, I believe I do. You are one Jacob Comer, known more generally as Jack Spot because of that unsightly blemish you have on your cheek. You have accrued your fortune largely by intimidating turf accountants, and it may be you suppose all others to be similarly cowed. If that is so, there is a danger that you have misunderstood our situation here. I shall repeat to you, I am not from the city that you know. My origins are in the other place, and it is not my well-being that's under threat in these negotiations. It may be you are in need of a display, to settle your uncertainties. That being so, then Mistress Shilling will perhaps obtain for me a kitchen knife, if such a thing is to be had.'

Spot was now shaking his head furiously, trying to retain some vestige of control on circumstances that were suddenly and inexplicably slipping between his nicotine-stained fingers.

'No! No, no, no! A fackin' knife? You think I'm fackin' simple, do yer?'

Bark-deep furrows creased the indoor mountain's forehead as he studied the unnerved and spluttering gangster.

'My opinion on your intellectual prowess is beside the point. What I think is that you are frit, believing that I mean to harm you with this implement when, as I have already told you, it is but for purposes of demonstration. And besides, the presence of a dirk makes not a whit of difference to your safety, when I could as well destroy you with my hands, or feet, or any other part of me. I am a hard man, Mr Spot, in ways you will not previously have encountered. Now, if Mistress Shilling will provide the object I have asked for, then we may sooner continue with our discourse.'

While the rest of her had stayed as motionless as marble, Grace's gaze had shifted back and forth between the villain and the vendor, trying to judge which way the winds of her predicament were blowing. With Spot incandescent but reduced to pop-eyed silence by the fruit-seller's unanswerable logic, it appeared she was decided. Face an apprehensive white mask as though all the blood had rushed to her extraordinary hair, she rose from the settee and went without a word into her tiny kitchen, coming back almost immediately with the requested knife, which she handed to Blincoe before once again resuming her position on the couch.

The instrument looked frighteningly sharp, with its steel blade perhaps eight inches long. As Blincoe gripped its handle with both hands, holding it upright like a ceremonial sword, the atmosphere in the cramped sitting room was charged with an uncomfortable electricity. Dennis and Grace were cringing, although neither was entirely certain why, and Solly Kankus's complexion had become as pale as whey. No one said anything.

It was so sudden. With one quick and forceful motion of his burly arms, the vegetable salesman drove the vicious length of steel three inches deep in his own brow between the barely inter-ested eyes, with a horrific, splintering thud. Everyone shrieked except Grace, who had clapped both hands over her mouth, and whose wide eyes seemed just about to relocate on to her blanching cheeks. Exhaling what was possibly a groan of mild discomfort, Blincoe took his hands away to leave the weapon jutting from his head as though he were a cutlery-draw unicorn.

Dennis let himself slump against the closed door, breathing heavily and slowly. The choleric rage had drained out of Jack Spot to be replaced by bilious greyness, and the shaken Mr Kankus said, 'I feel a bit sick, to be 'onest,' and sat back down on the kitchen chair he'd risen from when they arrived. Gog, with the murderous antenna sticking from his face, gave the ashen and speechless crime king an appraising look, content that he had made his point, which was just then embedded where Gog's forebrain should have been. The market-stall leviathan's small eyes contracted even further and he nodded, satisfied, initi-ating a faint quivering in the protruding kitchen knife.

'I issue, sir, not from the egg but from the acorn, and am thus insensible to injury. If you or your lieutenant should possess a fowling piece or barker, I must tell you that it would be no more use than this cake cutter that is giving me crossed eyes at present. In my back I have a musket ball, and in my thigh some lead shot and what I think may be a flint arrowhead, with none of it occasioning the least discomfort. I have had assailants think to burn me down, but being densely made, I am inordinately slow to catch, and so could strike my death blow while they were still fiddling with their tinderboxes. And, should it occur to you to publicly unmask my hidden nature, I shall ask to whom you might announce this revelation, and just what it is that you'd reveal. That there's a stall in Berwick Street run by a chap made head to toe from wood? Perhaps this is a titbit you might share with those policemen sympathetic to your cause, or, otherwise, amongst your loyal fellows in the criminal fraternity, who surely would not see such ramblings as a sign of instability or weakness.'

Spot stood voiceless and as still as ditchwater throughout all this, with all the fight gone out of him, flipping for options through the cooked books of his agile mind and realising he hadn't any. Gog continued, confident that he and the crime overlord had reached a point of mutual understanding.

'Now then, if I have convinced you of my verifieds, we may at last procession to the kernel of our present business, being your request for conference with a dignitary from the other town, that you hope might alleviate your plights. Do I have the right comprehension of it?'

Blinking a staccato Morse of disbelief, Spot stared hard at the floor and didn't seem to want to look at his interrogator's pole-axed cranium.

'Yeah, yeah, look, can you take that chopper out yer nut before we start with this? It's givin' me the screamin' abdabs.'

Blincoe shook his head from side to side, which only served to make the startling protrusion wobble disconcertingly.

'No. I believe that we shall leave it where it is, that it may better focus your attentions on the seriousness of our discussion.

Furthermore, it will help to prepare you for the rendezvous you have demanded with a presence that, I promise, is more sobering than I. He is called Harry Lud, and it is the red-handed soul of crime itself that you make your appointment with. To this end, I have been instructed to relay the finer details of that gathering. It is to be in Arnold Circus at the confluence of seven streets, upon the first stroke of tomorrow's midnight. Should you harbour any apprehensions, then you may come armed, although as I have shown you, there is precious little use in it. If it should further reassure you, then you can as well bring this man here' – he briefly pointed the unsettling knife's handle at the seated Solly Kankus – 'as a bit of company. He's seen enough this afternoon, and seeing more does not present a greater risk to our security, when neither of you can say anything of this, even to those you love the best, lest it should see you dragged away to bedlam.'

Trembling so badly that his chair was rattling, Kankus looked appalled to be invited to the next night's gathering, and very likely knew the things that he'd already witnessed would be in his foulest dreams for the remainder of his life. He had the eyes of one condemned. Jack Spot, meanwhile, had listened to the vegetable man's address with fidgety unease, a misbehaving schoolboy called to reckoning before an unexpectedly stern teacher. He scratched his boiled-bacon neck and shuffled his expensive shoes, all the while darting glances at Gog's stainless steel appendage before once more staring fixedly at Grace's carpet. Blincoe quietly surveyed the nervous men, considering.

'One other thing, and then our chat shall be concluded. It has not escaped my notice that you have subjected my friends, Mr Knuckleyard and Mistress Shilling, to considerable duress. From this point on, there'll be no more of that, or I cannot describe to you the consequences. They are both of them in the protection of the other town, and must be left alone. If that is clear, then you and your associate may take your leave of us until tomorrow midnight, after you have made fair recompense with Mistress Shilling for her loss of earnings in the two days that she was kept prisoner. She is a woman of exceptionally fine appearance, and by my own estimate might have expected that her takings should be not far short of five-and-thirty pounds. Let us agree to call it forty.'

There occurred an interval of silent incredulity before Spot came to see that bargaining positions, with a thing of solid timber that had just deliberately impaled its face, were neither here nor there. With gritted teeth, the gangland boss produced a wallet, counting out four tenners that he passed indignantly to Grace, who took them with a sweet and grateful little smile that only served to worsen Spot's already thunderous disposition. Then, with Kankus green and ill, with Jack Spot glaring impotently at practically everything except Gog Blincoe and his stuck-fast tableware, the two men made their muttering exit, leaving Grace and Dennis to an awkward lapse in conversation and, apparently, an ambulatory tree. In the ensuing hush, it was a moment before Grace came to the rescue.

'Well, that was a right how-d'you-do. Would anybody like a cup of tea?'

Dennis, belatedly removing his damp coat, accepted gratefully, but Blincoe shook his blade-augmented head.

'Why, thank you kindly for your offer, but I must decline. I'll take my nourishment when I'm home after work tonight, where I can put my feet down. With that said, there is one service you might do me, which is to assist in the removal of this blessed nuisance from my otherwise distinguished countenance. I will concede, I stuck it in with too much force, that I might make a more severe impression on the pair of dips or dragsmen that have lately quit our company. It is perhaps a good inch further in than I'd intended, and will likely be a bugger to pull loose. Perhaps if I should set myself upon this chair so you can reach, it will be easier for you to find firm purchase.'

Even after all the starfish-spider popes, loquacious cats and severed heads in pot-pourri, what followed was an episode that Dennis didn't feel was truly real while it was happening, and even less so later when he'd had a chance to think about it. He and Grace spent the next quarter of an hour attempting to prise Grace's kitchen knife from Blincoe's forehead, trying out experimental grips and holds while the arboreal goliath gripped his seat's edge and endeavoured to stay still. Eventually they managed it with Dennis crouched behind the chair and pulling, arms encircling the giant's chest as far as they were able, while Grace braced one foot against Gog's belly and, grasping the hilt in both hands, threw all her weight backwards. When the blade came free, she stumbled like a film reel in reverse and, fortunately, fell back on to her complaining sofa, gasping with surprise and effort. Dennis narrowly avoided landing on his arse and dragging both the chair and Blincoe down on top of him, which would have almost certainly entailed a trip to hospital. Sprawled panting on the couch while she recovered, Grace looked dazedly from the unharmed utensil that she held in one hand to the piggy-bank-sized slot between the corkscrew curls of Blincoe's eyebrows, where a bead of amber sap or resin was accumulating. While no doubt relieved it wasn't blood, she sounded worried.

'You want something on that. It'll get infected.'

Blincoe lifted an exploratory finger to his wound before examining the sticky residue left on the digit's tip. He offered Grace a reassuring smile, barely perceptible amid his rigid features.

'Thanking you for your concern, but this mere pinprick does not risk infection, since my biological affairs are not the same as your'n. That said, a dressing, if you have one, would be handy. Otherwise, my juice shall trickle down my face and likely in my eyes, where, should it harden, it might be a year or more afore I got it off.'

As it turned out, Grace kept a small first-aid tin in her bedroom. Wiping up as much of the clear, oozing gum as she could manage using a warm flannel, she applied a pad of lint to the deep gash, secured by a white gauze bandage that wrapped twice around the fruit-and-veg provider's huge skull and was fastened with a safety pin. Checking himself in a hand mirror of pink celluloid that Grace provided, the admiring behemoth seemed not dissatisfied with his new look.

'Aye, that will do the job. I shall pretend to have received the blow by walking smack into a shop's low awning, which, although a lie, is not the blackest. Some of the establishments in Berwick Street have canopies too near the pavement to allow safe passage for a person of my stature.'

Shortly after that, Gog made his genial farewells, assuring Dennis that he'd be there for the meeting up in Arnold Circus the next evening. Showing him to the front door, the two flesh-and-blood youngsters watched him walk off, whistling, through a still-falling rain he seemed almost to welcome. Grace and Dennis looked at one another silently – what could you say about all that? – and then walked back along the hallway to the stuffy flat, to make that postponed cup of tea, and talk, and find out what was left of them.

Soon they were seated hesitantly on the sofa, with an extra person's space between them that was careful not to imply any intimacy. It transpired that one of Grace's captors, Solly Kankus, had brought cigarettes and biscuits when he'd turned up for his shift of guard duty and taken over from a similarly cordial Sonny the Yank. Both Grace and Dennis dunked their plain digestives in their teacups, each intent on not permitting too long an immersion, anxious to avoid an oversaturated morsel falling with a faecal plop into their laps. At last, after he'd wolfed down half the packet, Dennis wiped his lips on an unseemly jacket sleeve and tried a conversational opener.

'They treated you alright today, then? When Sonny the Yank was driving me across the river to see Spare this morning, I got the impression that both him and Solly had a bit of a soft spot for you. They didn't seem so keen on me, though.'

Grace laughed and sprayed crumbs across the coffee table.

'Yeah, well, that's because they still think you're my ponce. When I was in the motor with them while you had your private natter with their boss, I told them all about what happened to me as a young evacuee, forced on the game by circumstance and prey to … well, to vicious brutes like you, as I explained it to them.' She was laughing harder now, and half of a digestive ended in the seashell ashtray. 'I told them you like to whip me with great, rancid lengths of seaweed – it was just the first thing that came in my head – and when they fell for that, I told them that you like to do it when you're nude except for a sou'wester and a pair of wellingtons. I think that, funnily enough, they ended up with more respect for you, although they thought that you were a disgusting pervert. Oh, come on. It is quite funny. You should see your face.'

Luckily, Dennis couldn't. Even if he could, he'd not have understood why anyone should find his scolded-puppy look of hurt betrayal comical, although in fact, to an objective eye, it was. 'Why did you tell them that? I don't just mean the bit about the seaweed. Why did you make out I thrashed you in the first place?' It took Grace a minute or two to stop giggling, and then a little longer to stop coughing when some sodden crumbs went down the wrong way. Finally, she raised her watering eyes and gazed at Dennis earnestly.

'It was self-preservation, pure and simple. If it turned out that this "different part of London" business was just something that somebody said the last time you were in the loony bin, I thought that I might earn some sympathy by painting you as a Marquis de Sade dressed up like Captain Ahab.'

Dennis didn't know who either of those was. Grace carried on regardless.

'Listen, I'm not laughing at you, Dennis. What I'm laughing at is all of this, because it's either frightening or ridiculous, and I know which one I prefer. Besides, I see that you've been on the level with me. You proved that when you walked through the door this afternoon, with half of Birnam Wood behind you. I've seen some things in my time, but bloody Nora, Dennis, what's all this you've gotten yourself into? I know that you've tried to keep it private, and from meeting Mr Blincoe – who's a very nice man, incidentally, for saying that he's not one – I can see why you might do that. You were trying to keep it all away from me, and that was lovely of you. Really lovely.

'But if this stuff you've been telling me is true, how have you coped? I mean, just look at you: you've all the substance of a beanbag, but today you've been off on an outing with a black magician to what sounds like Wonderland, where you've apparently been able to sort out our bother with Jack Spot – Jack Spot, for God's sake – and then turned up back here with Pinocchio's big brother for a bodyguard. Although I'm not sure that it suits you, you've been quite heroic. I'm not going to let you shag me. I'm just saying that I'm moderately impressed.'

Respectively crushed and elated by her last two statements, he felt unsure what to say, scratching his bristly nape to buy time until the words came to him.

'Yeah, well, you were the one sat here all day with thugs who'd said that they were probably going to kill you. You're a marvel. I don't know what I'd have done if you'd not took me in.'

Seemingly out of nowhere, Grace proposed that she should make them both pilchards on toast for tea, then hurried off into the kitchen before he could see her quiet smirk of self-satisfaction.

Later on, after they'd eaten, they sat there on the last-legs settee and listened to the tiny fists of rain beating against the window, the subdued catcall and clatter of a Thursday night in Spitalfields, audial entertainment in the absence of a wireless. Having met Gog Blincoe and concluded that the less she knew about this other place the better, Grace's only question was what happened next.

'I've got no problem letting you kip here another night or two, until this is all finished, but where does it go from here? What's going to happen in this Arnold Circus place tomorrow night, and are you going to be alright? Who's Harry Lud?'

Dennis was circumspect in his reply.

'From what I can make out, there's, well, let's say there's people in the other place, and they're, like, templates, essences or something, for the things in this place. What's the word?'

Grace lit a cigarette and raised her eyebrows questioningly. 'Archetypes?'

'I've not heard of them, but yeah, probably. They're called Arcana in the other place. Tomorrow, there's a mate of mine I said I'd see at lunchtime, but then after that I might go straight to Arnold Circus for this set-to with Jack Spot and Harry Lud. He's one of the Arcana, and he's, like, the archetype of crime, if that's the word I'm looking for. That's why Spot wants to speak to him, to see if he can sort out all Spot's gangster problems. I don't know what's going to happen, but Gog Blincoe and another fellow, Ironfoot Jack, have said they're going to be there. I should think I'll be alright.'

He washed up while she made them both another cup of tea, and, following that, Grace produced a careworn pack of cards, inviting Dennis to join her in a few hands of whist, playing for matchsticks. After barely two hours, Grace possessed enough to build a reproduction of Westminster Abbey, leaving Dennis without even one to pick an errant flake of pilchard from his teeth. During that time, however, they'd agreed that he should stay at Grace's flat after whatever happened up in Arnold Circus the next night, and she had generously offered him one of the ten-pound notes that Blincoe had extorted from Jack Spot. 'No, go on, take it. I'd have not got half of forty quid for Wednesday and today. When the warm weather drops away, so does the trade. I'm serious, you have it. That way, if I should tell anybody else you're living off my earnings, you'll know there's a bit of substance to it.'

They sat chuntering until the clock in Christchurch's oppressive steeple chimed for ten, and then Grace left Dennis to his monastic couch while she went off to bed. Before she did, she thanked him for the racing forecast cards that he'd had Austin Spare make out to her, and asked if she could borrow Machen's book, *The Cosy Room*, to read before she went to sleep. She'd had a browse of it during the many lapses in her conversation with Sonny the Yank or Solly Kankus, and had thought that 'N' looked interesting. Since the story only quoted from Hampole's imaginary volume and was not the inconveniently solid tome itself, Dennis could see no harm in this and told her to enjoy it.

With a voice as clear and musical as a struck wine glass, she bade him goodnight and went off to her room, leaving the echo of her cheapskate scent behind her, a faint compensation.

Folded up to fit on the settee, Dennis slept only fretfully. His mind was filled with Inferred Saracens and pot-pourri, with talking cats and wooden men, and had no room for dreams. He half woke from his half sleep the next morning in an unexpectedly good humour, to the smell of cooking breakfast and the at first unfamiliar sensation of not feeling doomed. Grace was both up and dressed, and had already been out to the shops for sausages and a wrapped block of cooking fat, hence the tongue-torturing aroma from the kitchen. He felt guilty that she hadn't gone to work already, realising that he must be a financial inconvenience, and at the same time selfishly content to have her there when he awakened, and then guilty again about being selfishly content. None of this spoiled his sausages and egg, nor his enjoyment of Grace's vermilion waterfall across the kitchen table. With what passed for dash in Spitalfields, he cut his sausage into rounds and speared them on his fork to mash into the ruptured golden eyeball of his egg, as happy as he could remember being.

Overnight the rain had packed it in, although the pavements were still wet and glittering like sticklebacks in a rare outburst of October sun when Dennis reached the Strand. Bond's Coffee House was relatively underpopulated for the time of day, and only when the idling proprietor had seen him coming and had hurried to open the door did he remember that here, in this few square yards of London, he was a soap-flake aristocrat. Reminded of his station, Dennis improvised a glance that mingled shame at his impoverished circumstances with what he thought might be upper-class contempt. It seemed to do the trick, and the attentive manager nodded and smiled with gratitude to be in the receipt of such refined abuse. When asked for cake and tea, with Grace's tenner flourished as a guarantee of payment, the man lifted both palms in refusal. 'No, no need for that, your

Lordship. On the house. Your legal friend is at his usual table, up the back. I'll bring it over.' Putting Grace's ten-pound note away with what he hoped was a disdainful lip curl, Dennis essayed his ungainly way through a blue wall of cigarette smoke to the café's rear, where Clive was waiting for him.

'Well, I'll be a monkey's uncle. It's Lord Snooty, and practically on the stroke of one! How did you manage that? I've always thought of you as too hard-up to own a wristwatch. Does whatever hovel you're existing in at present have an hourglass or a water clock, for instance?'

Dennis sniggered and sat down at the two-person table, opposite the grinning lawyer.

'No. It's just that being closer to the state of animals, we tell the time by shadows, rabbit droppings and that sort of thing. How are you, anyway? What gripping legal business am I dragging you away from now?'

Clive flicked his fine blond fringe out of his eyes and executed a theatrically glum expression. He was dressed up in a different suit from the chalk-stripe affair he'd worn on Monday, this one plain black, but it hung upon his lean form just as stylishly, as though the skin that he'd been born into had got side vents and buttons.

'Dennis, you have no idea what torments we civilised people go through. It's been nothing else but family arguments about inheritances, and retired major generals who want to sue King George for spying on them using secret rays. To be quite honest, I'd give my right arm for even a good acrimonious divorce, but, no, it seems that all these ghastly idiots are perfectly contented with each other. Why don't interesting types ever get into legal trouble?'

Dennis shrugged.

'So, not the rush of crackpot killers that you were expecting, then?'

Performing an offended scowl, Clive shook his head.

'Nary a one, dear boy! The acid-bath blood-drinkers have all let me down appallingly. I mean, there must be dozens of them out there, and it's not as if they're difficult to catch: they always knock off the same type of victims, in the same way, or, like Haigh, they use the same way to dispose of the remains. They might as well just autograph a bottom corner of the murder scene. You'd think there'd be at least one nutcase with his head sufficiently screwed on to vary up the act a bit. If you ask me, their problem isn't that they're mad, it's that they're so bloody repetitive. Why don't they … Oh. Hang on. I think this is your manservant approaching.'

From the far end of the cafeteria, the patently intimidated manager of the establishment was picking his way carefully between the smoke drifts and the scattering of other customers, holding a tray with Dennis's requested tea and cake on up before him, head tipped back as if he were a footman or an equerry. With a mischievous look and admirable smoothness of delivery, Clive switched from his vexed monologue on the shortcomings of contemporary homicidal lunatics to a concerned and lawyerly interrogation of his put-upon aristocratic client.

'Hold on, your Lordship, let me get this right. You mean to say that those low-born intruders, after barring you from your extensive Oxydol estates, have daubed communist slogans on the ha-ha and have clipped the topiary into a copse of rampant phalluses? It's little wonder that you vomited your kedgeree. Hanging's too good for these marauders, and if I had my way, they'd be staked on anthills, right across the length and breadth of Hampstead Heath. In fact … Ah. Yes, put it by his Lordship if you'd be so kind, there's a good fellow.'

This last was addressed to the speechless proprietor who'd by then reached their table, bearing Dennis's gratis refreshments, and heard every word of the foregoing upper-crust indignities. The fifth Lord Oxydol fought to maintain a corpse-like impassivity while picturing regurgitated boiled egg, rice and haddock steaming on the sculpted penile privet, trying not to laugh until their disconcerted waiter was back at his counter and thus safely out of earshot. Throughout all this, Clive impaled his supposed client with a look of near-angelic sympathy, only the blue eyes sparkling with amusement as the trainee barrister piled detail on ludicrous detail in his unrelenting efforts to make Dennis laugh against his will. 'And, just to recap, you say that they flambéed all the peacocks, before urinating in a writing desk once used by Mary Tudor, although not in that way?' When at last the startled eavesdropper was at the far end of the coffee house and the pair were no longer overheard, Dennis allowed himself to giggle dangerously around a mouth crammed full of fruitcake, while Clive settled back into his chair and sipped at his black coffee with a smile of satisfaction bordering on the sadistic.

'So, young Knucklehead, what's all this mystifying nonsense you were telling me over the telephone the other day? You made dark references to being stalked by desperados, and to some formerly unexplored region of the metropolis. I take it you weren't simply drunk?'

Taking a moment to swallow his cake and wash it down with too hot tea, the temporarily mute Dennis wagged a lifted palm from side to side in flat denial before he eventually answered.

'No. I'd had a pint or two the first time that I went there, but the next time I'd not touched a drop. It wasn't drink or the DTs, it was just unbelievable. The way it started, that day I saw you in here, I'd just unknowingly been lumbered with this bloody nightmare of a book. Some people who were in the know told me that it had come from, well, this different area of London, and that if I didn't want to come a cropper, I should get it back there sharpish. This was right around the time I found out there were shady types wanted the book as well, gangsters who reckoned it would get them into this, this different neighbourhood. It turned out it was Jack Spot. Anyway, the next night ...'

Clive set his half-finished cup of stimulation carefully upon its saucer, and leaned forward.

'Did you say Jack Spot? What, *the* Jack Spot? Dennis, are you having me on?'

'I wish I was. That Tuesday after I'd seen you, I had a couple of his men clock me when I was out at night, and both came running after me. It was like in a film, pelting along the alleys and the backstreets with a couple of arm-breakers right behind. Just when I thought that they were going to collar me and carve me up, I had this, well, I had this sort of accident, and next thing that I knew, I'd landed in the other place, the other bit of London. I was only there about ten minutes before I found my way out again, but that was ten minutes too much. It nearly bloody killed me. And since then, it's just got worse instead of better. The night after I called you, I had Jack Spot himself catch up with me. He threatened to kill me and, well, this other person, somebody I know, if I didn't set up a deal for him the next time that I visited this, this location.'

Both his gaze and elbows on the table, Clive tapped pensively against his lower lip with steepled index fingers. He was still wearing the horse-head cufflinks that he'd worn on Monday, a realistically presented chestnut mare in brown enamel, glinting in the coffee house's low light. After a few moments he looked up at Dennis, his eyes serious and questioning.

'So, just to clarify, this other part of London, it's concealed in some peculiar way that makes it difficult to reach or even find, is that the gist of it? It's somewhere so exclusive that Jack Spot's prepared to kill you to make contact, yet you stumble into it by accident, and then, ten minutes later, you find your way out again. Which seems to indicate that this near-inaccessible region or district of the city is, perhaps, ten minutes' walk from streets and landmarks that were more familiar. How does that work? You'll forgive me, but it doesn't sound as if you're talking about just another neighbourhood of London, does it? Without wishing to appear indelicate, isn't it more the case that what you're telling me about is, in some utterly confounding manner, an entirely separate world?'

Thinking about it, Dennis realised belatedly that the foggy account of his adventures he had given Grace was never going to hold up under Clive's forensic scrutiny. The jeweller's-lens analysis of every word in an account was what his best mate did to make a living. Feeling slightly queasy at the idea that he might have let Clive figure out too much for his own safety, he nevertheless admitted to himself that being subject to his friend's impressed attention was extremely gratifying. Torn between the urge to act responsibly and the desire to show off, Dennis continued his attempt to walk a tightrope line between the two.

'Um. Yeah, well, I suppose you could put it like that. Look, Clive, it's not that I don't want to fill you in on all this stuff. I really do. It's just that even knowing about this place can get people killed, or worse. It is a part of London in a way, but it's another London, standing here where this one is, but so that nobody can see it. I've not got the foggiest idea how it can do that, but I know it's really dangerous, double-Dick-Barton dangerous. That's why I'm not supposed to talk about it.'

Clive laughed, banishing the earnest moment.

'Funny that, you mentioning Dick Barton. I was just now thinking that you should have your own theme tune, what with all this drama. No, I'm finding what you're telling me enthralling, but I can assure you, anything you say is in the strictest confidence and won't go any further. I'll treat it as if it were all under lawyer-client privilege, how's that? And furthermore, I promise that I shan't press you for details, if you'll only throw me a few more of these intriguing crumbs. For instance, how did this blood-curdling business with Jack Spot end up? What with you having brought his tantalising name up in the first instance, it's only fair that you must at least tell me that.'

He had a point. Dennis had dropped Spot's name in order to make his unlikely tale appear fraught with importance, and, having done that, couldn't just leave Clive hanging.

'To be honest, all the rigmarole with Jack Spot hasn't ended up as anything, at least not yet. The thing he wanted me to set up was a meeting with one of, you know, the people from this other London. That's meant to be taking place tonight, at midnight, up near Coffin Ada's bookshop at a place where all these different streets converge. You wouldn't know it. I don't really want to be there, tell the truth, but in a way I'm looking forward to it, because then the whole thing will be finished. I can go back to a normal life, I'm hoping, where I never have to think about what's happened this last week ever again.'

Clive smiled and raised his coffee cup to clink against Dennis's teacup in a civilised, non-alcoholic toast.'Well, here's to Knuckleyard recovering his screamingly dull proletarian drudgery as soon as possible.And, my dear fellow, please try not to do this sort of thing too often.We can't have you suddenly becoming hugely interesting without throwing reasonable society into hysteria. For one thing, if you brutish underlings were regularly fascinating, why would anybody need to visit the theatre or read novels? The entire of Britain's glorious literary tradition would collapse, and we should have no Shakespeare, Wilde or Buchan. Mind you, on the other hand, we wouldn't have George Orwell's miserable predictions, either, which might cheer things up a bit.'

Not having absorbed much of Shakespeare, Wilde or Buchan, Dennis fastened with relief upon a book and author that he'd genuinely read. Their small talk drifted to the ills besetting modern entertainment, and thus comfortably away from topics with which Dennis had begun to feel slightly uneasy. They agreed that *1984* was probably a fair reflection of contemporary anxieties, with everybody's minds still full of pogroms, concentration camps and atom bombs. In Clive's opinion, with the national imagination pulverised by near six years of showering incendiaries, Orwell's disturbing novel was unlikely to be the last slice of alienation to impress itself on public sensibilities. As an early example of a similar phenomenon, Dennis brought up the radio comedian Tommy Handley, who had passed away that January last. In *It's That Man Again*, Handley had conjured his outlandish deep-sea divers, German spies and charladies to spout their catchphrases without regard for plot, sense or the laws of physics; the irrational hilarity of a blitzed world where nothing was connected and where anything could happen without cause or explanation. After two hours and another cuppa each, they came to the conclusion that all the surrealism of the 1930s had a lot to answer for, and so had Hitler.

When at last Clive couldn't risk extending his long lunch break any further, he and Dennis exited the coffee house past the solicitous proprietor who, no doubt still considering the virile shrubbery and Marxist vandalism to the ha-ha, offered Dennis a pained look of outraged sympathy. Outside, in the persisting sunshine, the pair shook hands and clapped shoulders as they made their jocular farewells. As Clive was just about to set out for the courts and legal enterprises of the Strand's far end, he glanced back at his scruffy colleague with a look of genuine affection and regard.

'Good luck with all this business later, Knuckleyard. And well done. That has to be the most rewarding hour or two I've ever spent. You're a remarkable young ruffian, you know.'

Still basking in the compliment, Dennis stood watching fondly as his friend and idol walked away into the jostling Friday herd. Despite whatever shattering incongruities he might be witness to in Arnold Circus later, Dennis was inordinately pleased with both himself and how his day was going so far. He'd accomplished all the near-impossible things he'd been tasked with – the return of Hampole's volume to its place of origin, and his unlikely success in the rescue of Grace Shilling from Jack Spot – as if he was a competent adult and not the freakishly tall child that, privately, he knew himself to be. And then, of course, there were his improved fortunes with regard to Grace herself. Alright, he couldn't really claim she was his girlfriend, and in fact she'd made it clear that she would blind him if he touched her, but for two nights running Dennis had been sleeping barely fifteen feet away from an attractive woman, and that had to count for something. Finally, the cherry on the top of all these causes for smug self-congratulation, there had been the look on Clive's face, an intensity of fascinated focus that he hadn't seen before, and that he thought might herald a forthcoming mutual respect between the two of them. Long after Clive had dwindled to a black dot in the varicoloured throng, Dennis stood marvelling at his own new-found capability, and then remembered that he'd left himself with some eight hours to kill before his midnight meeting, cursing himself as a hopeless amateur.

In the event, he passed his empty shift with a surprising number of pointless activities. A couple of the hours were spent thinking of calling in on Tolerable John, or Grace – or even, for a nihilistic thirty seconds, Coffin Ada – then deciding not to. An unspecified amount of time was squandered walking aimlessly through London's intestinal maze, attempting to take in the notion that each street and building coexisted with a lurid, otherworldly counterpart, but failing. A considerable period went by in three or four identically dilapidated tea shops, or conceivably the same one visited repeatedly by accident, stirring too much sugar into weak infusions while mentally planning the autobiography that he would surely one day write: his birth in 1931; his father Brian called away to war when Dennis was just eight, shot down and killed when he was ten; his mother Irene gone with her angina four years later; then the purgatory of Lowell's Books & Magazines; and finally the things he couldn't ever speak of without being put away, and, therefore, the immediate abandonment of his projected memoir. He perused at length a day-old copy of the *Daily Mirror* someone else had left behind, tutting in pity at 4,000 dead from floods in Guatemala, not much bothered about the conclusion of Japanese war-crime trials in the US, nodding in grave appreciation at the David Low cartoon and skipping *Jane*, its personality-free heroine uninteresting now she kept her clothes on with post-war propriety. He counted all the buildings in Long Acre and Great Queen Street, dined from a convenient Covent Garden pie-and-mash stand and considered learning French. The seconds, in their tens of thousands, gnawed him past the bone of boredom, and at something after ten o'clock, for all his many apprehensions, he commenced a long, cold walk to Shoreditch almost gratefully.

Despite a sun-soaked day, the night encouraged frills of fog from out of the river, bundles of grey gauze rolling uphill to hang blurring coronas on the streetlamps, themselves sparser in accordance with remoteness from the city's centre, so that the increasing distances between them seemed the suffocating voids that separated stars. Climbing through half-demolished streets into the dark, Dennis found himself thinking of the countless eggs of iron and fire that had fallen in the last ten years, some of them not yet hatched. Curled metal embryos, they slept beneath the amniotic rubble, saving up their birth wails for an unsuspecting future. This was the whole problem with the past, that it was never really over, when the dreadful bricks of yesterday were what tomorrow would be built from.

Wading in half-hearted revellers and thickening mist, Dennis ascended Bishopsgate towards his inconceivable appointment. Passing Spitalfields and the by-now-familiar mouth of Folgate Street, where Grace lived, he resisted the temptation to just wander down and check whether her light was on, just see if she was home, because what was the point of that? That was just soft. He'd see her later, hopefully, when the encounter up at Arnold Circus was resolved and he went back to her place and her posture-altering settee. He'd have to see what happened after that, regarding him and Grace, although the same thing could be said about his job, or his address, or any other aspect of his wispy, insubstantial life. Like all the war-struck world, he'd have to see what happened. Shattered fragments couldn't be expected to have aims or plans.

On native turf in Shoreditch, where the vaporous miasma bordered on opaque, Dennis relied upon the instincts ingrained by his scabby urban childhood in those lanes, a kind of pavement radar steering him into Old Nichol Street, up Camlet Street, and so to Arnold Circus where, it being still some minutes to eleven, he turned out to be the only person there. The fog was for some reason thinner in the circle's empty centre, perhaps ventilated by the seven streets that happened to converge there, with their intervening buildings become wedges of a monstrous and intimidating brickwork pie. Other than Dennis, there were only two old cars and what looked like a builder's truck, all evidently parked there overnight, so as a circus it was something of a disappointment.

Loitering in the murk and wanting for a better entertainment, he unpacked his memories of the place, the things he'd done there and the things he'd heard about it. He recalled a memorable fight in Arnold Circus when he'd been ten or eleven, probably a punch-up started over his pugnacious surname or the fact he didn't have a father any more. He hadn't won, of course, but, as he saw things, had been only narrowly defeated, making it the high point of his pugilist career. As for the circle's wider history, this was a narrative of ugly rumour and lamentable established fact, a penny-dreadful shocker writ in virid seams of moss between the district's stones. Back in the nineteenth century, this vacant ring had been a vortex of Victorian crime, an open plughole that half of the city's stolen goods were circling. A proper rookery, it had lent Arthur Morrison's *A Child of the Jago* its appropriately pungent backcloth, and had been the lair of the Old Nichol mob, whose murderous procurers had ripped more Whitechapel women than their better-known contemporary who, according to Gog Blincoe, had been an absconded Pope of Blades. He thought of Grace with an unhappy wince he didn't really have a right to, wishing that she hadn't been forced into such a bruising trade, or that she had a less-traditionally lethal place than the East End in which to ply it.

He constructed a compelling fantasy wherein, despite having no visible means of support himself, he rescued Grace from her at-least-rent-paying job, a fiction which ignored the fact that so far, Grace had rescued him. He'd just reached an important plot point, where the sudden and horrific death of Coffin Ada had revealed him as the unexpected beneficiary of her surprisingly large fortune, when a sound out of the clouded dark shredded the half-built daydream into flakes of tinsel. It was a harsh, grating noise, repeated at brief intervals, and drawing closer. As his heartbeat stepped on the accelerator pedal, Dennis wheeled round in a startled pirouette, attempting to identify which of the seven radiating lanes the din was coming from. Off down one fogbound passageway – he'd lost his bearings, but he thought it was Navarre Street – the unnerving racket was not only louder, echoing in the occluded row, but had a visible accompaniment of showering sparks, hot specks of burning orange on the churning greyness, an infernal mechanism clanking nearer in the smog.

It was Jack Neave. Hunched like a terrifyingly large crow in long, black coat and battered homburg, the backstreet entrepreneur limped from the swirling damp, his iron shoe scraping fireworks from the cobbles. His cravat was white tonight, bunched in the same elaborate silver ring, and his know-it-all smile was friendly, albeit dabbed with melancholy at the corners.

'Sorry, boy, I didn't mean to make yer jump. But if a little bloke who's got a dodgy leg turns you into a bag o' nerves, wait till you see what we've got comin' later. You'll be in a right state.'

Somewhere in the roiling shroud, a distant place of worship chimed eleven. Ironfoot chatted amiably as he circumnavigated their hazy arena, checking its security for the forthcoming interchange, casting an eye over the stationary cars before inspecting the open-backed builder's truck which, unsurprisingly, had nothing of more value than a heap of empty sacks left in it overnight. The pair elected to stand sheltering by the parked vehicle, where Dennis shivered and Neave lit a cigarette.

'I 'ad a word with our friend Mr Blincoe earlier. E's off in the Great When now, sortin' out the other end o' the arrangement, but 'e said as 'e'd be 'ere by midnight. It should all go off alright.'

Tightening his raincoat collar, Dennis raised an issue that had been perturbing him.

'What if somebody wanders by? I know it's foggy and it's late, but it's a Friday night ...'

Exhaling a long plume of smoke to further decrease visibility, Jack shook his head.

'They won't. With the Arcana, everybody looks the other way. Y'see, with normal people, they can't let themselves see things like that. Admittedly, you'll get yer artists, poets, nutters some- times, but not normal people. If there's somebody tonight who's thinkin' about walkin' 'ome through Arnold Circus, there'll be somethin' that comes up, some little incidental thing, and they'll decide to go another route. Nah, passers-by, least of our worries, that is. You'll find out.'

At around ten to twelve, the same tan Morris that Sonny the Yank had driven Dennis out to Brixton in nosed hesitantly from the fog bank blocking Club Row, grumbled to a halt a few yards from the builder's lorry and killed its anaemic headlights. After a mistrustful pause, the forward doors clunked open and Jack Spot climbed out, followed by Solly Kankus from the driver's side. While Spot seemed jumpy and on edge, Kankus looked genu- inely ill, the man's whole body cringing inwards in its effort not to be there. His unsettled boss, meanwhile, was glaring warily at Ironfoot.

''oo the fack are you? An' where's blockhead, the other chap? 'e said 'e'd be 'ere.'

Neave shrugged his thick lower lip in unconcern.

'I'm Ironfoot Jack, and I'm king of the Needies. Mr Blincoe is escortin' Mr Lud from the superior London, and they'll both be with us very shortly. Until then, my best advice is that we should compose ourselves, so as there won't be any untoward behaviour when crime's embodiment arrives.'

Spot scowled a simmering acceptance and then stood beside the motor, muttering beneath his breath to the unravelling Solly Kankus. No one else said anything, and Jack Neave's cigarette, sizzling brighter with each inhalation, was their only light- house in the curdled night. Then something happened: there was an elusive shift of atmosphere, and one by one, the four men noticed that the mist pooled in the circus was withdrawing, creeping back to crowd into the several street mouths, leaving the central enclosure dark, but clear as crystal. Dennis took a step back, Spot was made as still as marble halfway through an uncompleted gesture, Solly Kankus started to recite what was perhaps the Lord's Prayer in a quavering whisper, and the very windows, doors and drains of the encirclement gaped open-mouthed into a gathering mystery.

Jack Neave took a last quick pull on his fag, then ground it out beneath an iron boot heel.

"'ere we go.'

6

## *Behold Him, Gemmed with Larcenies*

And, like an opening rose or an explosion, it came rushing in. Diametrically opposite the builder's truck, across the suddenly pin-sharp expanse of Arnold Circus, double gates – with flaking emerald paintwork and their worn planks chewed at either end like pencils – were padlocked and chained against the Shoreditch midnight. As seen from the circle's far side, there appeared to be a fault or interruption over on the picture's right, between the stout green gatepost and the brick wall it was set into, a widening chink of colour rippling in the clarified-glass darkness. At the edges of this wavering flaw, both wall and gate seemed to be acting like a gas or liquid, shimmering and bending, momentarily deformed by something reaching through the shifting absence from beyond. The four men looking on at last identified this as a large and mobile human hand, fumbling in the shining gap to hook thick fingers on the sturdy post, which bunched between the digits without splintering or breaking, hard wood seemingly become as soft as velvet. In a swish like that of wind but with more echo and more sibilance, the pair of solid gates rucked into fabric curtains and were pulled aside, boards become billowing folds upon which padlock, chain and hinge were only painted. The strong hand that had accomplished this reveal turned out to be that of Gog Blincoe, head still bandaged, who stood silhouetted with a motley of hues behind him, then walked out into the eerily illuminated circus and stood to one side, impassive eyes fixed on the radiant aperture as though he were a compere silently awaiting the main act.

Jack Spot backed up against his motor, while Kankus sank moaning to his knees, his legs made into corrugated cardboard. Dennis, only a few nights before, would have been in the same condition but, now formed of sterner stuff, he merely trembled and made a concerted effort not to close his eyes. Beside him, Ironfoot leaned in confidentially and spoke in a stage whisper, to be heard above the mounting soundtrack that seemed to accompany the escalating dance of coloured light.

'Don't shut yer peepers. This is it, the thing it's all about. It's what they call perichoresis. It's an interpenetration, an' it's 'ow the Great When works, but you don't see it very often.'

The drab pudding of the cement round's reality hung heavy from its every crack and crevice, and was in the hardness of its paving, its toe-stubbing kerbs. The blunt, inarguable factuality of the ringed buildings was apparent from the circus's residual smell of stone and smoke, of people and their enterprises, evidencing the continuous and ordinary surround of being, but ...

*the cobbles are now staining with aurora, and from out a tunnel into brilliance an ungraspable form coalesces as it lumbers closer, each slow earthquake step rumbling its imminence ... about it is an auditory halo of policemen's whistles, gunshots, ambulance bells, victims pleading, frantic knocking-shop piano, breaking windows, weighty parcels falling into rivers, screeching tyres, a multitude of missing men and women bawling their surprise, or fear, or anger, and*

... Solly the Turk had curled into a foetal ball, down at the feet of a still-paralysed Jack Spot. It was as if the empty intersection was scene to a shattering collision of enormous bodies, to a catastrophic pile-up that could not be seen or heard, and only registered deep in the stomach or the screaming nervous system. Nor was this sense of emergency and crushing impact over in an instant, but went on and on, the moment of intolerable disaster like a held note, stretched out and interminable.

Dennis realised that his nose was bleeding, trickling warm and viscous. In the curly crown of his plucked-looking head, there was the high-pitched whisper of a wireless dial that wandered back and forth between two alternating frequencies, a squealing fluctuation as opposed eternities came into violent contact with each other. Flattened between crashing cities, Dennis clung tight to the tailboard of the builder's truck in his endeavour to stay upright. Cautiously, he raised his squinting gaze back to the blazing interruption on the circle's far side, where ...

*congealing from the colours, a shape previously uncatalogued collects itself, and in his mounting fanfare of undone lives, he is almost here, the general of ruin ... incompatible with human vision, the emerging mass is edited by Dennis's perceptual limitations to a bulbous rect-angle, bulging in space and time, some nine feet high and twelve feet wide, and yet with mannerisms and a measured gait as the illicit's absolute approaches entity, and unmistakeably he's Harry Lud, none other and no less ... around him, as his mantle, a gold glow with no apparent source ... his perfume is Bay Rum and Brylcreem, tarts and dogs, cigars and marzipan ... the heavy coat he wears is furred with rustling layers of banknotes, blackmail letters, compromising snap-shots, ransom messages, appalled newspaper headlines, flash-blanched mugshots, warrants and forged documents ... crowbars for cufflinks, and his tiepin is the head of a decapitated rat ... he's Harry Lud; he's all of infamy ... the brow is easily a yard from ear to ear yet still seems disproportionately small, topped by a broad-brimmed hat whose ostentatious band is pornographic film ... white hair like sisal hanging to his shoulders and a jaw that pokes out challengingly from amid his several chins ... four long scars that converge between the straggling eyebrows slice the face into a radiating sundial of antique hostility, a Union Jack of settled grudge and grief ... with dainty lips fastidious and great indifferent eyes the eerie grey of X-ray plates, a monarch of corruption lifts one plump hand in a signal of expectant invitation, and*

... heaving a sigh of resignation, Ironfoot Jack propelled himself in scrapes and showering sparks across the dumbstruck circus as he formally commenced negotiations.

'Most feared and beloved 'arry Lud, beside whose majesty earth's potentates are fuckin' little toerags, gratefully we welcome you to our unworthy manor. May your rackets all be lucky, and may snouts avoid your mention. We've got someone 'ere who seeks your blindin' counsel.'

Almost filling the arched entranceway behind the drawn-aside theatre curtain that had been a pair of gates, and with the shine of the Great When spilling its painted rays behind him, the disquieting statement that was Harry Lud wrinkled a sharp hummingbird nose as he considered this entreaty. Tilting his hat's cartwheel brim down, villainy's unpardonable saint gazed in deliberation at the ground, where ...

*caught on shoes like getaway cars that have radiator toecaps is a dragging train of smuggled bottle and explosion-blackened strongbox, bodies bound and naked, torture garages, guns in their hundreds braceleted as though unlucky charms, a winding torrent of dire consequence extending back into the maddening glare from which the street-wide figure is projecting ... and at length, the abstract principle of felony tips back his Cinemascope head to speak, his voice the rattling undertow of a dredged riverbed ... 'Then let the cunt be brought to me, that I may render the once-over unto him' ... about Lud's feet, the trailing stream of vice and victim shudders, moaning in the noir cacophony that is iniquity's continuous accompaniment, at which*

... an evidently strained Jack Neave glanced back with hollow eyes across his shoulder at the gangsters, cowering by their motor.

'I can't keep this up for long, so be warned. Mr Comer, this is what you asked for. My advice is, if yer can, walk over 'ere yerself and say yer piece to Mr Lud, or I'll 'ave Mr Blincoe drag yer.'

Jack Spot's gaze, fixed on Lud's mountainous physique, was full of naught but horror at the gold impossibility of everything. He sagged against his car, tinted by foreign colours washing from the aperture directly opposite, and made a whining sound, high in his nose. His mental processes writ bold on his contorting face, he visibly considered simply staying where he was and then glanced over at Gog Blincoe, looming in the mist-choked mouth of Calvert Avenue with those gigantic arms folded across his sackcloth smock. Blincoe returned the glance and shook the great boll of his head, as if to say that sitting all this out was not an option. With what looked to be the final resignation of the scaffold, Spot stepped awkwardly over the crumpled, sobbing mound of Solly Kankus and began his tottering advance towards a furnace mouth where stood the gilded figurehead of wrong.

Eventually, drawing level with Jack Neave and only feet off from the widescreen spectacle of Harry Lud himself, Spot fidgeted, and wrung his hands, and couldn't find his voice. And when he did it wasn't his but that of someone's mum, high-pitched and wheedling.

'I-I didn't know. I didn't know that this went on. I shouldn't be 'ere ...'

He trailed off into a helpless silence, while ...

*within a shifting Fort Knox spotlight, law's anathema tilts his three-foot boulder of a head and dons a frown of patient sympathy, his voice reverberant and subterranean as a sewer main, his tenor frighteningly gentle ... 'That's as may be, sunshine, but 'ere's where you are in our eternal dance of planets and police cars, aincha? Ask yer tawdry favour of extortion's ultimate, then fuck off out of it, there's a good boy' ... the words hang hefty as a ten-stretch on the diamond air and are in no way a request, so that*

... the quaking turf baron had no choice but to state a case that he'd become increasingly unsure of since the incident with Blincoe and the kitchen knife, in Spitalfields. He stammered, stalled and startled. 'My, my, my, my name's Jack Spot, and I'm, I'm in a bit o' bother, look, it's nothin', nothin' that I should 'ave troubled you with, you don't wanna 'ear about it, I'll just go. I can just go.' A pace away and in another world ...

*the prayer of scoundrels shakes his meaty face from side to side, almost regretfully, and once again the voice, a buried river of black syrup ... 'No, son. No, yer can't. Not until I've put my two penn'orth in, as you demanded when you called me from my glorious subterfuge. I know 'oo you are, Jacky. You're a criminal, and as such are a shitty little particle o' me; a bit o' dirt beneath my priceless thumbnail. I know all your form and all your previous. I know what name you called your teddy bear, and I know what you want me to sort out, which is to say the sour grapes between you an' Billy 'ill' ... the name drops like some squealer from a bridge, and in result*

... a burst of last-ditch desperation seemed to grip the formerly subdued and shaken gangster, a determination to at least get what he'd come here for.

'I know. I know I've mucked things up, but if you could just get it back to 'ow it was with me an' Bill, to 'ow it was before, that's all I'm askin'.'

Arnold Circus held in its collective breath, assuming that Gog Blincoe breathed. Whimpering on the blunt discomfort of the cobbles, Solly Kankus had both hands up, covering his eyes, while Dennis swayed unsteadily against the builder's wagon and saw a great deal of merit in the writhing thug lieutenant's tactic. At the epicentre of the dazzle were the two Jacks, Neave and Spot, their stretching shadows flung across the ring behind them, stark and black on its prismatic mottle. The audial collage of gunfire, faulty brakes and belching slot machines that laced the ambience was rising in its pitch, corkscrewing up into dog-whistle altitudes, while at the focal point of everybody's rapt attention ...

*the sublime of sin turns flickering-newsreel eyes to his despairing supplicant, delivering his verdict in tones that are grave and Stygian, but not unkind ... 'That's not what's gunna 'appen, Jacky. You know what you've done. You made yer play while Billy was in stir, the London airport job that was supposed to put you in the top seat for when 'e come out. Only it was a right dog's breakfast what you made of all that, weren't it? And now the mutations of the day are acted, do yer see me point? You've set a thunderous process into motion, an' it all works out 'ow it works out. There's nothin' to be done' ... felony's emblem sighs, like half the globe's last breaths at once ... 'Just over five years, you've got, till it 'appens. You'll be doin' bad by then, with up-and-comin' villain twins employed to bolster your decreasin' reputation. Billy and a couple of 'is friends will duff you up an' stripe yer, practically on yer front doorstep, with yer missus lookin' on an' givin' it the waterworks. This is what's on the cards, Jack, and you knowin' in advance about it won't change nothin'. Afterwards, you've got another thirty years. You'll outlive Billy, if it's any consolation, and you'll be a little Jewish chap called Colmore, with a stitched-up face and lots o' fascinatin' stories, 'oo*

*works in a bacon-packin' factory. The judge's summin'-up was jotted on*
*your mother's womb, with time itself your penitentiary, and there might*
*be a second-hand-shop paperback or two for 'eadstones. Now, you keep*
*yer nose clean, and you'll not see me again while you are living' ...*
*reaching from his burnished universe, Lud lightly touches Jack Spot's*
*arm with one manicured car door of a hand, a mournful pat indicative of*
*interrupted camaraderie ... tipping the barest fraction of a nod to Neave*
*and Blincoe, the summation of misconduct starts to turn his panorama*
*of anatomy away, which action*

... seemed to cut Spot's puppet strings. His face a motionless
wax mask of loss, he folded slowly to the stony ground and
never noticed that the left sleeve of his jacket was now bleached
unevenly, and smouldering.

Ironfoot looked down at the kneeling mobster, unimpressed,
and ...

*in the treasure glimmer, terror's author takes mastodon steps, glacier*
*slow, into a colour-saturated background, with his barbershop-floor*
*spoor and cataclysmic sounds ribboning after him, the almost oblong*
*outline dwindling in unfixed perspective, until*

... with his eyes already aching, Dennis had to look away.
When he forced himself to look again, Jack Neave was shear-
ing red-hot iron filings from his heel as he stamped back across
the circus, leaving Spot there on his knees with all his dreams
gone; with his sharp suit smoking and discoloured. Hollowed
out of point or purpose, the dismantled gang boss didn't even
budge when ...

*businesslike, Gog Blincoe strides right by him, seizing up the thick*
*folds of the curtain that are gathered to the left and dragging them*
*back over the fluorescent opening, their soft material hardening to*
*scored and splintered planking as he does so, before himself vanishing*
*around the drapes' end like an unobtrusive stagehand ... finally, with*
*a metallic clink, the painted padlock becomes real again, and so the*
*gaudy rupture between Londons disappears*

... and had, within an instant, never been there. Timid mists,
that until then had stood and quivered nervously in the conver-
gent streets, not wanting any trouble, now crept hesitantly

back into the centre ring and, like most witnesses to violence, behaved as if it hadn't happened.

Shrugging off the reconsolidated fog, Neave scraped his way to Dennis and peered in disdain at Solly Kankus, bundled embryonic at their feet with his paroxysm subsiding into shivers. Ironfoot pulled the ornate fastening tighter on his silk cravat, and sniffed before he spoke.

'So, Mr Kankus, is it? Mr Kankus, you're all done 'ere. I was you, when I was fit to walk, I'd get your gaffer in the motor so 'e can collect 'imself before one of yer drives the other 'ome. This is the finish of it. See as everybody understands that. Come on, Dennis. Let's be on our way, and leave these two to ponder on the marvel of existence. We've all 'ad, I'm sure, a very tryin' night.'

With Dennis, Neave limped noisily and pyrotechnically up through the grounded cloudbank filling Calvert Avenue, and by the time they were on Shoreditch High Street, the dense little bulldog of a man was grinning, eyes alight like gypsy fires beneath the trailing hedges of their brows.

'I think that was a decent evenin's work. I can't imagine you or your young lady gettin' any further interference from that quarter, shall we say? So, that the first time, was it, you'd seen one o' the Arcana? What it's worth, I thought you 'andled yerself very reasonably.'

Although Dennis was aware that 'reasonably' only meant he'd managed not to scream or soil himself, he took a certain warming pride in Ironfoot's compliment. This must, he thought, be what it would be like to have a job, discussing the success or otherwise of your endeavours with your colleagues, at the end of a long working day. It felt, he had to admit, very satisfying.

'Thanks. Yeah, well, I've seen the Inferred Saracen and Her Train, but that was the first time I'd heard one of the Arcana talking, back there.' He thumbed back over his shoulder towards Arnold Circus, deathly silent in the fuming shadows at their rear. Neave lit another fag.

'There's only one or two of 'em as can talk. 'arry Lud, 'e's one, an' Broadstair the Prime Monster is another, Slender' orse as well, but the majority do all their signifyin' by just bein' what they are. Beauty o' Riots, she sometimes sings, I'm told, but if we're lucky, we shan't live to 'ear it. Now, young man, I think this is where we part company. I'm 'eadin' on up Kingsland Road, and you'll be off down Bishopsgate to see yer girlfriend. It's been nice to meet yer, Dennis, an' I dare say we'll run into one another down life's byways now an' then. Ooh, that reminds me – I 'ad word from our mate Awstin, said to tell yer that 'e's got a show on at the Temple Bar in Walworth Road, a week today. Said you'd be very welcome if yer fancied droppin' by.'

Slightly ashamed that he had not, so far, corrected anybody who'd referred to Grace as his young lady or his girlfriend, Dennis said he'd try his best to be there. The two men shook hands, and Dennis watched as Neave lurched off, top-heavy in the marbling grey and sparking like a foundry, the Stoke Newington Hephaestus. Only when he was halfway to Spitalfields and heard a clock strike once for half past twelve did Dennis realise that the interchange between Jack Spot and Harry Lud, for all its detailed incident and doodlebug intensity, had been no more than ten or fifteen minutes in duration. Lazily, he entertained the notion that all aspects of the Great When, from its characters to its evinced emotions to its very sense of time, existed as some sort of concentrate, like orange squash. If it could only be diluted in some way, he dreamily construed, it might be easier to swallow. By the time he'd noticed that this train of thought was neither interesting nor practical, he had arrived at Folgate Street.

The fog in Spitalfields was constitutionally just the same as all the other fog, but much more threatening because of its location, soured by top hats, butcher's knives and all the Gladstone baggage of a dozen props departments. Dennis shouldered through the gaseous veils and somehow found the right front entrance. Letting himself in using his borrowed key – with a slight pang of melancholy that he might be called upon to give it back soon – he performed a haunted-house walk down the creaking hallway and tapped near inaudibly on Grace's door. He hoped she was still up.

'Is that you, Dennis? Come on in. I'm decent.'

'Decent' turned out to be a long navy dressing-gown, ridiculously big on her and probably a man's, its sleeves rolled back, although he had to admit that it went wonderfully with Grace's fireball hair. Completing the ensemble, she wore silky-looking slippers of ice blue and a faint smile that hovered unresolved between fond and amused. Even the rabbit-hutch proportions of the flat seemed cheerier and more welcoming, and Dennis realised that she must have simply swept and tidied up a bit. She very likely did this every Friday, but he still allowed himself the flattering delusion that her ordinary domesticity was just for him. She padded to the kitchen and returned with cups of tea for both of them, and they sat there at each end of her sofa, cosy in the paraffin stove's smelly halo.

'So what happened, then? Did Jack Spot get the meeting he was after?'

Dennis stared at a fixed point above the picture rail and thought how best to answer.

'Yes and no. He got his meeting, yes, but from the state of him when it was done, it weren't the one that he was after. Harry Lud ... I can't describe him. He was wider than a lot of houses, but the size of him, that was the least of it. It was, it was as if he was all swollen up and fit to burst with what he meant, but what he meant weren't something definite, and it kept altering, depending on the way you looked at him. He was more like, I don't know. More like a frightening poem than a person.'

Grace regarded him, lighting a Craven 'A' and squinting to prevent the floating curlicues from getting in her eyes. She nodded in approval.

'Very well put, Knuckleyard. I shan't press you for details, but you say the trouble that we had with Spot, that's finished now? And all the other business, too: I won't be called upon to pull my kitchen knife out of the heads of any more of your peculiar friends?'

He laughed, and sipped his tea.

'I shouldn't think so. I think it's all done with now. With any luck, we can forget about, you know, the other place, and just go back to being who we were before. I can get out your hair, first thing tomorrow morning, and go back to my exciting life at Coffin Ada's.'

Obviously, he was expecting her to say she wouldn't hear of it, that he must stay in Folgate Street to share her dreams, her life, her bed, and, just as obviously, she didn't. For the seconds that it took for this to be apparent, there was a taut silence in which the astonishing erotic future Dennis had been whittling since breakfast time that morning could be heard collapsing into hopeless dust, at least by him. Eventually, attempting not to show what he at least knew to be childish disappointment, he ended the crushing hush by thinking to ask Grace what her day had been like.

'Not bad at all. I done brisk trade because the sun was out, and knocked off early. Had some fish and chips on the way home, got in here around eight o'clock to have a bath, and since then I've been looking at the book you lent me last night. Have to say, that Machen, he's a cracking writer.'

She inclined her head towards the coffee table, where belatedly he noticed his near-mint edition of *The Cosy Room* in its sepulchral white-and-green wraps, resting near the seashell ashtray. Dennis was still thinking about how unfair it was that Grace still didn't fancy him after the terrible ordeal they'd shared, which he, admittedly, had been the cause of. Worse still, he was wondering if, with him back at Coffin Ada's, he and Grace would ever have a reason to meet up again. He didn't, at that moment, have a lot of interest in the literary skills of Arthur Machen, but still managed to ask her if she'd read 'N', so that it wouldn't look like he was sulking.

'I've read all of them, from front to back. I finished "N" about a half hour before you got home. So that's the one that landed you in this mess, with its made-up book that somehow turns up in your Persil box, or whatever it was? It's the best story in the collection, for my money – you can tell he's really serious with what he's saying, like there's something dead important that he's trying to get across – but all the others in there are good yarns, too, don't you think?'

Still steeping in self-pity, Dennis grudgingly confessed to having only looked at 'N'.

'I thought the others looked a bit sedate for my taste. I mean, just the title put me off, *The Cosy Room*. It's hardly the most gripping subject for a story, is it?'

Grace looked at him through smoke and very slightly narrowed eyes.

'Dennis, it's what's called irony. The cosy room is a condemned cell. You'd do better not to make your mind up about matters before you've completely understood them. Same with people, same with everything. My policy is, don't dismiss things, but don't swear them your allegiance either, not before you're sure that you've got all the facts. It saves a lot of trouble.'

She ground out her cigarette in the remains of a sea creature which could never have anticipated that its exoskeleton would one day suffer this indignity. Had that last thing she said been telling him to not get too attached to her? Dispirited already by imagined intimations of finality, Dennis elected to say nothing in response to this, but fixed his stinging eyes upon the paraffin stove's tennis-ball-sized dome of glowing wire mesh. Grace studied him, her bottle-green gaze thoughtful, weighing up his obvious dejection and deciding that she'd better say something companionable.

'You know, for all that this has been a bloody nightmare, I expect we'll miss it now it's over with. I liked the atmosphere around it, and the fairy-tale stuff like your Mr Blincoe. And when we weren't both in terror for our lives or else administering first aid to monsters, it was quite nice having you about, although quite frankly, you're starting to smell a bit. I like you, Dennis. You don't know it, but you're interesting. You recommend good books, even if you're too lazy to have read them properly, and I was very grateful for those racing forecast cards, so that's another thing you've introduced me to, this Spare chap's work. I shall be looking out for him.'

Though still rapidly sinking in his quicksand of despond, Dennis dimly perceived that Grace's well-intentioned sympathies might offer him a lifeline. It was one he clutched at desperately.

'I've just thought. When I was saying cheerio to Ironfoot Jack tonight – you've not met Ironfoot Jack, but he's a proper human being, he's not made of iron or anything, he's just got a bad leg, he's not like Blincoe – anyway, Jack said that Austin had invited me to this show that he's having in a pub, the Temple Bar on Walworth Road, next Friday. If you wanted, you could come along. I'll, I'll, I'll have a bath by then and, you know, smarten myself up.'

Her smile was like a buried earthquake victim's glimpse of daylight, so delightful that he wondered for a moment if he hadn't wanted that more than the sex. Also, unlike his probably inexpert first attempts at coitus would have done, this seemed to have thoroughly pleased her.

'I should like that. That would be a proper treat. And the Spare exhibition sounds alright as well.' She giggled at her own joke, and when Dennis at last got it and looked hurt, she reached across and jabbed him in his nearer shoulder. 'Dennis, I was kidding. You don't really smell that bad, although you're getting there. No, I should love to come and see his show with you. I've never seen real art before, not in the flesh. You come and call for me next Friday afternoon, and we'll go over there together. An art exhibition! Don't know about you, but I'm feeling more civilised already.'

His emotional death penalty commuted thus to a suspended sentence, Dennis found he was in a much better mood. They laughed and chatted for a good half hour before they noticed it was nearly two o'clock. He fished out the spare key and gave it back to her with nothing like the pang of loss that he'd expected, and then Grace and he went off to their respective bed or knackered couch. Like a compressed spring, with his head against one of the sofa's hard, unyielding arms, he slept only in fits and starts, and, for the fourth or fifth night running, had no dreams he could remember. He thought it might be

experiences like the recent spectacle in Arnold Circus that had
squeezed all the imagination out of him, or possibly that his
unconscious mind had become constipated, though this last
thought only led him to anticipate a large and painful dream,
tomorrow or the evening following. His last night under
Grace's roof was passed in an ambiguous grey drift of dustballs
that weren't quite ideas, until he could no longer tell where the
fog tumbling in the gutters outside ended, and the fog in his
part-shaven skull began. He'd had a busy week.

Saturday came with the free gift of yet another sunny morning hidden in its dreary cardboard cornflake packaging, inner
and outer mists all burned away long before Dennis prised
his eyelashes apart, blinking with unfamiliarity at the almost
forgotten benison of a weekend. Again, Grace was already up
and dressed, practically shovelling a plate of egg on toast down
Dennis as she made it clear that this was the financial high point
of her week, and that he'd have to leave the house when she did.
He remembered to retrieve his copy of *The Cosy Room* that he'd
had Gawsworth sign, shoved it into its carrier bag, shrugged on
his mac and followed Grace out of her sardine-suitable accommodation. It was all a bit rushed, not at all the lingering farewell
that would have been his preference: there on her doorstep,
with the yammer of the nearby market ruling out whatever soft
exchanges he'd been hoping for, there was a moment where
he wondered whether she might kiss him, or if he should kiss
her, but at last he stuck his hand out, whereupon she shook it
awkwardly and he felt like an idiot.

Pathetically, at least in his own estimation, he gazed after Grace
as she tick-tocked away down Bishopsgate, heading for Cheapside,
Ludgate Hill, and ultimately her accustomed pitch in Bride Lane.
Eyes like an abandoned dog, he watched as she reduced into the
French Impressionistic stipple of weekend pedestrians, her hair
with all the colour and potential of an unstruck match. Caught up
in the theatrics of thwarted romance, he heaved a self-indulgent

sigh and sulked up Shoreditch High Street, making for Gibraltar Walk and his upsetting landlady, a destination that he understood was nearly as unpalatable and as necessary as the place that Grace was making for. Slumping along, his carrier bag dangling, he dragged the ball and chain of his desire to turn and follow her behind him, like a comic-paper convict.

Making his unwieldy way through shoaling shoppers, shitting dogs and unexploded schoolkids off on Saturday adventures, Dennis thought about the previous five days, realising he still didn't quite believe they'd happened. Now it was all over – or, with luck, all over except him and Grace – he reckoned he could come to see it as a good thing, that it was concluded in so short a space of time, however hectic and traumatic those five days had been while they were going on. Perhaps their breathless pace would make them easier to wrap up as a brief, uncanny stammer in his life, a spasm of improbable events that he might one day, hopefully, dismiss as dreams or, better yet, forget entirely. He supposed it was a bit like London and the war, with nobody pretending that those seven years hadn't occurred, but everybody keen to put it all behind them and not look at it again. He even wondered if at some point in the unimaginably distant future, both he and the city might eventually become nostalgic for the terrifying times they'd been through, although, just then passing the rock garden of Great Eastern Street, he knew that the concept was laughable in either instance. He could see how London harboured sentimental feelings for the 1920s, when there wasn't yet a war, or how he could look fondly on his infancy for the same reason, but nostalgia for the Blitz or severed heads in pot-pourri was clearly never going to be a trend, for London or for Dennis. Some things, surely, were too raw to finish up in souvenir shops, or he hoped they were.

Crossing Commercial Street and still attempting to find something positive in the deranging horror of the last week, he decided that he must at least have gone through all the strangeness allocated to a single human being in their lifetime, and that from here on, speaking statistically, the rest of his existence should be free of funny or peculiar incidents. He was congratulating himself on this reassuring possibility when something funny happened – not Gog Blincoe funny, but still funny nonetheless. As he turned into Bethnal Green Road, Dennis registered a figure on the far side of the busy street, doggedly striding west, its gait familiar though glimpsed only in instalments through the intervening cars and horse-drawn carts. It was Clive Amery.

They both spotted each other at the same time and stopped in their tracks. The trainee lawyer's eyes were momentarily inhabited by blank surprise before his face lit up with a broad grin of recognition and he waved enthusiastically to Dennis, waiting for a break in traffic to dart eagerly across the road towards his younger, shabbier acquaintance.

'Why, Lord Oxydol! The very chap that I was looking for! Do you know, I've been wandering the grounds of your dismal estate for a good fifteen minutes, hoping to catch sight of you? I'd just popped up and squinted through the window of that picturesque Dickensian hovel where you work, but, failing to find you there, had given up the ghost. And now, as if from nowhere, here you are! Nature must give you guttersnipes your colouration so that you can blend in with the gutters when you're sniping.'

Dennis laughed, while inwardly still reeling with astonishment. Other than their first meeting, when Clive happened to call in at Lowell's Books & Magazines, he'd never previously known his stylish pal to venture so far from the law courts. Shoreditch, for a city boy like Clive, he thought, must seem like a safari into a dark continent of rationing, with tin advertisements for Oxo bolted up on its end-terrace walls. The young legal apprentice even looked a little worn and windswept after hacking through the urban undergrowth: still dashing, naturally, but with a couple of his blond hairs out of place, and a few minor wrinkles in the same dark suit that he'd been wearing yesterday. He didn't have his tie on, and the points of his unbuttoned collar were spread like white wings across the black lapels.

It wasn't that he was what anyone would call dishevelled, but, on Clive, anything other than impeccable tended to be more of a cause for comment.

'Clive? What are you doing all the way up here? Aren't you afraid you'll pick up commonness or beriberi?'

Giving Dennis an indulgent smile, Clive wagged one slightly grubby palm dismissively.

'Good Lord, no. If you're going east of Holborn these days, they give you injections against both those things, hadn't you heard? No, it was just a Saturday and I had nothing planned, so I thought that I'd take advantage of the weather, and trek all the way up here to see my old mate Knuckleyard. Especially after that business you were talking to me about yesterday. God, Dennis, what a yarn! I promise you, I thought about it all last night, and then this morning I decided that I'd better come and check on you to see how it all went, the episode with Jack Spot and his quaking henchman that you were expecting when I saw you last. Since you appear to have no obvious bullet holes, I take it that things didn't go too badly?'

Dennis raised an eyebrow, but then wasn't sure what he had done it for, so lowered it again.

'Oh, yeah. Yeah, everything went fine, and I don't ever need to think about that stuff again. I mean, it was sort of exciting, I suppose, but I'm not someone who's cut out for it. Somebody cleverer or tougher, perhaps they could handle it, but me, I've had enough.' Clive nodded, it seemed sympathetically. 'But I'm chuffed that you came here to make sure I was alright. You said you'd keep an eye on me when I rang up and asked on Wednesday, and you have. You're a good mate, Clive. Thanks for doing that. Had you got anywhere in mind where we could go? I was just heading back to Ada's after all this time away, but, obviously, it's not something that I'm looking forward to, and a chat in a Lyons Corner House with you would at least put it off a little longer. We could probably find somewhere on the high street, if you fancied it. My treat.' He'd still got most of Grace's tenner.

Clive made an apologetic grimace.

'Dennis, if I'm honest, it was just you and your welfare brought me up here. Now I've satisfied myself that you're still with us, there's most probably a lot of casework that I should be reading up on over this weekend. We'll have to save our badinage for a further occasion.'

Despite a fleeting cloud of disappointment, Dennis saw the logic in what Clive said, and was anyway too heartened by his comrade's gesture of concern to make a fuss about it.

'Yeah. Yeah, that makes sense. Perhaps we could meet up in Bond's next week sometime?'

The fledgling barrister sighed heavily and shook his head.

'No can do, I'm afraid. Something's come up, and I'm anticipating that I'm going to be exceptionally busy for at least this coming week. I'll tell you what, why don't we put our meeting off until the evening of the Monday after next, when I get out of work? And, strictly entre nous, I'm getting rather sick of Bond's, aren't you? The way that sweaty idiot manager fawns over both of us is starting to make even me uncomfortable. There's a nice café up in Farringdon Road, near the bottom. It's called Franklin's, and stays open late into the evening. You can't miss it. Shall we say Monday the thirty-first, at eight?'

Although it seemed like a long wait, Dennis accepted it resignedly. The two shook hands and clapped each other on the shoulder, while a passing coalman's horse evacuated its gold-green and fibrous load on to the tarmac not three feet away. Clive sauntered off in the direction of Old Street and Clerkenwell, and Dennis stood and watched him go, still marvelling at the unreality of their exchange. Something about it felt a bit wrong, almost, but this minor itch was wholly overruled by Dennis's elation that the bond between him and his friend seemed to be deepening, as he'd hoped. For Clive to have come all the way to Shoreditch because he was worried about Dennis felt like a tremendous honour – almost cancelling the doomsday of his forthcoming reunion with Coffin Ada, but not quite. Afflicted by a sinking feeling that itself had sinking feelings, Dennis steeled himself for the encounter with his landlady, now only a few minutes up the road and in his future. He drank in a mighty breath to fortify himself, and only then remembered the proximity of the fresh horse shit.

He dragged out his climb of a largely conceptual Gibraltar Walk as much as he was able, which was hardly any time at all. On his procrastinating way, he was obscurely cheered to notice that one of the chapters from Sax Rohmer's *Dope* – **Night-Life of Soho**, as it happened – was still holding on for dear life in a gutter of the cancelled street, despite last Thursday's rain. Dennis considered fishing it out of the drain that it had blocked and giving it a read, just as a further tactic for postponing the inevitable, but then told himself he was a better man than that, and anyway, the pages, save for their bold headings, were too sodden to be legible. With concrete in his shoes and heart, he carried on towards the walk's top end and its remaining stalagmite of brick and slate, its desolation show home.

Saturdays were always the best days for trade, and therefore Lowell's Books & Magazines was resolutely PEN according to its ghostly, hanging door sign. Carrier bag in hand, he pushed his way into the shop with a defeated jingle from its customer-alert bell, where he found that he and Ada Benson, possibly because it was still relatively early, were the only people there.

Standing beside the till, Ada looked up at him and all the colour would have drained out of her face if there'd been any to begin with. She attempted what a scream would be with very little breath behind it, like the death squawk of a strangled hen, and sagged forward across the counter, clutching at her chest, gasping for breath and with her varicose eyes bulging. She was obviously dying, more than she was normally, but when he lurched across the shop floor to his landlady's assistance, she threw up one trembling hand to ward him off and screamed again, although with even less force and conviction. Holding herself up with one palm braced against the counter and the other held out in refusal like a traffic bobby's, her distended eyeballs seemed about to launch themselves towards her underling from her slack, corrugated face.

'Dennis? I thought you were a cough cough cough cough cough cough fucking ghost! How are you cough cough cough cough fucking cough cough still alive? If you've still got that book there in your cough cough cough cough carrier bag, then you can cough cough fuck off out of it.'

Startled and stunned by the extremity of Ada's almost cardiac reaction, Dennis stuttered as he fumbled in the bag to pull out and brandish aloft Machen's *The Cosy Room*.

'No, no, no, I got rid of that. I, I, I took it back to where it came from, like you told me. All I've got in here's that Machen book with "N" in it. I, I, I got the editor to sign it for you.' Dennis paused and blinked as his internal filing system finally caught up with what his spluttering employer had just said. 'Hang on – you thought that I was dead?'

In her ambiguous maybe-tartan slippers, Ada stamped out angrily, without a sound, around the counter to confront him, although whether she was furious with him for having asked a question or for not being dead wasn't an easy matter to establish. He thought it might be a bit of both.

'Don't change the fucking cough cough cough cough subject! I had fucking Jack cough Spot in here, looking for you! If you're cough cough cough telling me that you've took back the Hampole book and seen off cough cough cough Jack Spot, and haven't come out of it inside out or fucking cough cough dead, you must think I'm as fucking cough cough cough cough daft as you are!'

Dennis, bag in one hand, Machen memorabilia in the other, was beginning to feel somewhat put upon. He was also discovering that after all the Popes of Blades and wooden men and talking cats, his landlady was fractionally less frightening, though only by a petrified and rigid hair. He wasn't ready yet to stand up for himself with Coffin Ada, but thought that he could perhaps manage a seated posture. His cowed apologia now had undertones of dignity, and even sounded slightly cross.

'Ada, I sorted it all out. I had help doing it, but everything you wanted me to do, I did it. I got Spot to hold off killing me until I'd taken Hampole's book back to the other place, and then I brought somebody home he couldn't argue with. He won't be giving either of us any trouble from now on, and neither will the other London. Plus, I'm now on speaking terms with all the top magicians, if you're after occult rubbish, and I got your copy of *The Cosy Room* signed by its editor and publisher. Not blowing my own trumpet, but I think for once I've done a pretty decent job. All I want now is to move back in here, and get on with my work, and put this bloody awful week behind me.'

Ada stared at him without especial malice, as if actually considering what he'd just said. She snatched the Machen volume that he was still waving, flipping through it to the flyleaf with John Gawsworth's signature and dedication, then looked back at Dennis.

'Dennis, I've cough cough cough cough cough sold your bed.'

He opened and then closed his mouth two or three times in quick succession without making any sound, his feelings evidently inexpressible. Ada seemed irritated by his look of hurt betrayal and the criticism of her character implied therein.

'Don't cough cough cough cough look at me like that. With you not coming back, keeping the cough cough bed seemed cough cough cough cough fucking morbid. Cough cough cough. Dennis, there comes a time when cough cough people have to let go and move cough cough cough cough on.'

He stared at her as if no longer sure what he was staring at.

'Ada, you saw me Tuesday. I've been gone four days.'

She carried on, as though he hadn't spoken.

'Anyway, the chap I sold it to refused to cough cough cough cough take the mattress, so it's not all cough cough cough cough cough cough doom and gloom. Think yourself lucky that I didn't cough cough cough cough fucking burn it, because I was cough cough going to.'

She paused as if in thought, perhaps considering the sheer unlikelihood of what her clueless lackey had accomplished. Unexpectedly her angry granite features softened.

'Well, you've spoiled my cough cough morning good and proper now, coming in cough cough cough cough here, and nearly giving me a fucking heart attack. I'll have to shut the shop until this after cough cough cough cough noon. I don't want anybody seeing me like this.'

She shuffled in her plaid or puked-on slippers and her three-week-dead flamingo of a dressing-gown across to the shop door, turning the hanging cardboard sign from PEN to LOSED, looking exactly as she did at every other point in all the years Dennis had known her, with her skin like puckered tripe, and fire-risk hair. She'd left it a bit late, he thought, to not want anybody seeing her like that, much as he both endorsed and understood her wishes. Having closed her business at what must have been around ten in the morning, Ada swivelled to regard her prodigal employee, briefly holding up *The Cosy Room* with an expression of airily unimpressed disdain.

'Not that it's any of your cough cough business, but I used to know John Gawsworth. He once served me coffee what had cough cough cough poor old Matty Shiel's ashes in it, the disgusting cough cough cough cough cough cough fucker. I knew Shiel as well, when he was living up that cough cough tree in Hyde Park. Lovely chap. Ah, well. I've shut up for the cough cough morning, so shall we go in the kitchen for a cup of tea and a cough cough cough cough cough fucking chinwag?'

This disorienting mood reversal offered Dennis no appropriate response except to mutely do as she'd suggested. It was like the grillings that he'd seen in films, where there was usually a threatening copper and a sympathetic one, to break down all a suspect's psychological defences, except in this instance, both interrogators used the same vinegar-shrivelled lips. He followed Ada through into the kitchen, where she made them both the promised cup of tea and even furthered Dennis's sense of unbalance by providing a half-finished pack of finger biscuits.

It was certainly the longest and, in its odd way, the most convivial conversation that the two of them had ever had. It wasn't that his landlady was any nicer to him, but more that she was suddenly subjecting him to the same level of unpleasantness that she reserved for peers and other grown-ups. Even when he told her about trying to take the Hampole book to Flabby Harrison's when he was drunk and consequently getting noticed by Jack Spot's men, the way Ada gave a phlegmy chuckle and called him a cunt felt something like affection. And when Dennis started to describe the chase through Soho that had ensued, she held up a crenellated finger in the most polite of interruptions.

'Cough cough cough cough. Dennis, if at any point soon you're about to tell me how you got into the cough cough other place, or what you saw there, then for cough cough cough cough fuck's sake don't. I only want the outline. You can cough cough cough spare me the fucking details.'

This was fine with Dennis as it meant that Grace could be one of the fucking details that he spared her. He told Ada about Monolulu pointing him in Austin Spare's direction, and about Jack Spot's unwise demand to meet with someone from the other London, but he didn't breathe a word about Gog Blincoe, heads in glass jars, or where he'd been sleeping for the last four nights. And once Ada was satisfied that Hampole's book was gone and with it the attentions of Jack Spot, she didn't press him further. They sat talking in a kitchen that was sunlit but still ugly, and their chat moved smoothly from the shaky ground of mystery to matters more immediate. Ada told him that if he'd serve in the shop when it reopened in the afternoon, then she'd put bedding back on his unwanted mattress and pop to the high street and obtain a piece of haddock for their supper. Other than the still-upsetting fact that he no longer had a bed, Dennis agreed that this all sounded very reasonable. He chatted to her about Spare and Ironfoot Jack, the latter of whom she had heard, and she belatedly remembered that someone had called in at the shop for Dennis while he'd been away.

'It was that cough cough nice cough cough cough John McAllister. This was the Wednesday, and he seemed quite worried that you might be cough cough cough cough dead. Well, cough cough cough we both were, obviously, but he wouldn't cough cough cough fucking shut up about it. He said he'd be out the cough cough cough cough office until next week, but if you got back in cough cough touch, he said that you could meet him in the Cheshire cough cough Cheese, next Monday night. Cough cough cough cough.'

All of his friends had been concerned about him, then, both Clive and Tolerable John, and he allowed himself to think that Ada, in her own way, had been worried, too. Although, of course, she'd sold his bed, which, possibly, was Ada's idiosyncratic means of dealing with bereavement, but inside he knew it wasn't and that Ada was a brutal, heartless travesty of an old woman, plain and simple. Finishing between them the half pack of finger biscuits, they concluded their conciliatory tea break, and she told him to go and unlock the shop while she set out to dress the corpse of his expired mattress and to do her bit of shopping. She also instructed him to watch out for that woman with the funny eye, who Ada would swear blind was pinching racy murder paperbacks.

Unlike the days that Dennis had experienced recently, Saturday passed much as predicted: when they'd opened up the shop again, Ada had coughed away to Dennis's lately unfurnished room and at least made it look like somewhere one might quarantine a dying animal. She'd put on a fur coat that had less hair than Ada had herself over her dressing-gown, and gone to fetch the haddock. Dennis watched the shop with its handful of customers, and, sure enough, at roughly half past three, a woman came in who had the brisk manner of a district nurse and one eye that was rolling uncontrollably in its ill-fitting socket. When he noticed her pick something from the shelves of the Detective section and stepped from behind the till to take a closer look, she put the book down hastily and fled the premises with her afflicted eye rotating like a compass needle at magnetic north. Just out of interest, he inspected the American crime paperback that she'd been coveting. Its cover had a painted brunette, naked save a near-transparent negligee, sprawled on an unmade bed with a trilby-clad shadow angling between her arguably pre-mortem legs, and bore the title *The Tomato Had a Toe Tag*. On reflection, the persistent accuracy of his landlady's bleak worldview was what made it so enormously dispiriting.

After they'd LOSED, Ada prepared the haddock with peas, boiled potatoes and a knob of butter, and when they'd had that, they both sat in the kitchen listening to the wireless. Ada coughed and cunted her way through the sports results, checking her Littlewoods pools coupon to see if she'd won a fortune, verbally abusing entire football teams when it invariably turned out she hadn't. Then, at twenty-five past six, she seemed to have her evil spirits raised by forty minutes of *Those Were the Days*, where Harry Davidson and his radio orchestra performed tunes from when Ada had still been alive. Following that, they had a quarter-hour of 'Quintin cough cough cough cough fucking Hogg' with dull impressions of his week in Parliament, and then, at eight o'clock, came *Music Hall* and the tired patter of its host, Ted Ray. At last, when Ada had begun to croak along with an old Marie Lloyd routine, Dennis could take no more and went off to his cheerless, bedless bedroom.

This turned out to be as physically and psychologically uncomfortable as he'd anticipated. With no bed supporting it, his mattress was a pancake rectangle – no springs save those that had been built into the absent bed frame – that raised him no further than two inches from the spider-haunted floor. Whereas he'd previously sat on his bed's edge, the room lacking a chair, other than standing up, the only posture now available to him was lying down, which meant he couldn't reach his bedside table any more, and that his main view of the place he slept was now that of an insect. It was miserable. Fully dressed and glaring at the crack map of the ceiling from a skirting-board perspective, Dennis fumed, flat on his back, and tried to work out how the thrills and terrors of the previous week could have boiled down to this cold cup of sick. He lay like that an hour or two, until he'd heard Ada's tubercular typhoon rage up the stairs and into bed, and then he removed everything except his once white vest and pants, turned off his bedside lamp and slid himself like luncheon meat between the stale bread sheets. Peacefully nodding off, as an eighteen-year-old, was usually not accomplished without physical exertion, and for several minutes he attempted to imagine Grace with lower standards, but this made him feel like a psychic intruder or a séance-medium peeping Tom. Eventually, he thought about the maybe dead brunette he'd seen on *The Tomato Had a Toe Tag*, who was painted and who therefore had no rights, and soon thereafter Dennis managed the Big Sleep.

Sunday was worse, what with the shop not being open and Saturday's sun revealed as a demoralising propaganda exercise arranged by the resurgent rain. All that was pleasurable about his life was paused until a future time which, from that Sunday's vantage, appeared geological in its remoteness: he'd still got four days of limbo before he saw Grace again and took her to Spare's show on Friday, while his postponed rendezvous with Clive was yet another three days after that. He read his tattered hoard of *Picture Show* and *Radio Fun* from front to back, and even took to counting Ada's coughs, but gave up in despair at the first thousand. Mostly, he consoled himself by looking forward to tomorrow night's meet-up with Tolerable John, if he could only get through until Monday without strangling Ada as she slept, then hanging himself with her carefully unpicked and braided hair. As Clive was always pointing out, this was the era of the murderous lunatic. No one would blame him.

Mercifully, it didn't come to that. Surprisingly, they boasted an unusually steady flow of customers for a wet Monday, leaving Dennis very little time for doleful reverie. The workday's only memorable event came in a lull during the afternoon, when Dennis plucked his courage up and recklessly asked Ada if there really was a dead man buried underneath the flowerbed in her backyard. She looked at him in silence for a moment, then said, 'Yes, Dennis, there is. And there's cough cough cough cough cough cough always room for more.' They didn't speak a further word to one another before he struck out that evening for a fleeting taste of liberty.

Much as he ached to see Grace, Dennis was relieved to find the puddle of weak lamplight at the top end of Bride Lane deserted.

Possibly she'd gone home early or, given the weather, not come out today at all, but either way it spared him the discomfort of encountering her during working hours. How would he talk to her, and should he even let on that he'd seen her? Grateful that he could leave these decisions for another day, he soldiered on through Fleet Street's dark and drizzle, dodging barging cars and weaving journalists, towards the alley mouth providing access to Ye Olde Cheshire Cheese.

Inside the windowless retreat, where dawn and sunset were at best a rumour, the same endless sixteenth-century day was going on. With the inevitable hanging skeins of smoke affording their traditional low visibility, it was too easy to imagine that the lumbering and occluded forms one passed between the backyard toilets and the bar were those of Samuel Johnson, W. B. Yeats or shuffling Carmelites from the old monastery raised here in the twelve hundreds. The two indistinct shapes playing dominoes at their secluded corner table might be an embittered grudge match between Gerald Kersh and P. G. Wodehouse. The unfathomable monologue from the vicinity of the end barstool was perhaps Alfred, Lord Tennyson checking his lines for scansion. Well, why not?

He somehow managed to find John McAllister's accustomed seat without recourse to a lighthouse or foghorn, and on sighting Dennis, the professionally joyless pressman's face broke open in a radiant beam of what was only mild unhappiness.

'I don't believe it! Dennis! I was just this second thinking that I'd very likely not see you again. How did you ever sort out all that bother you were in up to your neck? Hang on – let me get you a pint to celebrate, then you can tell me all about it, within reason. I shan't be a minute.'

Dennis was by now becoming used to the unsettling phenomenon of close acquaintances expecting him to have been murdered, and at least John hadn't screamed or taken Dennis for an actual ghost, like Coffin Ada had. Now that he thought about it, that was possibly because John hadn't ordered Dennis to his almost certain death and, being thus less weighted down with guilt than Ada, hadn't seen him as a vengeful and accusing Banquo come to shake his gory locks at anyone. Dennis was vaguely annoyed that nobody he knew had rated his survival chances higher when, after the things he'd done, he knew he wasn't the inept and fragile hatchling everyone assumed, naïve and wet behind the ears. He thought about this for a moment, then ran an exploratory finger up behind one ear to check, dismayed to have it indeed come back glistening and moist. He'd walked here in the rain, of course, but didn't know if that was a sufficiently extenuating circumstance. It was then that John came back from the bar with a fresh, foaming pint of beer for each of them. Setting the glasses down, McAllister reclaimed his seat and leaned across the table, wearing a peculiar expression that Dennis eventually recognised as warm enthusiasm on a visage that had never been designed to handle it.

'Come on, then, tell me all about it. Though when I say all, I mean don't tell me about anything unnatural. If you have to talk about, you know, the other place, then call it Birmingham.'

To Dennis's astonishment, he found this ploy made it much easier to relate a narrative that he himself did not completely understand: 'So, anyway, I had these gangsters chasing me through Soho, and the next thing that I knew, I was in Birmingham.' 'Then Austin Spare, he took me halfway across Birmingham to meet the City Heads. Of Birmingham.' 'When I got back, Jack Spot had to do everything we said, because I'd brought home somebody from Birmingham.' 'And so, after that night in Arnold Circus, it's all finished, and I hope I never have to go to bloody Birmingham again.'

As the long tale at last reached its conclusion, John sat back in the well-padded chair and shook his morose head in marvelment. 'So it's all true, then. I suppose I've always had a feeling in my stomach telling me it was, but if you've been there, then I can't deny it, can I? Birmingham is real.' One of John's fellow journalists was just then wading through the dream sequence of smoke around their table, and he gave McAllister a startled frown, as if this fact was news to him, too. Ever since the V-bombs, life in London had just been one unbelievable surprise after another.

When no more could usefully be said regarding Birmingham, the two men's conversation drifted readily to less unearthly territory. Dennis thought to mention Spare's forthcoming show in Walworth Road, and John said that he'd be there if he got the chance. 'I could even try putting it on my expenses as an article for the *Express*. "Bombed Black Magician Puts Perplexing Paintings in Pub", or something like that.' Dennis fetched them another pint, then asked McAllister how the reporter's own last seven days had gone. John's answer was a drawn-out sigh expressed in words.

'Well, I suppose you could say it's been tolerable, though only just. From what I'm hearing, the man on the Clapham omnibus is starting to object to being robbed and murdered on a nightly basis. Since the war, the crime's been shooting up all over, for all sorts of reasons, and one of the editors at the *Express* thought we might get a feature out of it. That's what I've been assigned to, although frankly, I'm not optimistic.'

Dennis laughed involuntarily into his beer foam but disguised it as a fit of choking, and made a recovery by lifting both his eyebrows in surprise and saying, 'Really?' Seemingly oblivious to mockery, McAllister's hands, face and shoulders synchronised into a gloomy shrug.

'The problem is that everybody's looking for a simple reason why all this is happening – it's the Labour government, it's the bent coppers, it's the foreigners – when, far as I can see, the war put paid to simple reasons and we shan't be seeing 'em again. It's complicated reasons these days, in the world that we've got now. Everything's tangled up with every other thing, and it's all got a million different causes, not just one. And all these complications keep on multiplying until soon the average person won't be able to keep up, or to make proper sense of anything. England's a different place now, Dennis. Everywhere's a different place, and crediting the rise in burglaries to Clement Attlee or Dick Barton isn't going to make it otherwise.'

The mention of radio's special agent put Dennis in mind of Clive, who'd jokingly blamed Barton for what Clive saw as the post-war rise in homicidal madmen. He decided to ask Tolerable John for his opinions on the subject, which seemed pertinent to their discussion.

'I was hearing someone say the other day about these nutcase killers we've had since the war, like Haigh and Neville Heath and that. This person reckoned we'd be seeing more of 'em in years to come, due to the psychological condition everybody's in from being bombed.'

John nodded in unfortunate agreement.

'Yeah, that sounds about right. Being bombed, and all the complications of life nowadays, like I was saying. You can see how someone might go a bit strange. O' course, we had our maniacs long before the war. Been part of human nature, I suppose, since Jack the Ripper's time, at least.'

Though privately unsure that human nature had got anything to do with Jack the Ripper, Dennis merely nodded and let John continue.

'Like, before him, in the late seventeen hundreds, you'd got Renwick Williams, who they called the Monster. He was a mad slasher. And then, not long after that, you'd got your Ratcliffe Highway murderer, who slaughtered a young draper and his missus, alongside their boy apprentice and three-month-old baby, with a mallet and a ripping chisel. He got buried at a cross-roads on the Highway with a wooden stake banged through his heart, like Dracula. His name was Williams, too. John Williams. What is it with all these blokes called Williams? Are the family all murderers?'

Dennis didn't think that he could get away with saying he'd been talking to John Williams's severed head only the other day, even if he maintained that this had taken place in Birmingham. Instead, he opted for a humorous deflection.

'What about Vaughan Williams, who did *Lark Ascending*?'

John looked up at him and, it goes without saying, didn't crack a smile.

'A poisoner, from what I've heard.'

Caught out by the deadpan delivery, Dennis guffawed while John just twitched the corners of his mouth and said, 'Hmuh,' which was his equivalent. Completely undeterred by this derailment to his dogged, journalistic train of thought, McAllister continued with his thesis.

'No, but what you heard about there being more mad killers since the war, with more to come, I think that's definitely on the cards. In my job, they're the kind of cases that I tend to notice, ones where there's no purpose and no motive for the murder, where they don't make sense by any rational standards. I'm not talking about any of the big names, Haigh or Heath, the ones who make the front page of the paper. What I notice are the little stories, buried on page eight and never mentioned after that because there's nothing known, there's nothing anyone can say. Like, I don't know if you'd remember, but the Kenneth Dolden murder back in 1946 was one that I could never figure out.'

Dennis frowned, searching through his memory but to no immediate avail.

'The name rings a vague bell. Perhaps I read it in the papers at the time, although I couldn't tell you now what it was all about. Refresh my memory.'

Before he did that, the reporter volunteered to first refresh Dennis's glass, and so there was a brief hiatus before John returned with beer and picked his story up without missing a beat.

'Right. Kenneth Dolden. He was this young feller, twenty-three or thereabouts, ex-service and on his demob leave from the RAF. He's in a car with his fiancée, parked up for a snog there at the edge of Epping Forest down in Waltham Holy Cross. Suddenly, out of nowhere, this chap with a muffler covering his face pulls open the car door, shoots Dolden four times to make sure he's killed him, then he scarpers and is never seen again. No clues, none of the other courting couples in the clearing could remember seeing anyone, and no apparent motive other than the killing of a total stranger. Hasn't been solved in three years, and probably it never will be. That's most likely why it's stayed with me, the pointlessness of it and that there won't be a solution. There'll be no murderer's name made famous in the headlines, but there's been no end of nasty little stories like that since the war, so what you heard is right. The mental cases spring up where the bombs fell, like a dangerous variety o' London rocket.'

Dennis bobbed his shorn head gravely in agreement. Not having McAllister's professional involvement in such matters, he had always tended to assume that murders hadn't happened if he hadn't heard of them, forgetting that celebrities like Heath and Haigh were just the tip of a red iceberg. There must be a dozen or more slayings like the one that John had just recounted every year, that never even registered as mysteries before they were swept out with the statistics. He supposed that in a way, the stories everybody was familiar with, from Heath and Haigh to Jack the Ripper and the Ratcliffe Highway murderer, were stories written largely by the papers of the day, assembled from whatever facts were known with a large helping of imaginative surmise. The bigger murder narrative, bigger because it was comprised from all the countless cases that were little and ignored, was hiding in plain sight while everybody gawped at John Haigh and his acid baths. It was as if— Halfway through an entirely unconnected thought, Dennis remembered where he'd first seen the name Dolden.

It had been in Clive Amery's notebook, when he'd left it briefly unattended at Bond's Coffee House last Monday – Gordon Bennett, had that only been a week ago? – and Dennis had contrived to have a gander at it: Dolden, Green, Dorland & Lockart. A firm of solicitors, as he'd assumed, and very probably that's what it was. There must be, after all, a lot of men called Dolden, and he couldn't work out why his stomach had dropped when he'd recognised the name. It must, he reasoned, be the hideous fantasia of his last seven days that had conditioned him to look for hidden jeopardy in the most trivial coincidence; the jittery legacy of Birmingham. It was like demobbed soldiers jumping when some schoolkid burst a crisp bag. He needed to calm down and accept that he'd been through a lot and, like the soldiers, wasn't finding it as easy settling back into a normal life as he'd expected. All the same, it was a funnyosity to not have come across a name in eighteen years of life, and then to hear it twice in the same week. He sipped his pint and tried to listen to what John was saying.

They talked for another hour or two until the landlord called time, at which point they put their coats on and expressed the hope that they might meet up at Spare's exhibition on the coming Friday. Only when they were about to leave did Dennis, feeling privately ashamed of being such a nervous nelly, give in to his apprehensions and ask Tolerable John if he could have a nose around and dig up anything about the three names Green, Dorland and Lockart. 'It's just that I saw the name you mentioned, Dolden, on a list with those three others, in the notepad of someone I know. I'm thinking that it's probably a legal firm, but anything that comes up, I'd be grateful.' John said that he'd see what he could do, needlessly adding that he wasn't optimistic. They shook hands outside the alley entrance of the Cheshire Cheese, then headed off down Fleet Street in their opposite directions.

As he laboured up past Spitalfields to Shoreditch, Dennis thought of Grace and how he only had three days to wait until he saw her, and then three days later he'd be seeing Clive. Much as he felt encouraged by these future treats, he was aware that the six days skipped through so lightly in his sunny forecast would be spent at Lowell's Books & Magazines with Coffin Ada Benson. In the still-obtaining drizzle he slogged back home to Gibraltar Walk and his slab of a mattress, wondering about those half a dozen nights, and how he'd ever manage to survive them.

Nonetheless, in what seemed like no time at all, he found himself arriving in Farringdon Road to make his long-delayed appointment with Clive Amery. Dennis couldn't for the life of him think when he'd last been up that way, but when he turned into the street, at dusk, he felt a rush of warm familiarity as he remembered the location, scarcely able to believe that he'd forgotten it. Farringdon Road, he now recalled, was the place built to look almost exactly like the Strand, maybe to make the area less unfamiliar to visitors such as himself. He drifted down the twilight avenue with a cosy nostalgia for the countless times he must have been there previously, perhaps during his childhood.

The café halfway along, where his friend had arranged for them to meet, was placed so as to reproduce the same position Bond's held on the Strand, which was most probably the reason Clive had chosen it. The name above the door was Compton's, which he didn't think was the name Clive had given him, but since it was so obviously the right place, he didn't see that this would matter.

He was just about to push the glass door open and go in when his attention was seized by activities across the street, on Farringdon Road's other side. It was two men, one of them drunk or in a state of some sort, and the other evidently trying to help him. It was difficult to make them out at first, what with the failing light, but after a few moments' squinting, Dennis realised with surprise that it was Solly Kankus and Jack Spot, both standing on the road's far side and peering back at Dennis with identical expressions of insufferable dread. Kankus seemed to be weeping, possibly in terror, and at the same time was shaking his whole body with convulsions that appeared exaggerated and theatrical, as if the sobbing mobster were miming an earthquake during his turn at charades. Beside his henchman, Jack Spot was apparently attempting to help Kankus get himself under control, all the while shooting frightened looks across Farringdon Road at Dennis, as though Spot was desperate to get as far away from him as possible, but was delayed by Kankus and his overstated trembling. Having no wish to exacerbate the recent problems between him and the two gangsters, Dennis thought it prudent to enter the cafeteria and thus remove himself as the direct source of their agitation.

The interior of Compton's was, as he'd expected, laid out very much the same as Bond's, with its long counter just inside the door. The stout proprietor was hurrying already from behind the till to welcome his illustrious customer, the way he always did, and for a moment Dennis thought that it was the same chap who managed Bond's, but quickly spotted that it was in fact the very similar-looking Flabby Harrison, who bustled up to him in beaming welcome.

'Why, Sir Dennis Nayland-Smith, how good of you to visit us. Everything's on the house, of course. I'll bring it over to your Lordship's table in a minute.'

Dennis found himself surprisingly relieved and pleased to meet with the pot-bellied book dealer again. He knew that Harrison had, for some reason, closed his bookshop in Charing Cross Road, and Dennis thought there'd been some sort of setback at the dealer's home address in Berwick Street, although he couldn't recollect the details. Either way, it was good to see Harrison back on his feet again, and Dennis was cheered up to see that Flabby had retrieved his dust-encrusted model aeroplanes from Berwick Street and had them dangling from the ceiling up behind the counter.

Awkwardly – there were, for some reason, large cardboard boxes full of books crowding the café's floor – he made his way towards the rear of the establishment, where he found Clive reading an evening paper, while the clutch of secretaries grouped at an adjacent table giggled and looked on admiringly. Absorbed in his newspaper, Clive did not appear to notice Dennis's arrival, and, not wanting to disturb him, Dennis sat down in the vacant chair across the table while he waited for Clive to look up and spot him. Idly, he perused the headline on the broadsheet that Clive held up in front of his face, which read 'Night-Life of Soho', probably a scandalous exposé. As he sat there, he became aware that one of the young girls at the next table seemed to be intently staring at him, before understanding with a guilty start that it was Grace. The disappointment with which she regarded him was plain, and Dennis realised suddenly that if this was the night that he was meeting Clive, then he'd completely missed the Spare show that he'd promised to take Grace to. He was trying to think how he could possibly apologise when she leaned over to him, whispering in a flat monotone.

'He didn't know you were at mine, but should have known you weren't at Ada's.'

Was she talking about Clive? And where was Flabby with his tea and cake? Starting to feel uneasy, he looked back at the young lawyer opposite, who was still engrossed in his reading. Was his pal deliberately ignoring him? Looking around, it struck him for the first time that the unoccupied tables at this back end of the café all had dirty burlap sacks piled up on top of them. He wasn't certain he was in the right place any more. Returning his attention to the figure sitting with him at the table, face concealed behind the open newspaper, he was no longer even sure that it was Clive. What he had taken for a smart black suit turned out upon inspection to be folds of membrane, beaded here and there by milky perspiration. Where Clive's hands were visible as they held the obscuring newsprint up before him, they weren't hands at all but things that ended in unfolded knives instead of fingertips, and there were three of them. As he began to stand up from the table in alarm, Dennis said, 'Clive?' in an unsteady voice, and by way of response heard only click-click-click-click-click ...

And woke to Monday night on his unleavened mattress, not entirely knowing what had scared him so.

# 7

## *Self as Hitler*

He was still thinking about his not-quite-nightmare on and off over the next few Shoreditch days. The bad dream tangled itself in amongst the furniture of Dennis's routine existence, wrapped around his spells of serving in the shop or helping Ada do the laundry, a strung bunting of unexplained details, of suggestive dialogue, of something being wrong, that threaded glinting through the dull detritus of an uneventful week. He was still being haunted by it intermittently come Thursday night, when Dennis took the bath he saw as a contractual obligation of his not-quite-date with Grace the following day.

Ada had taken the zinc tub down from its bent nail on the kitchen wall, lit the copper boiler for him and creaked off to her room, because 'nobody wants to cough cough cough cough see you naked, Dennis'. As he partly filled the bath with boiling water from the copper and judiciously reduced its temperature with a few saucepans full of cold, he bitterly reflected that his landlady's dismissive words were probably a fair assessment of the broader public sentiment. He stripped to his malnourished waist and kneeled beside the steaming vat to wash his hair. With Ada's second-best jug, he scooped up enough hot water to first drench his head, then, after rubbing up a lather with the dwindling bar of Lifebuoy soap, doused it a couple of times more to rinse away the suds. Inevitably some went in his eyes, and so he dried them with a scratchy towel before removing shoes, socks, trousers, underpants, and stepping gingerly into the by-now-only-lukewarm tub. Pale as a lily, he sat down as best he could, his freshly shaved chin

233

almost resting on his knees, and thought about his dream while wiping himself with a semi-rigid flannel.

The most puzzling thing about it was that he was puzzling over it some three nights after the event. It was a dream, and if its nonsense seemed unusually burdened with significance, that was a dream as well. Like most such night frights, it was clearly a collage of otherwise prosaic elements selected from the week just gone, assembled randomly by his subconscious into an unsettling new context. Dreams, almost by definition, felt like they were bursting at the seams with meaning, when in fact they had none. All the same, this one was nagging and insistent, its strange details surfacing at inappropriate moments such as talking to a customer, brushing his teeth with table salt or sitting in a tepid bath while watching islands of dead skin and soap scum gathering on its grey surface. Why had he dreamed Solly Kankus virtually shimmying, and where had all that burlap sacking come from? What had Grace meant by her indecipherable aside? Knowing that it would yield no answers, knowing there weren't any answers there to yield, he still persisted with his useless fretting until he was textured like a prune and on the draughty outskirts of pneumonia.

At last he prised himself out of the miniature gunmetal tub and dried as best he could with the abrasive towel, already damp from where he'd used it on his hair. Donning his mac as an impromptu dressing-gown, he carefully conveyed the half-filled tub of dirty water out into a freezing cold backyard, depositing it over Ada's problematic flowerbed where there at least was nothing left to kill. One of the few advantages of having no surviving neighbours was that he could stroll nude save his raincoat in the middle of the night without obtaining an unsavoury reputation, so he took advantage of the outdoor lavatory before he hurried back into the house with his teeth chattering. He hung the bathtub back on its bent nail, grabbed his discarded clothing and raced upstairs to his bedroom before Ada could emerge from hers to tell him that nobody wanted to see Dennis naked with a cough cough mac on, either. Having turned the

light out, writhing on his mattress and reflecting he'd do better
with a fakir's mat, he tried to strew his path to sleep with petal
thoughts of seeing Grace tomorrow, but kept finding himself
there in Compton's café, worrying about what was behind the
newspaper.

He got to Folgate Street a little after one o'clock on Friday afternoon. On hearing of the Spare show at the Temple Bar, Ada had
generously given him the rest of the day off, or, as she'd phrased it,
told him that he could fuck off and join the cough cough Foreign
Legion for all she cared. With his heart and hormones leaping like
a spring lamb, Dennis knocked on Grace's front door and then
shuffled restlessly while he waited for her to emerge. The day
was something of an anti-hero, weather-wise, neither completely
good nor absolutely villainous. The pipework of the sky was
lagged with white fleece to prevent it bursting in a cold snap, but
at intervals there was a prettier season visible through gaps in the
celestial insulation. He was in the process of convincing himself
that he should have rapped in a more masculine and forceful
manner when the door swung open and she came out smiling,
with her hair tied back and a sea-green coat that he hadn't seen
before. In the five days that she'd been absent from his life, she
had mysteriously become more beautiful, more mesmerising, and
a few years older. Smartly dressed and with her scarlet ponytail
caught up in a black ribbon, Dennis wondered if she might even
be twenty-four or twenty-five, and worried that this yawning age
gap might prove insurmountable. Still grinning, she stepped out
into a burst of sudden sunshine, leaned in close to sniff and say,
'You'll do,' before taking his startled arm and marching him away
to Walworth.

They decided that they'd go by bus to Elephant and Castle
and then walk from there. They sat together for the ride across
the river, Grace claiming the window seat, and chatted with
surprisingly good humour about the inadequacy of their bombsite lives. He managed an exaggerated take-off of his landlady

that made Grace laugh, and told her he'd be moving out as soon as he found some way to support himself, floundering when she asked him what that way might be. Only a fortnight back he'd told her that he thought he'd make a first-rate secret agent, and although he wasn't nearly as grown up as Grace, he had at least in those two weeks matured enough to wince at what a schoolboy dolt he must have sounded; must have been. Almost before he knew what he was saying, he had blurted out a passionate desire to be a writer, that he hadn't previously believed that he possessed. This seemed to impress Grace much more than had his earlier career choice, and so there and then Dennis resolved to have a literary life rather than the romantic death in the Vienna sewers he'd been planning. In response, she told him of her own fierce drive to one day be a dancer, an ambition that she clearly hadn't made up just five minutes back, like Dennis had.

'I've got a decent body, and it strikes me as a better move to show it off than lend it out. I've never taken proper classes, but I think I've got a feel for dancing, a lot more than for the work I'm doing now.' She gazed through the bus window at the rushing Thames. 'One day, young Dennis, I shall be London's sensation. I'll be much too big by then to talk to you, of course, but if you're lucky you might get work writing some of my reviews, ay?' She smiled sweetly and he wished, not for the first time, that he knew when she was joking.

They got off at Elephant and Castle, where they were relieved to find the Temple Bar was not far down the Walworth Road, a nice three-storey building in good nick that had exposed black beams against white plaster, in a style that Dennis thought was known as 'Brewer's Tudor'. Entering, immediately swallowed by the public house's atmosphere, it struck him that the London pubs he knew were very much like dogs, each with their own smell, their own friendly growl, their own sharp bark when things had gone too far and their own toilet habits. Once inside, the Temple Bar turned out to be both warm and spacious, with occasional long rays of sunlight through the tall front windows even lending it an airy quality. The lounge, with Spare's work hanging everywhere about its walls, seemed to be going through a crisis of identity, unsure if it was a South London pub that had both educated and refined itself, or an art gallery that had unfortunately turned to drink. A sizeable crowd near to filled the room, but it was difficult to say if they were art enthusiasts or lunchtime alcoholics.

Peering between the intellectuals and inebriates – assuming there was any difference – Dennis spotted Spare's shabby but striking figure on the room's far side, in conversation with Jack Neave. It was the first time Dennis had seen the two men together, but they talked to one another like old friends, or possibly survivors of the same disaster. Ironfoot Jack appeared to have dolled himself up for the occasion, at least relatively speaking, in that his cravat this week was yellow silk with no conspicuous stains. Spare, on the other hand, had not altered a single mucky fingernail since Dennis had last seen him, still in the same scruffy layers and patched-together shoes that seemed to be his only clothing; the apparel that he lived and worked and conjured rain and slept in. Gently seizing Grace's arm, perhaps the first time that he'd dared deliberately touch her, Dennis guided her between the jostling art drunks and across the lounge to show off his illustrious new acquaintances to her, and, naturally, vice versa. Having an attractive woman by one's side was, after all, surely a universal language of esteem, at least for men, even when hobnobbing with sorcerers and lopsided bohemians.

Spare was the first to notice them approaching, and nudged Ironfoot's higher shoulder.

"'ere, Jack, 'ave a dekko over 'ere! It's Dennis and a woman 'oo's too good for 'im. Smashin' to see yer, young 'un. Jack tells me you done alright the other night, with Spotty and 'is spear carrier in Shoreditch. An' are we to take it this is your Miss Shilling, 'oo our mate mahogany-bonce Blincoe was considerably impressed by?'

Before Dennis could reply on her behalf, Grace had stepped forward and stuck out her hand.

'Yeah, I'm Grace Shilling. And you're Mr Spare. Thanks ever so for signing your surrealist cards for me. I think that you're a brilliant artist, and tell Mr Blincoe I was dead impressed by him as well. He frit the life out of me, obviously, but he's a lovely chap, or whatever you want to call him.'

After shaking hands with an amused and, from the look of it, delighted Austin Spare, Grace turned and did the same with Jack Neave, who seemed just as taken with her.

'And you're Ironfoot Jack, I'm guessing by the iron foot. Thank you for looking after this big bugger with the business in Shoreditch last Friday. I don't want to know about it, but thanks all the same. After I'd met your Mr Blincoe, Dennis here was quick to reassure me you weren't made of iron, but having seen you, I think you most likely are. It's a great honour meeting both of you.'

Neave grinned at Dennis from beneath his hat brim, his eyes twinkling like wet lumps of coal.

'Bloody 'ell, Dennis, where did you find this one? I thought that my Jinny was a box o' fireworks before she evaporated, bless 'er soul, into the elements. But this one 'ere knocks Jinny into a cocked 'at for bleedin' cheek. You want to watch she don't 'ave you for breakfast, boy.'

They were all chuckling now, a still point in the circulating drift of pub goers and patrons. If art exhibitions were as relaxed and convivial as this was, Dennis wondered, then why hadn't he attended one before? Probably lack of opportunity, he reasoned. He couldn't recall there being any culture back before the war, and any since still had its hair on fire and its ears ringing. Spare's show, on the other hand, seemed somehow straightforward and natural, for all of the undoubted strangeness in the images themselves. Despite all his misgivings, Dennis found that he was thoroughly enjoying this. Ironfoot and Spare, apparently, had both taken a shine to Grace and she to them, and although Dennis wasn't really involved in this amity, he felt inordinately proud and pleased to stand there basking in its warmth. They talked for a few minutes, and then Grace demanded that Dennis accompany her in a circumnavigation of the lounge bar and the pictures that they'd come to see. The artist and the dispro-portioned hawker both seemed to have other matters that they wanted to discuss, and cheerfully encouraged the young couple on their way, saying they'd see them later.

Wandering through the subdued rhubarb of the modest crowd, Grace gave Dennis a nudge and nodded to a well-dressed old man with a neatly trimmed moustache and beard, then holding court on the impromptu gallery's far side. She dropped her pure and vulgar voice to a stage whisper.

'I think that's old what's-his-name, the painter who did Lawrence of Arabia and all them. Augustus something, if I've got it right. It might be John, something like that. Augustus John.'

Dennis, predictably, had never heard of the much-vaunted Post-Impressionist, but deftly concealed this behind his genuine astonishment at Grace's breadth of learning.

'How are you so brainy, Grace? I mean, compared to me. From what you've said, you can't have spent a lot of time in school. I expect you paid more attention than what I did.'

Guiding him towards a corner where the exhibition seemed to start, she glanced up and afforded him a smugly satisfied quirk of her lips.

'Well, hardly. I was barely there for long enough to pay atten-tion, and I found the Luftwaffe a bit of a distraction, to be honest. Still, at school they taught me how to read and told me what a library was, and, as it turned out, that was all I needed. I mean, it's not like there's any subject I know inside out, but I know little bits and bobs about a lot of things. Now, if you can just leave off buttering me up for a few minutes, we can have a proper look at your mate's pictures.'

The first one of these that they inspected was a pencil drawing on buff paper, and according to the catalogue that Dennis later spent five shillings on for Grace, was titled *Theurgy*. The image was remarkably compelling, although neither of them could have said at first precisely what it was or what it represented. At the upper left was an exquisitely presented female head, a handsome woman who directed her expressionless gaze off the portrait's far side, as though not wishing to be involved with the unusual illustration's other content, or else unaware of it. The drawing's right-hand side was occupied by what looked like a single line, that twisted in a coiling and recursive smoulder from the picture's lower reaches to its upper edge, where it performed a writhing tailspin down again. Along the way it warped itself into a flickering column, at once smoke and fire, that seemed to be a melting totem pole of coalescing faces: ageing and patrician at its summit, diabolically licentious in the middle reaches and a wry daydreamer at its base. The lovely and impassive woman faced these conjoined wraiths, though it appeared she was not looking at them. Underneath this, at the bottom of the frame, was a hand-lettered text in English that was, even so, inscrutable, embedded as it was with cryptic runes in place of punctuation. Nearby, a bird's wing, feathered with flames, revealed itself to be the artist's signature, while down below it were three grovelling forms that looked like cartoon pigs fashioned from dough or wax. Dennis was mystified. He didn't understand it and was disinclined to try, but Grace strong-armed him into it.

'I think that what he's doing is, he's trying to cast a spell over that woman. It looks like a picture that she's sat for, judging by the pose, and from her face I'd say that she was putting up with the experience rather than enjoying it. He knew her, then. She was somebody in his life, and I'd lay odds that all the funny writing and the devil faces are a sort of magic that's meant to attract her, or to keep her with him, or to win her back. Whichever one it was, I'm not sure that it would have worked. She looks as if, inside, she thinks that she's a cut above it all.'

Dennis saw straight away that she was almost certainly correct about the work being intended as some kind of sorcery – it reeked of magic, with its half-real shapes and made-up hieroglyphics – but he privately suspected that her love-charm theory was just Grace misreading everything as being about women because that was Grace's gender. Slightly cross that she was so much more assured and confident than he was, probably through being that much older, Dennis felt he needed to assert himself and demonstrate that he was, sometimes, almost capable of insight.

'What are all these faces on the right, then? Is it demons that he's conjuring up to make her fall in love with him? I mean, from where I'm looking at them, they could be just about anything.'

He found it flattering that Grace appeared to take his comment seriously and give it her consideration before, as he saw it, pointing out why Dennis's interpretation was completely wrong.

'Hmm. I suppose it could be demons, evil spirits and all that, but if I were to make a guess, I'd say it might be different parts of him, parts of his personality. This one down at the bottom here, perhaps that's what he thinks of as his basic self, one that finds all the other business funny, half the time. Then, up the top, the one that looks all venerable and solemn, that might be his highest self, the part of him that understands it all but seems fed up about the whole thing. As for the face in the middle, where it's like a dragon or a bird but with a really lecherous expression, that's his dirty devil. That's his cock, in my opinion, and it's looking at the woman like it wants to eat her.'

Which shut Dennis up, if only through Grace's deployment of the word cock and her succinct account of how they look at women gastronomically. This was an observation that struck far too close to home, so rather than say anything, he gave a thoughtful nod and allowed her to bundle him impatiently towards the following exhibit. The boozer-cum-gallery was starting to fill up, with wide lassos of cigarette smoke twirling over the perusing and pontificating herd, the clink of glasses starting to compete with the low murmurs of appreciation. Next on Grace and Dennis's itinerary was a piece so different from its predecessor that Dennis at first suspected it of being work done by a different artist that had been included by mistake.

Rendered in charcoal and pastel on textured board that Dennis judged to be around ten by fourteen, it was the head-and-shoulders portrait of a man, the features oddly tilted in a manner that he couldn't, to begin with, put his finger on.

The man's face radiated so much predatory criminality that the appended title scrawled in at the bottom – *Spiv Rex* – seemed wholly unnecessary. It was a distinctive look that had become ubiquitous in London since the conflagration, with the fag-end burning down to perilously near the corner of the curling lips; the heavy-lidded eyes slid sideways in covert appraisal of an opportunity or a potential victim. Modelled in soft browns and flesh tones, slightly underlit against the pale blue of what might be a club's backroom or gents' urinal wall, long eyebrows in a straight line, directional arrows following the shifty, calculating gaze ... belatedly, Dennis realised what it was about the tilting face that had evaded him before: the picture's point of view was subtly distorted, so that the man's face was stretched out laterally, as if it were drawn upon the skin of a balloon that had then been inflated. Even now that Dennis had seen through the painterly illusion, he could not say what it was about the image that unnerved him, or of what it had reminded him. He therefore stood back cautiously to view the picture from a distance, even as Grace tottered right up to it for a closer look. Studying both the drawn spiv and the equally absorbing rear view that he had of Grace, he failed to hear the clunk and thud of Jack Neave limping closer until the misshapen figurehead of lost bohemia was right behind him, and his opening remark made Dennis jump.

'Put you in mind of anybody, does it?'

Neave was grinning, and it took Dennis a second to take in that Ironfoot was referring to Spare's picture rather than his voyeuristic glimpse of Grace. Frowning in puzzlement at the distended mug of the black marketeer, he couldn't see what Jack was on about. Something about the face had taken him aback, he would admit, but it hadn't reminded him of anyone. Or had it? Staring, squinting, tilting his head first to one side then the other, finally the tenuous resemblance hit him, and he turned to Neave with a gone-out expression.

'Is that ... does he look a bit like Harry Lud?'

Jack cackled like a mucous fire that was just getting going.

'Well, no, it's not 'arry, but I reckon that it's 'arry what give Awstin the idea, don't yer think? A villain with 'is mush all spread out sideways, even if this chap 'ere is an understatement o' the three-foot-wide original. 'e gets a few of his peculiarities from the Great When, does Awstin.'

Their hushed conversation was at that point interrupted by a sudden peal of laughter from Grace Shilling, who turned from *Spiv Rex* still giggling, but tried to get herself under control when she saw that Jack Neave had joined them.

'Sorry. I weren't laughing at the picture. It's a knockout. I was laughing because I just cottoned on and got the joke. I didn't know why Mr Spare had drawn this feller with his face stretched out, but then I thought, "Of course! *Spiv Rex!* This chap's a wide boy!" I just weren't expecting, with him being such a brilliant artist, that he might be having a laugh sometimes, too.'

Ironfoot and Dennis both laughed heartily as well, not having recognised the obvious visual pun themselves. Jack shot a glance up at the younger, taller man, his turtle-skin eye corners crinkling.

'Well, I'm still not givin' up on my 'ypothesis, but I'd say that this copper-locked enchantress o' yours was bang on the money. Awstin, 'e likes pullin' people's legs, 'avin' 'em on and that. Sometimes it's 'ard to get a serious word out of 'im. Ask 'im about 'is life, an' like as not 'e'll make up somethin' for the fun of it. Like 'ow 'is governess seduced 'im when 'e was a boy an' taught 'im magic in the bargain, or 'ow 'e was trapped under a load o' corpses back in World War I. I s'pose 'e's like a lot of us mob when it comes to 'is biography. You take ol' Monolulu – 'oo's been in a proper two-an'-eight since goin' on your expedition with yer, incidentally – 'ow 'e'll tell yer 'e's an Abyssinian prince, when 'e wouldn't know Africa from Pimlico. Nah, all us crowd, we're all a lot o' fantasists. Apart from me, o' course. I'm 'onest as the day is long.'

Grace snorted, although not without regard.

'Well, that's not saying very much. Ain't it about now that the clocks go back?'

Jack laughed again and intimated that Grace was a cheeky little bleeder, although, once more, not without regard. The three of them moved on together through a beery hall of marvels, wading amongst exhibition goers of such different social backgrounds that it was astonishing to think they shared a city, let alone a lounge bar. Grace and Ironfoot fell into easy dialogue about their differing but not dissimilar experience of post-war London's lower rungs, while Dennis, not so conversationally adept as either of them, thought about what Neave had said regarding fantasists.

When Jack had spoken about 'us mob' or 'us crowd', Dennis assumed he was referring to the infinitely small minority of London's citizens who were familiar with the Great When, such as Neave himself, Spare, Monolulu and, more lately, Dennis. Was he also a tall-story merchant, then? A fantasist, just like the others? He had never seen himself as such, but now he thought about it, he remembered the procession of defenceless kittens, frightened infants and blind nuns that he'd led from the blazing ruins of Cripplegate when he was nine, as well as the long stints of being Desperate Dan or Harry Lime or Winston Smith that he had served across the years since then. Perhaps he did have an imagination, after all. Perhaps his recently adopted lifelong urge to be a writer could be something more than just another ineffectual tactic to engage Grace's attention.

Then, of course, there were the wider implications of what Ironfoot had said. His comments had suggested that an individual's ability to pass into the different London was dependent on their being prone to make-believe, on having a degree of distance from normal reality. Dennis recalled that up in Arnold Circus, just a week back, Jack had said that category could include nutcases, too – presumably nutcases with imaginations. Perhaps that's why everyone had been so adamant that the imagination-free Jack Spot could never be admitted to the other place. It underlined, for Dennis, the perturbing fact that having an imagination wasn't just a means of landing a career that might impress good-looking redheads, but could also be a milestone on the road to mental instability. Uncertain where this left him, he tuned back into the conversation between Grace and Ironfoot, where the latter was currently holding forth on London life and lowlife since the nights of burning sky.

'A thing what weighs on my mind is 'ow everythin' as was is bein' done away with, an' shall soon be vanished altogether, from what I can see. Since I was a young man who still 'ad both 'is legs, I've travelled all about the country. Sometimes I'll be with the gypsy people or else I'll be with the Needies: with the tinkers, swindlers and theatre people in between engagements. Used to be that we could go from place to place, doin' a bit o' this, a bit o' that, floggin' our trinkets, tellin' fortunes or whatever, so that we could scratch a livin' and thus solve the Problem of Existence. Since the war, increasin'ly, you can't do that no more. This welfare state what Bevan an' them 'ave brought in, it's an amazin' benefit, an' very necessary. All the same, it means things 'ave to be more regimented these days, and there's not the loop'oles that there was for a bo'emian like me to squeeze through. All the characters, the way o' life, the world I recognised, it's all goin' the same way as the dodo.'

Grace sighed as she agreed.

'I'm too young to remember much of how it was before, but all the older women on the game that I know, they all say that it's gone downhill since the bombing started. In the blackouts, they'd be in shop doorways shining torches on their tits to drum up custom, but they say it's not much better with the lights on. These days you get more rough customers, more mad blokes, or that's what the other girls all tell me. I think that the war blew up a lot of buildings, but it blew up our behaviour as well, I reckon. Even though it's over, it'll leave its mark on things for years and years to come.'

They'd come to rest before another of Spare's portraits, this one being a bizarrely elongated but immediately recognisable attempt at Bette Davis, or at least how the actress had looked some several years ago. There were two images of Davis, both in a green dress with fiery orange hair which, although beautiful, was not a patch on Grace's. One of these portrayed the film star with her head tipped back in profile while the other had her meet the viewer's gaze, but both were stretched more radically than Spare's depiction of the spiv had been, and this time vertically rather than horizontally. What Dennis was surprised by, though, was Spare's decision to transform a popular screen idol into proper art, something he didn't think that he'd seen done before. Grace, meanwhile, had come to her own annoyingly informed conclusions.

'I think I know what it is, this sort of art. It's something-morphic. Is it anamorphic? It's, like, where you have to look at it edge-on to see it in the right perspective. It was in this book I read on Holbein, him who painted all the Tudors. It said in there it was a technique he used.'

She stepped closer to the picture to examine it, allowing Dennis a quiet interchange with Jack.

'That's like those wave things in the other London, isn't it? The anamorphic spasms that keep happening. He said I should ask you about them, Mr Spare did, if I got the chance.'

Neave pulled a sombre face.

'That might be because Mr Spare is as reliable as fairground rifles, an' 'e likes to put about a lot o' fairy tales, like I was sayin'. In this instance, 'e was probably implyin' that the tragic accident what knackered up my leg was brought about by me 'avin' incautiously stepped in an anamorphic fuckin' spasm on my earliest visit to the 'igher city, when o' course I'm far too sensible to ever do a thing like that. 'e's got a very cruel, low-minded sense o' 'umour, 'as ol' Awstin. Personally, I don't think "appallin'" is too strong a word.'

Dennis wasn't entirely sure how he should take this, and as Grace rejoined them, he was treating Ironfoot with what, out of context, must have sounded like profound insensitivity.

'So, then, how did your leg get so messed up?'

Neave smiled around the fag that he was lighting.

'Well, I'm very glad you asked. It was a run o' bad luck, weren't it? After being mauled by blood'ounds while I was escapin'

246

Dartmoor and then by a tiger in an 'untin' misadventure, I got caught in this Tibetan avalanche, an' then 'ad the misfortune of gettin' run over by a car when I was rescuin' a toddler. I'll tell yer for nothin', by the time I 'ad it bit off by a shark while I was divin' for these whopping great pearls, I was glad to see the back of it. It's like I say, yer can't believe a word what Awstin tells yer. It grieves me that I 'ave to say this, but 'e's a compulsive liar.'

Trying to keep a straight face, Grace asked how the shark had bitten off his leg but left the foot attached, and Jack gravely informed her that, after a lot of haggling, he'd managed to persuade the shark to give him at least that much back, and then sold it a watch that didn't work. Grace was forced to concede that this, at least, sounded believable, and Neave was gleefully further embellishing his hard-luck story when the three of them were joined by an ebullient and handsome chap who looked to be in his mid-forties, and whose face lit up the moment that he saw Jack Neave.

'Ironfoot, you lovely man! What are you doing all the way down here? Don't tell me that you're running fiddles in the art world now. Is nowhere safe from you and your infernal ingenuity?'

Hearing the voice behind him, Jack turned and said curtly, ''oo are you?', before fissuring his weather-beaten features with amicability. The two men clearly knew each other well.

'Gor bless my soul, it's Mr 'ickey! Lovely to vada yer dolly old eek, mate. Dennis, Grace, this is my dear ol' pal, Tom Driberg, currently pretendin' to be Mr William 'ickey in the column what 'e writes for the *Express*. 'e's also the MP for Maldon, if yer can Adam an' Eve it, but I s'pose it's just an indication o' the shockin' state the country's in at present. Tom, these are my young associates Mr Dennis Knuckleyard and Miss Grace Shillin'.'

Driberg, with his charm, his confidence, his wavy black hair centre-parted and his beautifully tailored suit – all things that Dennis hadn't got – shook hands with Grace first, and was so attentive to her that Dennis's spirits sank. Why couldn't he talk to a woman the way this bloke evidently could?

'My God. Ducky, you have to be one of the most attractive women that I've ever seen! God, look at her! Darling, you could have stepped out of a Titian. I expect you're on the game, yes?'

Dennis's mouth fell open, partly because he was unsure what a Titian was, partly affronted on Grace's behalf. He felt that he should say something defending Grace's honour, or perhaps punch Driberg, even though he hadn't thrown a punch since he was twelve. Luckily, her amused and clearly charmed response to the MP for Maldon's over-frank enquiry made him hesitate in this decision.

'Yeah. It pays the rent, 'cept when it don't. Ta for the kind words, incidentally. Very discerning and appreciative, I'm sure. I don't know about you, though. You don't look so much like a Titian as you look like competition.'

Driberg howled, then threw his arms around Grace, hugged her, kissed her hair and told her she was priceless, while she merely giggled. Dennis had no idea what was going on. At last, the suave Lothario released his hold on Grace and turned to Dennis, raising his arched eyebrows as if in surprise and dwindling his lips into a silent 'ooh'.

'My goodness. Where have you been keeping this one, Jack? Imagine him without the haircut and he's rather dashing, don't you think? And Knuckleyard! What an extraordinary name you have, young man. Just hearing it, it makes you sound like you're a bit of an adventure.'

Dennis shook hands numbly and, painfully slowly, started to take in the surely unbelievable idea that the MP for Maldon was not only 'one of them', but that he didn't care who knew it. Was that even possible? And if it was, did Driberg's rakish smile mean that he fancied Dennis? Dennis hadn't knowingly met anybody queer before and became paralysed for want of an appropriate reaction. Both disturbed to be for once the object of somebody else's amorous attentions, and also obscurely flattered, he was thus relieved when Ironfoot intervened in his ambiguous discomfort.

'Oi! 'ands off the merchandise! Besides, I think you'll find 'e's spoken for. What'd Clem Attlee say if 'e knew you was chasin' young lads round South London?'

Driberg shrugged. 'Oh, Clem would probably just thank God that I wasn't doing it in Westminster, and giving Labour, socialism and Joe Stalin a bad name.' He turned once more to Dennis, this time seeming genuinely penitent. 'Don't mind me, Dennis. I'm just a disgraceful commie poof having a bit of fun. It really is a pleasure to meet youngsters like Grace and yourself, who've got some life in them. It's something that I'm rather starved of, between the *Express* and Parliament.'

Grace was now smirking at Dennis, and he had a strong suspicion that his ears were turning pink. Recovering somewhat from his panic, Dennis laughed it off as Driberg finally released his hand.

'Haha. No, you're alright. It's nice to meet you. As it happens, I've a mate on the *Express* who said he might be coming by here later. John McAllister, I don't know if you know him?'

Driberg nodded, with what Dennis took to be a fond expression.

'John? Known him for years. He's easily one of the nicest chaps on the *Express*. Straight as a die, of course, but none of us are perfect, are we? No, I wouldn't trust him with my confidences, he's a journalist, but I think I might trust him with my life. Very dependable, much like our Mr Neave here. Did you know that this confabulating rogue opened the first – and I hope not the last – queer club in Soho? When he dies, I'm going to have him melted down and make a statue of him.'

Ironfoot flapped one stubby-fingered hand as if waving away a gnat. He grimaced with distaste, while giving the impression that this gruff dismissal had within it a quiet, secret pride.

'You bloody shan't. I'm makin' it a stipulation o' my will that when I'm gone, I'm to be flogged for scrap. An' anyway, my club weren't nothin' o' the sort. It was an 'aven for bo'emians an' artists, an' the rest was a vile calumny invented by the newspapers an' the authorities.'

He shuffled noisily about, so that he was addressing Grace and Dennis.

'What it was, gettin' on fifteen year ago, I'd 'it a snag in my ongoin' difficulties with the Problem of Existence. I'd been doin' well, sellin' this Indian scent called "Russian Aura", but I knew that it weren't gunna last. For one thing, I was feelin' worn out with it all, an' wanted nothin' more than to buy me an' Jinny a nice little caravan an' a nice little 'orse, so we should 'ave somewhere to live what nobody could take away from us. Now, back then, you could get a lovely caravan for 'undred quid, but 'undred quid was a fair way beyond my means in 1934. So, what I thought was, I should open up a club what might financially support my open-road ambitions, to be decorated in a sumptuous Oriental style an' called the Caravan Club, for the reasons I've just mentioned.'

Neave paused to pinch his cigarette out and secreted it behind one ear before continuing.

'So anyway, we found this place what we could rent in Endell Street, an' done it out with these exotic odds an' ends I'd picked up on me travels: tapestries and Indian curtains what 'ad little bits o' mirror stuck all over 'em, silk cushions, Chinese rugs, an incense burner I 'ad 'angin' from the ceiling, this big chair from a Burmese pagoda what 'ad all carved dragons on, primitive wooden masks ... it was like the Arabian Nights, but further east. All sorts we 'ad down there, amongst our clientele. Lords, ladies, doctors, writers, one or two dodgy MPs' – Neave cast a haughty sideways glance at Driberg, who was snickering – 'celebrities, musicians, tramps off the Embankment, and occasionally some figure from the underworld what drifted in. And, yes, it may 'ave been, as our friend 'ere suggests, that unbeknownst to me, some queer chaps had popped in for somewhere they could 'ave a kiss and cuddle without interference, which, as a bo'emian, I felt no inclination to deny 'em. Course, it got in all the newspapers, it caused a public outrage, and instead of me gettin' me 'eart's desire, I ended up with twenty months' 'ard labour served in Wormwood Scrubs. So I can do without the statue, thank you very much. A few quid for a caravan would have been quite sufficient.'

They stood talking for some minutes more as the bemused or beaming human currents of the Temple Bar swirled all about them, until Grace noticed that Driberg had an exhibition cata-logue tucked under one well-tailored arm, and asked him where he'd got it from. 'What, this? They're on that little table over where the show starts, going for five bob a throw. Hardly extor-tionate.' The MP gestured languidly at a far corner of the room, and Dennis realised he and Grace had not commenced their tour from its official starting point. Still finding himself slightly tense in Driberg's company, he volunteered to pick a copy up for Grace and launched himself into the press of tipsy critics and enthusiasts, bobbing away from her and the two men across a sea of better haircuts.

Moving through the gathering more by Brownian motion than his own volition, Dennis observed that the crowd was shift-ing in its composition as the afternoon wore on. The balance between locals and more smartly dressed outsiders now favoured the latter category, and he found himself borne by the jostle past a conversation between the Grant couple that he'd met a week or two back, and the stylish older man that Grace had thought was possibly Augustus John. Intent upon what the distinguished-looking chap was saying, neither Ken nor Steffi Grant appeared to notice Dennis as he struggled by them, although since their chat was loud in competition with the lounge bar's hubbub, he was able to hear most of it. Surprisingly, it didn't seem to be about Aleister Crowley.

'So, did you two see that thing with Terry-Thomas in, the other night? Quite novel, I thought.'

'No. We've got the television, but we didn't know that it was being shown. What was it?'

'Well, it was like one of those comedy programs that you get on radio, *Much-Binding-in-the-Marsh* or something of that nature, only, being television, you could see it. I suppose that's why they'd featured dear old Terry-Thomas; looks as funny as

he sounds. *How Do You View?* they'd called it. Terribly amusing.
But to get back to what you were asking about my portrait of
Crowley ...'

At this juncture, the convivial continental drift that Dennis
was caught up in, took him out of earshot, though it struck him
that this was the first time he'd heard anybody talking casually
about television. Yes, there had been televisions since the 1920s,
but nobody that he knew had ever owned one. There were
several thousand sets, he thought, distributed through London,
but it hadn't seemed as if the trend was ever likely to catch on.
Now, however, after overhearing what might be the chatter of
the future, he was not so sure. Heavily influenced by having read
George Orwell's frightening book so recently, he could imagine
that a time might come when there were television sets all over,
perhaps in a hundred years' time, after he was dead. People would
have to carry televisions with them everywhere they went,
presumably strapped on their backs in some variety of harness.
This was Dennis's disturbing social vision as he progressed
incrementally across the room: of populations bent and crippled
under bulky sets, deformed by entertainment.

Finally, he buffeted his way towards the table that Driberg had
indicated, where he found to his relief a small stack of a dozen
catalogues that were as yet unsold. They were beside a cardboard
shoebox with a paper note attached that read '5/-', and, beneath
that, a hand-drawn Egyptian hieroglyphic eye, no doubt to
watch over the trove of half-crowns, florins, shillings, sixpences
and thrupenny bits already gathered in the battered oblong
carton. Five bob was a lot of cash, but Dennis had concluded
that he couldn't buy Grace flowers without risking derision,
and thought that a slender volume of unsettling pictures as a
love-token might be the better option. Conscientiously depositing two half-crowns in the untended receptacle, partly through
fear that the Egyptian eye might be a curse on pilferers, he took
a copy and flipped through it briefly before once more entering the logjam of humanity that he hoped would convey him
back across the lounge to Grace's side. There was an essay in

the catalogue by Kenneth Grant, describing Spare as though he were a villain from Sax Rohmer, 'one who has come face to face with all Evil', which Dennis thought was a bit *Boy's Own Paper*. Closing the nicely presented pamphlet, drawing a deep breath, he reimmersed himself in the slow, heaving whirlpool that was seemingly his only means of transport.

Roughly halfway through this session of pedestrian shoveha'penny, Dennis found that he was stalled before an exhibit he hadn't seen before, that fixed him to the spot as surely as the cultured crush surrounding him. Just under two feet tall and just a little over one foot wide, it was an obvious self-portrait in pastel and charcoal, with a younger Spare emerging head-and-shoulders from a background darkness mottled by rich blue and river-bottom green. It showed the artist as he must have been some ten or fifteen years ago, with a brushfire of russet hair and similarly hued toothbrush moustache. The arctic sapphire eyes burned through the surface of the picture and that of the viewer also, like a blue-hot knife through butter. Suddenly remembering he had a catalogue clutched in one hand, Dennis turned through its pages until he located the piece he was after. The accompanying description stated that the picture had been done in 1948 to reproduce an earlier version Spare had sold in 1936. The title of the work, according to the catalogue, was *Self-re-Hitler*.

At the top, where the blue-green was thinning to a wash, there was a passage of handwritten text, as with so many of the artist's pictures. This, at least, was all in English with no runes in sight, and seemed more explanatory than incantatory. Considering the startling title of the piece, Dennis remembered Spare's odd comment on the day that they'd first met, about refusing to paint Hitler's portrait. While he'd taken it to be a boast, delusion, or perhaps a leg-pull at the time, it now caused Dennis to squint back and forth between the writing in the portrait's upper reaches and the entry in the catalogue, until he thought he had at least a quivering smoke-ring outline of the whole unlikely story.

If he'd got it right, in 1936, before the outbreak of hostilities, some high-up at the German embassy had bought the work's original and, possibly because of the toothbrush moustache, had shown it to the Führer. Hitler, very much impressed, invited Spare to Berlin so that the South London sorcerer could paint his portrait, too. Spare's strangely eloquent refusal was apparently the source of the handwritten message floating there above the lightning storm of his delineated face, which ended, 'Only from negations can I wholesomely conceive you. For I know of no courage sufficient to stomach your aspirations and ultimates. If you are superman, let me be forever animal.' The rebuke was caustic, and it was no wonder Spare had spoken of the bombing raid that had disabled him and pulverised his studio as Hitler, out of spite, getting his own back. If that was, for fancy's sake, the case, then he'd undoubtedly done Spare considerable damage, although Dennis noted that it wasn't Austin Osman Spare who'd blown his brains out in a bunker. Dennis doubted there'd be space for anyone to blow their brains out in Spare's bunker. There was barely room to blow your nose.

It was a powerful and peculiar story, but that clearly hadn't been what had arrested Dennis in his crowd-propelled traversal of the lounge, nor what still held him frozen where he stood before the picture's stern and unforgiving majesty. The impact of the image, he decided, was all somehow caught between its title and its subject's fierce and questioning blue gaze, although Grace would have put it better. His first thought on viewing the self-portrait, other than the undeniably strange story of its sale and recreation, was that Spare was asking himself whether he had anything in common with the Führer; any aspect of his character or 'atavistic personality' that might, in the right circumstances, be a Hitler. It also occurred to Dennis that the depiction's penetrating stare seemed to be asking the same question of the viewer – was there any part of Dennis that could bring about a vast human catastrophe, could unloose dreadful horrors on the world? Worse still, wasn't the picture asking the same thing of everybody? Wasn't it implying that we all, at least, shared a biology with the Reich chancellor, and thus that anyone whom we encountered, from the best beloved friend to the most fleeting stranger, might contain the seed of concentration camps or gas chambers within them? The idea was chilling, and when someone spoke behind him, Dennis all but leaped out of his skin.

'An 'andsome bleeder, don't yer think? Very distinguished, from the look of 'im.'

Dennis spun round to find an older and world-wearier version of the portrait's subject standing at his shoulder, as though stepped from thin air with the aid of elemental spirits. Although shabbier and with the colour firebombed from his hair, this version wore a grin of satisfaction and, without the tache, was not demanding anyone consider their resemblance to the architect of World War II. Embarrassed to be caught transfixed in worship by the work's creator, Dennis dimpled sheepishly and spread his hands in admiration, shaking his short back and sides with wonderment.

'All this, it's just bloody amazing. I don't know how you can do the work you do, when you're … you know. When you're …' Dennis trailed away to mumbles, but Spare laughed.

'Come on, boy. Spit it out. "When you're stuck down an 'ole no bigger than a coal scuttle and can't sit down for cats", is that what you were gunna say? 'ow do I unpack all o' this out of a tiny little box like that? It's a good question, Dennis, and yer needn't look as if you've farted by just askin' it. The answer is, that's where the magic comes in. William Blake, at Fountain Court, 'e lived in little digs off boiled bacon, an' from that 'e bodged up an 'ole universe. O' course, we can't take all the plaudits. Both Bill Blake an' my good self, we weren't entirely unacquainted with those areas o' London what 'ave caused you so much grief o' late. The Great When's 'ad its part to play in both our oeuvres, I dare say. Credit where credit's due, ay?'

It was then that Dennis thought to ask a question that he should have asked a fortnight earlier.

'Mr Spare, what … the Great When. What is it?'

The artist regarded Dennis with a sympathy that bordered the paternal.

'Well, for a kick-off, it's Austin. Or Awstin, should you prefer. Or even Zos, for when I've got me magic 'at on. But the Great When … for my money, son, it's the imaginary o' London. It's the place what people think of when they 'ear that name, a London all made up o' bits an' pieces what they've 'eard or what they can remember, that bears no resemblance to whatever shit'ole's goin' on outside these doors. It's the eternal London, if you like, and as such it's a truer place than this is, 'ere one minute and bombed flat the next. It's the imaginary, like I said, so it's what the material city's founded on, and in that sense it's realer than what we are. It's an 'idden attic o' mankind's imagination, what's only accessible to them 'oo's stairs go up that 'igh. Sometimes I think of it as like a metaphor what's put on weight an' substance, or a matter-phor, as yer might say. It's been built up across the centuries from dreams o' London, which are often more endurin' than a place put up wi' bricks an' mortar. All the same, mate, it's not Butlin's. It's not somewhere you can visit for a laugh.'

Dennis agreed with this assessment, and especially the last part.

'You're dead right there. I don't ever want to see the place again. I don't want anything to do with it. I don't know how you've managed for so long, or got to know those parts so well. How do you even find your way about, with everything continually changing into something else?'

Spare fingered his pugnacious chin and pondered.

'Well, it's like with everythin', it all gets more familiar if you've travelled there a time or two, although I 'ave to say it's easier once yer've 'ad a gander at an Oxtercross.' Interpreting Dennis's interested nod as obvious camouflage for blank incomprehension, Wynne Road's warlock ventured him an explanation. 'What the Oxtercross is, it's a map o' the Great When, an' the street names in its index are all alphabetical. For some unearthly reason, it's arranged accordin' to the 'ebrew alphabet, so rather than it bein' A to Z like normal, it's aleph to tau, or ox to cross, therefore the name. O' course, you only see 'em in the other place. If one turned up 'ere in Short London, it'd be a cock-up bigger than your 'ampole book, you mark my words. Fuckin' disaster, that'd be.'

Having apparently concluded his deliberations on the subject, Austin looked once more at Dennis, this time wearing an expression of concern.

'Dennis, what you were sayin' about 'ow you never wanted to 'ave anythin' to do wi' the Great When again, it's only fair as I should tell yer it's not up to you. Yes, I'll allow that givin' it a wide berth is yer wisest policy, but you should bear in mind that the Great When is finished with us when it's finished with us, not before. Again, it's very like the artistic imagination: you may think you're lucky, stumblin' upon a vision, but it's better that you understand right from the get-go, it's the vision that's the one what'll be givin' all the orders. It's the vision what's in charge.'

The rest was pleasantries – Dennis repeating his appreciation of Spare's art, and Spare saying he hoped Dennis would keep in touch – conducted in the baleful glare of *Self-re-Hitler*. In the end, the artist spotted Steffi Grant gesticulating at him from the room's far side and, grunting his apologies, went off to see what was the matter. Catalogue in hand, Dennis continued his progression down the slow conveyor belt of murmuring faces that might hopefully deliver him to Grace.

When finally he found her, she was by herself, Driberg and Ironfoot having wandered off, and she was weeping. This shocked Dennis to his core. From the first moment that they'd met, Grace had been perfectly composed, despite the life-or-death ordeals that she'd been made to sit through, and he couldn't begin to imagine what bereavement or what tragedy had taken place in the last twenty minutes to undo her so. Immediately anxious and at a much higher pitch than he'd expected, he asked what was wrong, but she was plainly still far too upset to speak. Instead, she shook her head and gestured with the hand that wasn't crushing a white hanky to her wet eyes, mutely indicating the exhibit they were standing by, which, in his sudden panic of concern, he hadn't registered.

In landscape ratio and perhaps eighteen inches wide, smaller than many of the other images, it was an equine portrait that was rendered once more in pastel and charcoal. Signed and dated in the upper right – AOS '48 – this was apparently a recent work, and following a hurried consultation of his catalogue, Dennis discovered that its full title was *Horses to the Slaughter: Railway Horse.*

In browns and greys against a ground of charcoal smudge, the horse's head was almost a right profile, elderly and at what was presumably an auction block, waiting to find out who its meat and glue were being sold to. Muzzle roped and bandaged shut, preventing any fuss, the animal's untended mane fell lank across its brow to frame a sole visible eye. This was a cobalt planet of despair, its gaze directed flatly at the artist, at the viewer; an expression without fear and speaking only of exhaustion, of a final resignation that was awful to behold. Beside him, Grace had at last tamed her tear ducts and was once more capable of conversation.

'Sorry. It's the eye that got me. He puts such a lot into his portraits' eyes, your mate. That poor horse, how it's looking out at us. It's like it's saying, "Yeah, I know that it's all up for me, but don't forget, you're part of the same queue." It made me come over a bit unnecessary, that's all.'

He could see why. The creature's bleak acceptance of its fate said all the things to him that it had said to Grace, but also seemed to resonate with his own lingering dread concerning the picked carcass of his days-old dream; the same centreless feelings of approaching doom, of horses to the slaughter. It was with considerable relief that Dennis allowed a recovered Grace to lead him from the *Railway Horse's* mortal scrutiny and into the remainder of the exhibition.

She seemed thrilled when he eventually remembered to present her with the catalogue, and also greatly cheered up by the opportunity to have a go at Dennis over his reaction to Tom

Driberg. 'Honestly, you should have seen your face, pink as a baby's bum. At least you know now what I feel like. It's a burden, Dennis, being irresistible.' Laughing and chatting, they continued with their circuit of the lounge, eventually arriving back at *Theurgy* with its detached muse and her stack of gaseous faces. Both agreed they'd had a smashing afternoon, but that it might be time to get back to North London, with perhaps some fish and chips for tea on the way home. Deciding that she'd better use the ladies' toilets at the Temple Bar before embarking on a reasonably lengthy return journey, Grace left Dennis just inside the pub's front door to wait on her return, and was therefore not there to witness Tolerable John McAllister's belated entrance.

Dennis greeted the puffed-out journalist warmly, but explained that he himself was just about to leave, at which McAllister nodded morosely and said, 'Yeah. I knew that that would happen. I've had a right day of it at work, and couldn't get away till now. But still, I'm glad I caught you. I dug up some information on those names you asked me to look out for.'

It took Dennis a few seconds to remember his embarrassingly jittery request to John upon the Monday night just gone, about what he'd seen written in Clive Amery's notebook. He was just about to laugh it off as nerves and tell McAllister that he shouldn't have bothered when the glum reporter pulled out his own notebook and looked up at Dennis quizzically.

'That mate of yours, whose book you saw this list in, am I right in thinking he's a copper?'

Thrown off balance by the unexpected question, Dennis's reply was guarded.

'Um, yeah. Yeah, he's with the law. Why? What was … ?'

John was flicking through the worn and compact jotter, filled with what at first resembled Spare's invented hieroglyphics, but which Dennis soon identified as Pitman shorthand. At length, John located the precise pages of scribble he'd been looking for, then read them out to Dennis in a tone that was too weary to be even mournful. 'Violet Green, believed to be a prostitute, was shot dead on the landing of her Rupert Street address in

Soho – this was 1947 – with what the police thought might be an American service revolver. Edith Dorland, 1948, still a young woman, thirty-one years old, she had her head bashed in and turned up on a bombsite at Mint Street, in Southwark.'

Prior to delivering his findings on the third and final name that Dennis had enquired about, McAllister raised his eyes from the indecipherable scratchings, shook his head defeatedly and sighed.

'The names are all in order chronologically, as it turns out. The last one, Eileen Lockart, I think she was strangled, later on in 1948. Her body was discovered by chance on another bombsite, this one up at Chiswell Street in the remains of Cripplegate. Eileen Lockart was five years old.'

Numbed by the information, Dennis couldn't think of anything to say. John closed the wire-bound pad and slipped it back into his pocket, brow still furrowed by the thought of the dead child.

'They're unsolved London murders from the last three years, the lot of 'em, with Kenneth Dolden as the earliest, in 1946. There's nothing else connecting them, as far as I can see. I should imagine your mate had them written down as part of ongoing investigations.'

Yes, of course. Of course that was the answer. Though Clive wasn't a policeman, he was with the law, as Dennis had evasively put it to John. He'd obviously jotted the names down in reference to forthcoming cases, or some other complicated legal process Dennis wouldn't understand. When Tolerable John had said that his imagined legal partners were in fact a list of unexplained dead bodies, Dennis had felt, unaccountably, a sense of vertigo, as if suddenly finding himself at the brink of an abysmal drop with no clue how he'd got there. Now, however, with his brief Dick Barton fancies so convincingly dispelled, almost before they'd formed, he told himself he couldn't even properly remember what they'd been, although that wasn't strictly true: his fears had been connected in some manner with the scalpel-fingered presence, clicking from behind the newspaper with its 'Night-Life of Soho' headline, there in his unpleasantly persistent dream. And though the names were clearly nothing he should worry himself with, the dream remained, an odd-shaped stain on memory's unswept floor.

Hugely relieved, although not sure what of, Dennis thanked John for all the trouble that he'd gone to, promising the melancholy journalist a pint the next time they were in the Cheshire Cheese, perhaps next Friday after work, the evening before Guy Fawkes Night? John solemnly noted this down in his Rosetta Stone of a reporter's notebook, and then smiled to see Tom Driberg blowing kisses at him from the lounge bar's open door. 'So Driberg's here, then? Red, queer and in Parliament. I don't know how he gets away with it. He was a mate of old Aleister Crowley as well, once upon a time.' Dennis was unsurprised. Who wasn't? He and John rushed through a farewell handshake, and McAllister went off in search of his flamboyant colleague. A few minutes later, Grace returned from her safari to the ladies', blaming her long absence on the toilet's solitary, permanently engaged cubicle. When Dennis offered no response to this, she frowned up at him, questioningly.

'Here, are you alright? You're looking a bit shaken up by something.'

Was he? He supposed it must be some residual reaction to the news from Tolerable John, even though that misunderstanding had been sensibly resolved. Annoyingly, her use of the phrase 'shaken up' had conjured an irrelevant vignette from Dennis's increasingly stale nightmare, with the gangster Solly Kankus trembling exaggeratedly on the far side of the Farringdon Road, his fleshy body rippling like a windswept flag. Dennis assumed that this bizarre and inexplicable internal image wasn't helping with the seen-a-ghost look that Grace had referred to, and so told her that his stricken countenance was a result of thinking about *Railway Horse*. Her lime eyes melted and she pinched her lips into a sympathetic pout. Believing Dennis to be a more sensitive and feeling individual than she'd previously suspected, she let him link arms with her for most of the long journey home, even inviting him into her Folgate Street flat for an hour, so he could eat his fish and chips from a clean plate instead of last week's *Daily Mirror*.

They talked, between mouthfuls, of the exhibition and the people that they'd met, and Grace described the personal impression Spare had made on her. 'There's sex not far beneath the surface in some of his pictures, but, from talking to him, I think that he might be shy.' After their meal was finished and washed down with a hot cup of tea, Grace thanked him for the catalogue and said she'd had a lovely day which, he concluded, meant that it was time for him to leave. On her front doorstep, she said he should call in on her sometime, and they made a tentative engagement for the Sunday evening after next. She stood on tiptoe to bestow a goodnight peck upon his startled cheek, and Dennis floated all the way back to Gibraltar Walk without once thinking of himself as Hitler, or of Tolerable John's grim list of unsolved homicides, or of his dream.

Over the following weekend, of course, without the scintillant distractions of a wonderment-crammed pub or Grace's company, he thought of very little else.

It wasn't simply that he had a cloud above him while he served an uneventful Saturday behind the till at Ada's shop, or idled in his bedless room throughout a rainy Sunday. It felt nothing like a cloud. It felt more like a train – black, loud and steaming – rumbling closer in his belly and his heart, although he didn't know from which direction, or what he could do to get off of the track. His bubbling and fizzing mind was an alchemic glass retort where unknown substances appeared to be reacting badly with each other: somewhere in the random slop of information that he took into his close-cropped head without examination, contradictory facts were screaming at each other, urgent and irreconcilable, but Dennis couldn't for the life of him tell where the increasingly panicked disagreement issued from.

Hardest to understand was why he should be in this fretful
mood when everything was going relatively well. He'd somehow
managed to get through the terrifying other London ordeal only
mildly scarred, and all that was successfully behind him now. He
thought that Grace was perhaps starting to warm up to him, and
then on Monday night he had the long-delayed appointment
with Clive Amery that he'd been looking forward to all week,
although admittedly less so since Dennis's nocturnal horror film
of seven nights before. That was what most annoyed him, that a
blatantly nonsensical assemblage of mental rubbish like a dream
should shadow this rare period of enjoyment, hanging over his
forthcoming rendezvous with his best mate. During the day on
Monday, working in the shop, there were even occasions when,
ridiculously, he considered telephoning Clive at work to call the
meeting off, then realised with a stab of shame how stupid he
was being. He had wanted nothing more than Amery's friendship and approval all this time, and here he was preparing to
reject it, all because he'd had a stupid dream. It was the sort of
thing a twelve-year-old might do, and Dennis was a man now;
could be called upon to do his National Service if the country
ever found out he existed or, worse, where he happened to be
living. He resolved to grow up and put all this nebulous and
morbid nonsense from his thoughts, but when he set out from
the shop that night at seven for the Farringdon Road, Dennis
learned that his thoughts had decided otherwise.

It was the last night of the month, pressing against the sharp
edge of November, and was much colder and blacker than he'd
been expecting. Making his way out of Shoreditch, leaving
vaporous parcels of his breath behind him in a bread-crumb
trail, he noted that the streets tonight were mostly empty, with
few cars and fewer still pedestrians. Most probably this was as a
result of the low temperature, but, then again, it was All Hallows'
Eve, the night when all the witches, ghouls and devils were
supposed to be about, and when sensibly superstitious people

didn't venture out of doors. At least, that's what his mum had told him, and he was beginning to think that he should have listened to her. Without the diversions of the shop, he found himself with no recourse except to dwell upon the things that he'd been trying not to dwell upon, and without Ada's coughing as a kind of background music, the dark lanes and empty byways seemed unnaturally silent. He could hear his every worry.

As he started up the drawn-out yawn of Old Street, Dennis tried to take his anxious self in hand, commencing a stern lecture on how there was absolutely nothing real that he should be concerned about. All he was doing, after all, was keeping an appointment made over a week ago with Clive, when Dennis had fortuitously bumped into his friend there on the corner of the Bethnal Green Road. Clive had been looking for him up at Coffin Ada's, to make sure he was alright, and Dennis had been walking home from Grace's after the preceding night's decisive interlude at Arnold Circus. He remembered how appreciative of Clive's concern he'd been, to think that the urbane young lawyer would walk all the way to Lowell's Books & Magazines, simply to check on his well-being. It was—

He was just passing the blitzed shell of St Luke's, a clot of deeper shadow on the other side of Old Street, its peculiar Egyptian steeple bayonetting the sky, when a thought struck him. It was no more than the tiniest of loose ends, dangling from his carefully embroidered memories, but like a schoolboy with an unpicked scab, he found himself compelled to pull the end of it: hadn't he told Clive, from the telephone box by the church in Spitalfields, that he would not be living with his landlady until his 'other district' difficulties were resolved? He felt sure that he had, and then reluctantly recalled the cryptic words that Grace had uttered in his dream, something about 'He didn't know you were at mine, but should have known you weren't at Ada.' But, of course, that made no sense. Why would Clive trek to Shoreditch if he'd known that Dennis wouldn't be there? It wasn't as if the bombed-out area had got anything else to offer a sophisticated trainee lawyer. And they'd met on Bethnal Green

Road, just as you'd expect if Clive had visited the bookshop before heading back along Gibraltar Walk, although, now that he thought about it, Clive had seemed surprised to see him.

He crossed the City Road, puffing his trail of baby ghosts, and, just past Bunhill Row where William Blake was sleeping, came upon the northern reaches of the wasteland that had once been Cripplegate. Out there in the night acres, down towards the stubs of Chiswell Street, a blaze was raging that he soon identified as a kids' bonfire, prematurely set alight before November 5th by rival children, as an act of sabotage. It spat and crackled, faintly echoing the greater conflagration of nine years before and, being Chiswell Street, put him in mind of Eileen Lockart, five years old and strangled, out there in the admixture of brick and willowherb. This wasn't something that he wanted to consider, and so he redoubled his attempts to reconstruct that Shoreditch corner and his unexpected run-in with Clive Amery. What had Clive said to him, exactly?

From what he remembered, it had mostly been about Clive's urge to make sure that he was OK after the trouble Dennis was anticipating when they'd previously met, his then forthcoming tryst with 'Jack Spot and his quaking henchman', as Clive had succinctly phrased it. This, predictably, sparked a repeat of Solly Kankus and his overstated shuddering in Dennis's still-unexploded dream, with on its heels a sudden notion that transformed his spine into a knobbly icicle: while he was pretty sure he'd told Clive that he wouldn't be at Ada's for some time, he was completely certain that he hadn't mentioned anything about Spot having an associate, much less a quaking one. He couldn't have said anything about it when he'd met with Clive at Bond's that Friday afternoon, for the compelling reason that it hadn't happened yet. In fact, the only way that anyone could know of Mr Kankus and his fit of trembling, that night in Arnold Circus, would be if they'd …

At his back, across the weeds and rubble, a great pile of broken furniture and branches – carefully constructed and maliciously ignited – was still roaring, an unwitting funeral pyre for Eileen

Lockart. Crossing Goswell Road, his pace slowed to a trudge, as if his bone marrow had been replaced by lead, when almost all his pennies dropped at once in a hard copper rain: the only way for anyone to know how Jack Spot's colleague had behaved that night was for them to have been there.

But Clive hadn't been there; hadn't even known the meeting would be taking place in Arnold Circus. Although Dennis was becoming rapidly aware that he'd told his friend about matters he should not have done, he knew that he'd avoided naming the location of Spot's audience with Harry Lud. All that he'd said was, it was somewhere up near Ada's bookshop where a lot of different streets converged ... which, Dennis realised haltingly, for anyone with access to a map of London and a pair of eyes, was practically as good as giving them the full postal address. He plodded onward automatically into the Old Street murk, simply because that was the way his feet were heading, and insisted to himself that even if Clive had deduced that Arnold Circus was the place in question, that did not alter the plain fact that Clive hadn't been there. There'd been only Spot and Kankus, Dennis and Jack Neave, and of course Gog Blincoe and Harry Lud. Other than that, beyond two parked cars and a builder's truck, the place had been entirely empty. But, having commenced to tug on the loose thread, he found he couldn't stop until his memory embroidery was an unravelled intestinal mess.

It came to him, for instance, that if Clive in some way *had* been there at Arnold Circus, it would at a stroke explain his earlier questions about bumping into Clive that afternoon in Shoreditch, although hardly reassuringly. This new scenario would mean that his friend wasn't coming back from having been to call on Dennis up at Coffin Ada's, having somehow not recalled that Dennis wouldn't be there. In the new hypothesis, Clive had been up at Arnold Circus all night long, both during the exchange between Jack Spot and Harry Lud, and afterwards, when everybody else had gone. But if that was the case, what was he doing there all night? And anyway, completely undermining this whole ludicrous conjecture was Dennis's certain knowledge that Clive hadn't been there in the first place. Then, dragging his heels across St John Street, he thought once more of the builder's wagon with its stacks of not-worth-stealing burlap sacking in the back, as in the cafeteria in his dream, and as the penny rain became a bruising torrent, Dennis finally had no choice but to understand.

Oh God. Oh God, Clive had been underneath the sackcloth, must have hidden there at some point earlier that Friday afternoon while Dennis had been idly frittering away the moments until midnight. He would have heard everything and no doubt seen it all, Kankus and Spot's arrival, Blincoe dragging back the previously timber curtain and the entrance of crime's essence, Harry Lud. Dennis stopped in his tracks at the worn kerb of Britton Street and let the awful truth sink in.

If his distressing theory was correct, Clive would have witnessed Blincoe opening an aperture between the different Londons. Did that mean he'd then know how to open one himself? Dennis felt sick. Was that where Clive had been that Friday night, exuberantly exploring the Great When? Starting to shiver now, he thought back to their Bethnal Green Road meeting and recalled that Clive had been ever so slightly rumpled and dishevelled, as though he'd just spent a night out on the town. It was a shame, in retrospect, that Dennis hadn't thought to ask which town. He slumped against the nearest brick wall, and the full enormity of what he'd done washed over him, a pulverising tide.

He'd blabbed. He'd done the thing that everyone had told him not to do, because he'd so much wanted to impress his older friend, and now the trouble he was in was terrible. This was worse, even, than his first encounter with the Hampole book, because then he'd had the assistance of Jack Neave and Monolulu, Maurice Calendar, Gog Blincoe, Austin Spare ... he couldn't turn to them for help with his current dilemma, because none of them must ever know that he'd betrayed the concealed city. What, he wondered with heart thudding, was he going to do? What if the City Heads, or even the horrific

Charming Peter, learned what he'd allowed to happen? Him and Clive would end up in the same condition as his landlady's book-dealer friend, eyes on the inside, staring at the backs of their own heads. And couldn't this put Grace in danger, too, just from the little that she'd seen? He leaned against the blacked-out brickwork, gasping, and he wanted desperately to turn around and hurry back to Shoreditch, wanted all of this to go away, but knew it wouldn't. God, what was he going to do?

His only option, it occurred to him, was to meet up with Clive as planned and force his errant friend to see that this wasn't some supernatural lark, and if they didn't both leave it alone, then it would get them killed, or worse. He didn't know if he could out-argue a lawyer, only that he had to. Straightening up and drawing a deep, quavering breath, he carried on to Old Street's end and then turned left into Farringdon Road. Despite his new resolve, there was still something bothering him.

Dolden, Green, Dorland & Lockart. Not solicitors, apparently, but unsolved murders that his chum had jotted in a notebook, no doubt as upcoming legal cases he was looking at. Descending the benighted road faster than he'd intended, borne now on an avalanche of pennies, Dennis suddenly perceived the flaw in his own reassuring explanation. Who was there to prosecute, who to defend, if these four murders were unsolved? And if Clive's listing of those names was therefore not professional, what was it? His unsettled mind was racing now, in an attempt to keep up with his feet. Was he suggesting that Clive might have killed those people? All of them? That he'd shot Violet Green and strangled Eileen Lockart? No. That was ridiculous, when Tolerable John had said that these were random slayings that had nothing to connect them up. Unless, of course, they had. He thought of Clive berating homicidal maniacs for their predictability, and of the lawyer's many monologues debating the post-war compulsive murderer. Down at the bottom of the almost empty road, on its far side, he could see an illuminated signboard that said 'Franklin's'. He was almost there.

Clive couldn't be a murderous lunatic. That couldn't have been what the clicking thing behind the newsprint in his dream, that he suspected was a Pope of Blades, was telling him. Because if that was true, then … then he'd done something much worse than to betray a confidence. If Clive killed people for the fun of it, then in his efforts to impress somebody posh and cultured, Dennis had set loose a monster in the city's secret and immortal soul. He'd unleashed unimaginable suffering upon both Londons, gifting them a killer that might move from place to place in the material world without detection; that might threaten the superior realm itself. Dennis alone had done this. *Self-re-Hitler.*

He was now outside the café, nothing like his dream, and found that he was pushing open its front door and entering, despite his every fibre telling him to run away. Why had Clive chosen somewhere so far from their usual haunts, and at so late an hour, for their meeting? Why, if Dennis's increasingly hysterical surmises were correct, would Clive want to meet up with him at all, once he had served his purpose by revealing the forbidden landscape? Was it because he was the one person who might possibly connect Clive Amery to the Great When? Manoeuvring through the unfamiliar premises, uneasily considering the implications of this final question, he jumped when he spotted Clive at one of the establishment's rear tables, smiling, his eyes twinkling.

'Lord Oxydol! I was just starting to suspect you'd stood me up.'

And Dennis's bad dream began.

8

*A Startling New Calendar*

There was a glint, a visual whinny, every time Clive's horse-head cufflinks caught the light. In Franklin's late-night café, the trapped air hung thick and still above the cup-ringed tables, most of them unoccupied, and in the hush, each stifled cough or rattled saucer was a nerve-testing percussion. Everything seemed smeared – the sounds, the atmosphere, Dennis's face inverted in the hollow of a teaspoon, his glazed feelings – glistening as though through a thin grease of apprehension. The establishment wasn't at all like Bond's and had no poor, dead Flabby Harrison behind its counter, yet felt less real than his dream had done. There were three other customers, two men and an impassive older woman, seated separately at their different wooden islands of preoccupation and apparently invisible to one another, silent funeral deities. Dennis was nailed there, held in place by the moment's impossibility and wondering how his best friend was going to kill him.

In a trance of fright he overstirred his weak tea, mesmerised by the slow, looping scrape of steel on chinaware, a tinkling soundtrack to his circling thoughts as he sat fixed by the oncoming headlights of extinction. Why wasn't he doing anything? Was he just going to wait for it to happen? His own end was just across the table from him, chatting amiably, and Dennis couldn't marshal a response to literally save his life. His panicked, fluttering attention lighted upon detail after detail as if in a miserable attempt to gobble up these last few crumbs of sight and sentience: stray grains like chiselled ice floes at the base of the salt cellar's crystal lighthouse; dead fly belly-up behind the sugar bowl; residual carbon bruises, black stars furiously ground into a currently unused tin ashtray. His well-spoken executioner's least incidental gesture startled the equestrian cuff-fastenings into a glittering steeplechase, while Dennis sat there and did nothing save recall the bleak acknowledgement in *Railway Horse*'s one visible eye, that knowing shared glance on the way to slaughter. No more than two feet away and yet as though from an immeasurable distance, Clive was saying something entertaining about Scotland that, to Dennis's ear, sounded now like the smooth, reassuring patter of somebody flogging sudden death on the black market like a pair of nylons.

' ... heard about their latest Highland fling, with the petition that they launched on Saturday? The sixth Duke of Montrose, quite possibly an Edinburgh cousin of your Lordship, was the first to sign this ransom note insisting that the Jocks should have home rule, as if we can just saw the country off at Newcastle. Wherever will it end? Next thing you know, we'll get the Welsh demanding independence, or the Cornish. It won't let up until Putney's a republic. I say, are you trying to tunnel through the bottom of that teacup?'

Made aware that he was still stirring compulsively, Dennis apologetically withdrew the spoon and placed it in his saucer. He was uneasily conscious that he wasn't holding up his end of the pair's customary back-and-forth; not chuckling at the one-sided jokes about the class distinctions that there were between them. Feeling like a condemned man, not wanting Clive to spot that there was anything the matter, he attempted a relaxed smile but could manage no more than a rictus.

'Haha. And, yeah, I mean, who'd be, you know, presiding at a Scottish parliament? They'd have, they'd have to have the, I don't know, the Loch Ness monster, or, or, or Macbeth. Somebody frightening and Scottish, Burke and Hare, someone like that. Haha.'

Which, even as the words were spilling from his mouth, he knew was frantic nonsense and nothing at all like repartee.

Nevertheless, Clive gave him an amused look that was only faintly questioning. 'Yes, I suppose they would. Perhaps in a black kilt that had a human head as a replacement sporran, playing bagpipes made from somebody's wee mother, something of that nature? You know, Knuckleyard, I've missed these chats of ours across the course of this last dreary week. You really are a tonic after all the chaps at work, who, I'm afraid, can be as dull as ditchwater. Perfectly decent fellows, I suppose, but, for all that, there's no one there who's anywhere near my own age, who I can talk to as a friend and equal. Nobody with your primitive allure.'

Down at the nearly silent cafeteria's front end, one of the other customers scraped back his chair, perhaps to make a visit to the lavatories. The older woman looked at the cartoon strip in her *Evening Standard* with a face free from expression. Dennis automatically said 'Ha' as a response to the remark and brandished once again his rictus grin, but inside he was crumbling. To hear Clive speak of them as equals, once his fondest dream, was like a hard punch in the stomach now he knew it for a tactic. Clive was going to kill him because Dennis was the only living individual who might associate the trainee barrister and trainee murderer with the Great When, and all this flattery was part of an insidious routine, a lethal courtship. Knowing this did nothing to reduce the amber bead of paralysing dread he was held fast in, like a prehistoric bluebottle. He found he was incapable of doing anything or saying anything that might prolong his brief and, thus far, largely wretched life, opting instead to babble more non sequiturs in lieu of conversation.

'We, we'll probably be more alluring when we've, you know, when we've come down from the trees and, and, and combed out all the nits and, I don't know, the bits of bark, or …'

Clive's fond smile, maintained throughout, now had an undertone of puzzlement.

'Dennis, I have to ask, is everything alright? It's just, you don't seem quite your usual self. You've not been having any more of your spine-tingling adventures, have you?'

Glancing as it was, this reference to Dennis's excursions in the other London sounded in him a profound peal of alarm, so that he recoiled from the question into mumbling improvisation.

'Yeah, I'm sorry. I, earlier on, I had something to eat that's given me a bit, you know, a bit of bellyache. It's nothing serious. You go on with what you were saying.'

From somewhere adjacent to the café entrance came the creak of a door swinging shut, and then another scrape of chair legs on linoleum, announcing the stray customer's return. Clive held Dennis's darting gaze for a few seconds, still wearing the same amused and interested smile, before he lounged back elegantly in his chalk-stripe suit, his orange tie, his racecourse cufflinks, and resumed his lulling monologue on the importance of their friendship. Motionless behind its sugar bowl, the fly held all its legs up as if frozen in the act of trying uselessly to push away demise.

'Well, I suppose what I was getting at is that, for all our differences in rank, we've got a lot in common, you and I. Both young chaps, keen to find our footing in the world, both with our parents gone, both with the same bomb-happy sense of humour – we should spend more time together, don't you think, and get to know each other? Tell you what, after we've finished here, why don't we toddle down and take a walk on the Embankment? You can tell me all your boyhood tales of life with Bill and Nancy and the Artful Dodger, and I'll top you with hilarious accounts of setting fire to servants.'

The pack-ice psychology that held Dennis immobile creaked and splintered as its grip upon him tightened. That was it, then. That was how his life was going to end, in a short stroll beside the Thames upon a freezing cold October night with nobody about. There'd be some soothing and placatory chatter, then a muffled noise of some variety, a splash, when he would be appointed a full partner in the company of Dolden, Green, Dorland, Lockart & Knuckleyard. And nobody would ever know, he realised. He'd kept Clive all to himself, in a compartment of his life away from all other acquaintances like Ada, Grace or Tolerable John: he hadn't mentioned Clive to any of these people, hadn't wanted to share Clive with them. Nor would Clive have mentioned him to anybody, it went almost without saying. His brief life and brutal death would both forever be unsolved, and here he was, on the front doorstep of his own mortality, and there was no defence; was no reprieve. Inside him, everything was caught in an accelerating spin, the vertigo of any clump of suds in its decaying orbit of a plughole. Distantly, he heard his own voice saying, 'Yeah. Yeah, that sounds great. I'd better just pop to the gents' before we go. It's that meal I had earlier, playing up. Shan't be a minute.'

He was somehow upright and making his way unsteadily towards the front of the café and its toilet facilities, a high-pitched ringing in his ears. Despite his desperate attempts to catch their gaze with eyes that shouted 'help me', neither the defeated-looking pensioner behind the counter nor the Three Wise Monkey customers would look up from their own dilemmas or acknowledge Dennis's. Was he so close to dying that the living could no longer see him? He was barely conscious of his actions, as if part of Dennis had already given up on his basic responsibility to keep himself alive, shuffling in the coffee shop's low-wattage twilight, a sleepwalker to the guillotine. He supposed that his pretended urgent visit to the lavatory was intended to buy him a minute or two's precious time, before accompanying his homicidal friend to the Embankment and their last appointment. Shambling in a stupor of the abattoir, he didn't see what else there was to do except proceed to the inevitable outcome and have all this terror over with. Off on his left now he could see the entrance to the ladies' and the gents', discreetly signposted, while a few feet in front of him, there was …

In an adrenalated scream of bone and fear and muscle, Dennis flung himself towards the cafeteria's front door before he realised he was doing it, yanking the heavy portal open with the frigid air outside smacking into his face and lungs. Behind him he heard Clive say, 'Dennis? Just where do you think you're going?', and his crisp enunciation wasn't jocular, it wasn't playful. It was cold, surprised and angry. Hurling himself out into the icy blackness, he glanced back and saw that the apprentice brief was standing, snatching a fawn raincoat from his chairback, with Clive's grey, unblinking eyes locked on to Dennis, staring, full of awful promise. Eerie as a waxwork tableau, no one else in Franklin's had looked up, or given any indication he and Clive were even there. The weighted café door swung shut behind him, but by then Dennis was pelting down the sparsely lighted road and praying to his dead mum he could disappear into the empty, echoing shadows under Holborn Viaduct before Clive reached the street and spotted him. That didn't happen.

Rhythmic and untiring footfalls slapped the bomb-cracked slabs behind him as he ran on into the truncated tunnel's denser darkness, where his friend and ending called to him again. Unnervingly, the tone was once more ribbing and good-natured, with its bark of a frustrated predator entirely absent, as though never there at all.

'Look here, young Knuckleyard, this is all very entertaining and mysterious, but can I ask what it's in aid of? Do you salt-of-the-earth scallywags end all of your social engagements with a hundred-metre dash? Or are you hoping the fresh air will help you with your rickets?'

Ludicrously, Dennis found that he was starting to compose a bantering rejoinder, and so pounded on beneath the viaduct, spurred by his own alarming vulnerability, erupting out into the glimmer of Farringdon Street on its far side. A car purred past but didn't slow, and although he could make out one or two other pedestrians through the miasma, in his thudding heart he knew that nobody was going to offer him assistance. Amery was smartly dressed while Dennis was a grubby scruff, and any intervention would be based on the assumption that Dennis had run off with Clive's wallet or said something unforgiveable about Clive's wife. If anybody deigned to notice the pursuit, they'd more than likely rugby-tackle him as an absconding miscreant. No saviours. No Samaritans.

He hurtled on into the London dark and heard Amery's steady and relentless pace behind him, but how far behind he couldn't tell. His own feet punched the pavement mercilessly, the repeated impacts jarring through his lanky frame, and though he knew with terrifying certainty what he was running from, he had no clue where he was running to. He raced across Stonecutter Street, and only then became aware that if he didn't change direction soon they'd be at the Victoria Embankment, where Clive wanted them to be. Dennis's ineffectual escape bid had only allowed his murder to occur slightly ahead of schedule. His breath burning in his throat, he swung around the next turn on the right, where he was momentarily surprised to find himself in after-hours Fleet Street.

His first thought was to take sanctuary in Ye Olde Cheshire Cheese, but that was too far down the road and his pursuer would be rocketing around the corner any second now, would see where he was going. Before Dennis knew what he was doing, he'd crossed Fleet Street at a frenzied sprint and darted, hopefully unseen, into the dark mouth of Bride Lane. Expecting with each step to feel Clive's hand fall on his neck, not daring to look back and check for fear of losing crucial instants, Dennis was committed to this new trajectory and only saw his error when it was too late: the other end of Bride Lane led on to New Bridge Street, only slightly further down the road he'd just turned off from, slightly nearer the Victoria Embankment and its wide, indifferent waters. Was this, then, his fate, certain and inescapable, where every effort to get out could only lead him deeper in, towards his river-bottom terminus? His headlong pace was slowing, perhaps fatally, his feet no longer sure of their direction or their destination. If he carried on towards the Thames, then Clive would kill him. If he went back, Clive would kill him. If he stopped, if he put up a fight, if he did anything at all, he knew his life was done. Caught helpless in the maelstrom of what were most probably his final thoughts, he'd not consciously recognised this as the exact spot where Grace had scraped him from the Bride Lane pavement, but his nearside arm was reaching out already of its own volition. His numb fingers hooked on something, possibly the stone edge of a window, and reality collapsed. A whole fifteen-foot section of brick wall swung out into the feeble lamplight, an impossible door now ajar, and without thinking, Dennis flung his body through before it could swing shut again, so that

*he is immediately somewhere else, amid skyscraper blossoms that have tender green stems bigger than the trunks of elms, and fragrance so thick he can cut it with a knife ... behind, the doorway inconceivable is closed once more, leaving a blacker black between the redwood irises, an interruption of decanted starlight ... he's back in the fit or seizure of the Great When, at what Maurice Calendar had called the Fisbo opening in Furious Alsatia ... still horrifically afraid and with his limbs still full of flight, he tells himself that even if Amery had chased into Bride Lane after him, it wouldn't have been quick enough to notice the miraculous two-storey entrance opening and shutting ... even so, he backs away from the concealed gate's distilled darkness, stumbling backwards up a slope of knee-deep grass to higher ground, his eyes fixed on the blank void of the portal, just in case ...*

*drinking the too rich air despite it hastening his pulse, he cautiously makes his reverse ascent through towering stalks, and petals shed like wedding dresses cast off in regret ... although this place could never in a million years become familiar, he starts to remember where he is, as if partly retrieving an elusive dream ... off to his left, viewed through the enlarged flora, is the edifice of sensuously contoured coloured glass, Westminster Abbey-sized, that he recalls from his previous visit to this cyclopean garden, a voluptuous immensity of tints and glints that might, he fuzzily conjectures, be a counterpart of St Bride's Church ... on its far side, seen through the bulbed translucence, Dennis briefly glimpses a long skein of floating smoke that he suspects to be the gossamer unfolding of Her Train ... the billowing Arcanum keeps its distance, hanging back, perhaps because Dennis's fear is at this point more aromatic than his poetry ... he's in the process of succumbing to the mental drift and mesmerism of the hidden city's atmosphere, its trilling sound effects, and when Clive steps out from the abyss bracketed by flowers only a little further down the gradient, Dennis's heart performs a sickening lurch, tripped up by the skipped beat ...*

*amongst the monster hollyhocks, lit by a night sky with too many constellations, the new breed of post-war murderer that Dennis has let into London's under-mind appears relaxed and in a playful mood, no longer running and no longer needing to ... tilting his head back, smiling up with satisfaction at the star jam overhead, Amery's stylish figure looks immaculate against the flaring vision of its backdrop; looks alarmingly at home ... when he returns his sparkling gaze to Dennis, his expression is one of disorienting fondness, his delivery amused, detached ... 'So, this makes two doors that you've shown me now – and from what I gather, I'm quite good at opening the things. It must be something in my carefree personality. I take it, after your peculiar antics at the café, that you've realised the mistake you made regarding Arnold Circus. But, I mean, look at it, Dennis! This place is just marvellous! I've been exploring little bits of it all week. You surely can't have meant to keep this Shangri-La all to yourself? To be quite honest, I'm a little disappointed in you, Knuckleyard. I ask you, where's the harm in sharing such a fabulous discovery with your best mate?'*

*unhurriedly, Clive strolls towards him through the stellar dapple, elegant in his fawn coat and looking like the hero ... every step that Amery takes forward is reflected by a pace from Dennis in retreat, as he backs up the incline with his sweaty palms held out before him, trembling and placatory ... his voice, when he can find it, is the plaint of a kicked puppy ... 'Clive, you kill people. I know you do' ... the other man now pauses in his casual advance, flicking his fringe back from a brow knitted in puzzlement, and, in the end, he laughs ... 'Dennis, you can't be serious. Wherever did you come by a preposterous idea like that? Is this some lurid fancy you've imagined while sat on a bombsite with your roughneck friends, imbibing gas and milk?' ... continuing his rear-view climb throughout this humorous interrogation, Dennis is now almost at the summit of the gently rising ground where it abuts the Great When's Fleet Street, or its Upper Scandals as described by long-gone Maurice Calendar ... his hushed reply to Amery sounds, in his own ears, tremulous and frightened ... 'Kenneth Dolden. Violet Green. Edith Dorland. Eileen Lockart' ...*

*the attorney's wry and cordial features melt into the face of someone Dennis doesn't know, the grey gaze narrowing, the finely modelled lips without a vestige of amusement ... shaking his blond head as though regretful, Clive resumes his patient and sedate approach, while Dennis sticks with his attempted backwards disengagement ... nonchalant, his hands deep in his raincoat pockets, the young lawyer's tone is level and straightforward, with its chummy camouflage unnecessary now ... 'Hm. It appears that I've misjudged the depth of your stupidity. I'm not sure how you found me out, but, then, that doesn't really matter, does it, when you must have also realised that you're next? Dreadfully sorry and all that, but I can't let you keep me from all this. The way it crawls and changes, the magnificent grotesquery – Dennis, it's what my dreams are like. This is what I was born for' ...*

*they're both at the slope's top end, facing each other in their awkward progress through the giant horticulture ... with a heavy sigh, Amery takes his hands out of his pockets, holding in his right what looks to be an Arab knife with a sharp, curving blade that glitters in the stellar downpour ... 'This is my Moroccan kris, the letter opener that I picked up in Portobello. So, what do you say, young Knuckleyard? Shall we peruse your contents?' ... with a choked cry, Dennis is delivered from his stasis, at last turns away from his tormentor, bolting for a madman's fantasy of Fleet Street ... through his shock and panic, he hears Clive's expensive, hand-tooled footfall close behind him and, as they burst out on to the Upper Scandals, hears Amery's cry of pleased surprise ... 'Good God! This pavement is all gold! There's more gold here than there is in the world!' ... not daring to look round, Dennis runs on in helpless dread, and only when confronted by the startling obstacle at Fetter Lane is he compelled to cease; is everything compelled to cease ...*

*four-storey buildings made of folded newspaper curtail their rustling, and the street's handful of baroque pedestrians seem halted in mid-stride ... Dennis himself is poised impossibly on one foot, all his weight thrown forward, and behind he hears Clive make a similar dead stop, with the world's motion suddenly suspended, its kinetic force held in abeyance ... at the centre of the burnished thoroughfare, facing both prey and predator, there is a thing of morbid and arresting beauty ... by its tingling aura, Dennis at once knows it for a representative of the Arcana, though it's one he hasn't seen before, a new variety of the Great When's disquieting fauna ...*

*stopping time, arresting the momentum of the moments with its presence, at the base of Fetter Lane there stands a spectacle ... a mighty steed made all from bone, and, sat side-saddle on its spine, a female form that isn't quite a woman, more a stylised swirl of luminescent pen strokes that implies the feminine ... with its component pieces polished to a white which borders on fluorescent, the articulated skeleton of a tremendous shire horse blocks the golden road and its chronology alike ... the fleshless hooves are massive and the fetlocks stout as silver birches ... the long skull seems broken at its muzzle, now the cartilage and velvet hide have gone, and in the emptied sockets is a watchful dark ... exposed ribs like a giant's xylophone gleam as if carved from moonlight, and it shakes a great head bare of everything except its bridle, whinnies with a hollow echo, both the graveyard mare and its outlined suggestion of a rider being seemingly exempt from the extended instant's immobility ...*

*on her sepulchral mount she is an animated pencil drawing, loosely crayoned in swipes of light ... the flickering arms are raised, and in one hand she holds aloft an iron key, while in the other is a jet-black handkerchief ... the dancing lines that sketch her face give the illusion that her scribbled eyes are fixed on Dennis, filled with intimations of significance he doesn't fully understand ... it comes to him that this might be the archetype Jack Neave has talked about, called Slenderhorse, but whether that be jockey, nag, or if the two comprise a single entity, he cannot say ... the key she holds, he somehow knows within his vitals, will unlock the mysteries of death, presumably his own ... the purpose of the handkerchief, however, is opaque to him until she drops it ...*

*parachute silk cut from night, its tumbling descent is languid, rivetingly graceful ... like a woven liquid or an opening bloom it falls, the thin black square slipping and crumpling into new and transient configurations as it swoops, breeze-borne, on its leisurely tailspin towards millionaire macadam ... his gaze frozen on its stately plummet, he considers how much horse racing has played its part in this disastrous undertaking ... Monolulu, Spot's illegal bookie empire, Spare's Surrealist Racing Forecast Cards, Clive's cufflinks ... with a cold flash of belated insight,*

*Dennis comprehends that he is looking at the signal to commence a fatal derby ... flittering and flimsy, the black hanky cartwheels and cavorts from shape to fluid shape in its gavotte with gravity, hovering, floating, flirting with the glistering ground until at last it touches terra firma, spreading its obsidian skirts out like the farewell curtsey of a ballerina, and time is resuscitated, and they're off ...*

*absurdist strollers at the street's far end complete paused paces and continue with their dazzling perambulations ... broadsheet buildings recommence their whispering flutter ... Dennis is flung forward from his freeze into a smooth resumption of his previous stampeding gait, without the fall or falter that he's been anticipating, and not far behind, hears Amery do the same ... the two men, game and poacher, make their dash along the Upper Scandals, kicking up the Eldorado dust as they shoot past the cemetery equestrian to either side ... although it isn't the greased lightning that he felt when he was being dragged by Maurice Calendar, Dennis discovers that he can run faster in this London than the other, perhaps due to a decrease in friction, gravity or air resistance ... he accelerates between the fish-wrap architecture, its façades of head-line smearing by him in the corners of his vision, Edward abdicated, Mafeking relieved ... the lead this buys him is short-lived as, at his rear, his adversary quickly picks up the same trick, with nearing shoe slaps ringing in the operatic resonance and, up above, the spatter of a billion lights ...*

*once more without a clue where he is running to, he only knows that Clive is going to catch him, gut him like a mackerel on these gilded boulevards ... he can't see any other way that this is going to end ... Amery's tougher, cleverer, has passed the week just gone in unrestricted exploration of the Great When, may already know as much or more than Dennis does, has all of the advantages, is holding all the cards ... although Clive hadn't known the centre of the higher city to be paved proverbially with gold, perhaps because it was outside Clive's radius of reconnaissance − but as he jets from a perfected Fleet Street into an apotheosis of the Strand, Dennis can't see how this fact is of any use to him in his mortal predicament ... probably corresponding to Short London's law courts, Amery's home ground, he passes on the right a soaring stone colossus, blindfolded but brandishing a sword and balance ... justice symbolised and yet, from Dennis's perspective, hardly evident ...*

*to either side, buildings boil up and simmer down as Dennis skids on the quintessence of the Strand, sizzling in and out amongst the slow drift of phantasmal boulevardiers ... men with the heads of pigeons, little girls with clocks instead of faces, stained-glass dowagers, and, gathered at the mouth of a sublime Arundel Street, grouped figures in Regency frock coats, wearing hose and periwigs and chalk-white gloves without a shred of flesh or skin to mask their grinning skulls ... they stand in conference to examine unrolled diagrams or take a pinch of snuff, wet eyeballs swivelling suspiciously in their dry cavities as they watch Dennis and his hunter streaking past ... does he remember Cromwell's head mentioning something about Barebones? ... but the thought is thrown away as he imagines Amery narrowing the gap between them, burying his letter opener between Dennis's shoulder blades ... refuelled by fright, he pulses forward and, near Surrey Street, sees once again the stocky form that Maurice Calendar had said was Arthur Machen, still in his viridian spotlight with his arms thrown up in ecstasy ... and Dennis charges onward through unending marvel ...*

*on the iridescent avenue, uncanny traffic still processions and parades ... helmets with headlights, tramcars that have gills and glide like trout, glass penny-farthings ... as with his first visit, this illuminated torrent forks about a great, marmoreal erection rising from the highway's centre, trailing rivulets of maypole ribbon, an unfathomable telescope of vast dimension balanced on the sculpted bulb ... he hears Clive's surprised bark of schoolboy laughter, ringing and repeating in the rarefied acoustic, still some way behind him but not far enough ... competing fireballs, they stream past a steaming analogue of Charing Cross at the Strand's end, where the Infanta de Castile's beloved body touched the earth and sprouted an ornate stone monument to stroke the busy firmament ... as he tacks right and surges through an ultimate St Martin's Place towards the Indices of Charing, Dennis realises that his chosen route is simply an unplanned reversal of his flight with Maurice on that first occasion, running in the one direction he can almost recognise ... it fleetingly occurs to him that this was not the wisest path he could have taken, but he has a madman with a dagger right behind him, and it's too late now, one more spilled-milk decision that he doesn't have the time to cry over ...*

*he leads their hectic dance of death into the Charing Cross Road's flipped-through, frilling immortality: a canyon of cracked spines with doorways where the imprint of a publisher should be, with walls of rippling page in lieu of shopfront or façade ... his chest is aching now, his legs and his adrenal gland exhausted ... knowing that he cannot save his life and very soon will not be even able to prolong it, Dennis hammers on into the unfamiliar scents and soundscape of an utter London, into the distended jaws of his forthcoming doom and disappearance without so much as a marker ...*

*he's eighteen years old and cannot bear the thought of suddenly and simply vanishing, with Grace and Tolerable John and Coffin Ada never knowing where he'd gone, his short duration ending in a puzzle and, thereafter, soon forgotten ... with him living off the record to avoid his National Service, will there be the flimsiest remaining trace of his existence? ... on the heels of this, he finds that he is thinking of Clive Amery, however much he doesn't want to ... thinking of the trail of slaughter that will certainly lead from his own, the other Kenneth Doldens and, oh God, the other Eileen Lockarts ... but there's nothing he can do about it except thunder on through the asylum lights ...*

*like beaded mercury he skitters on gold paving, Clive and Dennis both now only pulses of velocity, weaving at high speed to avoid collisions with the strolling wonders ... in the road, a seahorse of cast porcelain on wheels rolls by the other way, and vehicles that bounce, and a brown anaconda omnibus that slithers with the creatures on its open top deck taking the intoxicating air ... it seems to Dennis highly likely that the last impressions passing through his mind will be of things that he could never in a lifetime understand, an apex of monstrosity that no one save an ether-swigging fin-de-siècle poet could imagine ... when he can't resist the impulse any more, he risks a backwards glance across his shoulder, and discovers with alarm that Amery is closer than he'd thought ... the kris clenched in one pumping fist, fawn raincoat flapping like a harrier's wings, and on Clive's face that impish, playful smile of certainty, the storm-grey eyes locked hungrily on his escaping prey ...*

at *Shaftsbury Avenue Superior*, a river of bejewelled improbability, Dennis buys precious seconds with a reckless spurt in front of an oncoming transportation, a brass mechanism that conjoins the locomotive with the locust, leaving *Amery* paused briefly on its other side ... dear God, he thinks, don't let me perish here, beneath this herd of foreign stars ... gaining the foot-worn treasure of the pavement opposite, his thoughts are a consuming bonfire of irrelevance, sparks going everywhere ... an image of the clicking horror from his dream, concealed behind an evening paper with a nonsense headline ... *Clive's surprise*, back in the *Upper Scandals*, on discovering that there were fortunes underfoot: he's not familiar, then, with the *Great When's* interior ... torn pages of *Sax Rohmer* gradually disintegrating in a *Shoreditch* gutter ... out of nowhere, and before he knows what he is doing, Dennis finds his beanpole legs have made a unilateral decision to propel him out amongst the fuming, nightmare chariots that rumble on these *Indices of Charing* ...

he careers across the busy avenue, avoiding gaseous velocipedes, carts pulled by strutting metal peacocks, diamond humming tops ... there's a near miss with an impractically large roller skate ... he hears *Clive* shouting something, still not far enough behind, and races on into the last place that he'd ever hoped to see again, into the trachea of an *Older Compton Street* ... he doesn't have the first idea why he is doing this; why he is slavishly retracing his initial flight with *Calendar* despite its leading inexorably towards the very place that *Maurice* saved him from ... and suddenly, he knows ...

now galloping along what – one way or another – are his chosen track's home furlongs, he swerves north abruptly into the ennoblement of *Greek Street* ... blurry but explicit ferns, smut butterflies, a handful of mirages on their twilight promenades ... and, at the steep lane's near end, the deciduous gas lamp with its knotted ferrous roots sunk into precious concrete, where the shabby spectre of *Thomas De Quincey* slouches in eternity awaiting *Ann of Oxford Street's* return ... certain that *Clive* is close enough to see where he is going, Dennis darts across the relatively peaceful and unthreatening byway, making for the mouth of *Bateman Street's* tropic epiphany ...

and now it's rank outsider *Ada's Servant* in the lead, only a length or two, with bookie's favourite *Legal Murder* coming up on the inside

... *the sylvan squeal and chitter grows more evident, more resonant, and in his flaring nostrils, the exotic scent of petrol orchids now, the sour spoor of trash animals ... he's hoping he can get in fast enough, before the place wakes up ... he hoofs it over a delirium of Frith Street with Clive right behind him, hurdling the first carnivorous dustbin that rolls optimistically towards him, hoping Amery will take it for another of the higher town's outré phenomena, without considering its implications ... hoping Clive will not know what a vividistrict is ...*

*when Dennis spots cracks with the contours of a snout, fissured across the million-dollar slabs ahead of him, he's ready ... without breaking stride, he stamps down heavy on the paving gator's upper jaw before it has a chance to lift up, how Maurice had taught him, knowing that most of the inorganic creature's buried-cable muscles are designed for clamping shut, not opening ... he bats away spent-lightbulb hummingbirds that whir into his eyes, barely in time to notice that one of the busted fruit crates on his right is starting to stand up ... it's small, a youngster, only big enough for plums or tangerines, and Dennis kicks it from his path just as he hears Clive Amery scream behind him ...*

*running on a few steps more to make sure that he's safely past a sway-ing, snapping cardboard flytrap made of empty chocolate boxes, Dennis stumbles to a halt ... flapping away tin-tack mosquitos, he turns back reluctantly towards the now continuous shrieking ...*

*the gold-crusted crocodilian has taken Clive's left leg off, just below the knee, and now the well-bred homicidal lunatic is headlong on the teeming cobbles of Soho Entire, crawling and writhing, horrified amid investigating crate crustaceans, litter organisms, earwig hairpins ... painted mamba black, some fifteen feet of drainpipe lazily detaches from the brick wall where it's been sleeping, slithering and scraping noisily across the priceless stones to wind around the young solicitor's remaining ankle ... from the hungry rubbish, Amery lifts up his head and glares through angry tears, with sticky gumdrop parasites embedded in his cheek and brow ... 'Dennis, you worthless little oik, you come back here! You come back here and help! This filthy fucking slum is eating me! It's——' ... he breaks off to scream again as the constrictor drainpipe finds new purchase on his thigh, around his waist ... blood everywhere, the run-off gurgling between the iron teeth of grateful drains ... from a safe distance up the snarl of Bateman Street, Dennis peers nervously into the glimmering dark around him, looking out for any debris predators, but all the district's febrile scrap seems more attracted to the feeding frenzy down the way ...*

*one of the wooden crabs draws back as Amery flails with the kris, biding its time and waiting for its victim to exhaust himself before successfully impaling the offending hand with a sharp-splintered fore-leg ... there is what appears to be a mantis improvised out of a rusted penknife, sawing at Clive's ear ... the python pipe is now around the doomed man's chest and squeezing tighter every time there comes an exhalation or a moan ... unable to take any more of this unbearable display, white-faced and shaking, Dennis tears his eyes away and runs into the twitching shadows ... at his back, Clive's mounting screech is ceased and there is nothing save for scuttle, clank and munch as the Night-Life of Soho settles down to supper ...*

*skidding over Dean Street with its nest of yard-brush centipedes, with its discarded pairs of motorcycle gloves made leather bats, its tetanus cacti bristling with builders' nails, Dennis is speeding still, running now not from Clive but from what he has done to Clive ... he's killed someone, he's worse than killed them: had them eaten by a street ... he crashes on, still heading west through writhing shortcuts, backyards boiling with ferocious bric-a-brac biology ... he's killed someone ... he swipes the toffee-wrapper wasps away and treads hard on the levering, invaluable jaws of alley Caymans ... feral reels of filmstock roll at him down something more than Wardour Street ... he's killed someone ... barrows with hands on Berwick Street, Ingestre Place alive with cubist reptiles folded out of dirty postcards ... finally, in Upper Beak Street, where there are once more a few unearthly strollers and the wildlife seems restricted to less harmful breeds – French knickers billowing an inch or two above the gleaming kerbs like saucy jellyfish, or wriggling moray fishnets – Dennis shudders to a halt and makes an effort to collect himself ... he's killed someone ...*

*and, yes, the person that he's killed was trying to kill him, had killed four innocents already, would have gone on to kill dozens more, and, yes, he knows he's done the right thing, but he's killed someone, is now in that select minority of people who have taken human life and from that*

287

*moment on have known themselves for killers … he stands shivering, all the fear and energy drained from his legs into the ingot pavement, all the ugly electricity running to ground … his head swims, and he concentrates on keeping himself upright, focusses on not collapsing in a heap to the king's-ransom ground amongst the grazing lingerie … perused through quizzing glasses by hallucinatory night wanderers, at length it comes to him that what he has committed is perhaps the perfect crime … his earlier anxieties about not having talked of Amery with anybody else now show themselves to Dennis's advantage, and he also, with an inward wince, knows that they'll never find a body … worryingly, Dennis registers his fit of giggling at the same moment that he realises he is weeping, the effects of shock in a place wholly made from shock … above him, fruitbat brassieres make short leaps from lamp to lamp, cups swelling on the updraft …*

*after some few minutes' wobbling there at the western limits of Soho Entire, Dennis feels once more capable of motion, executing an unsteady stumble on the backstreet's alchemy-touched flagstones, with an eye to somehow getting out of here … the metaphysical pedestrians don't seem inclined to interfere; the drifting coelenterate underwear appear to be avoiding him … he numbly wonders where he's previously heard of Upper Beak Street, fuzzily recalling it as somewhere Maurice Calendar had lodgings, when he passes a shop window of vertical puddle water, rippling concentrically, and is astonished to catch sight of Calendar himself …*

*beyond a pane of liquid, the sartorial trailblazer is suspended, head down, by a fibrous white umbilical cord from the ceiling of a mostly empty premises, unfurnished and unlit saving the astral shimmer from outside, refracting through a wall of water … though on Dennis's last sighting of his erstwhile rescuer the fashion king had seemed unnaturally puffed and swollen, now his dangling outline isn't even human … a dirigible, a saveloy, a six-foot cylinder with rounded ends, the pulpy mass is only recognisable from the caricature of Maurice Calendar that has apparently been painted on its wrinkled surface … at its bottom end, the hanging sausage looks to have been dipped in tar, a viscous blackness following the shape of Calendar's contemporary haircut, with above that his inverted features, two-dimensional and crudely reproduced, cartoon*

*eyes open wide and staring ... torso, legs and feet are similarly rendered,
the fawn raincoat's arms and the protruding hands drawn flat against
Maurice's sides, the grey tube of the trousers, childishly delineated shoes
and socks there at the upside-down blimp's top ... the coloured epidermis, puckered and distressed, is blotchy; peeling here and there like
sunburn ... strewn about the shadows of the chamber's floor, akin to
sloughed-off sleeping bags, Dennis can make out the remains of empty
husks with bits of people painted on them, brittle, dry, unmoving, slowly
decomposing in the starry dark ...*

*he doesn't understand what he is seeing ... pummelled each new
second by signals and signs he can't decipher, he is overloaded with the
alien, incapable of a reaction or response ... if things in the Great When
are Symbolist precursors of phenomena in Dennis's own London, what
the hell is this ridiculous arrangement meant to represent? ... he struggles briefly with an impulse to extend his fingers through the sheet of
fluid hanging upright in its ornate window frame, but, not wanting to
lose them, thinks again ... he turns and shambles off from the incompre-
hensible display, continuing towards the west and Upper Beak Street's
end with no more sense of destination than a wind-up train ...*

*it takes perhaps an hour or more for him to navigate a path back to
the Upper Scandals, the one gateway that he's reasonably familiar with,
and in that time he's only intermittently aware of who or where he is,
much less what he is doing ... concussed in this ghastly paradise, he
totters down the length of a symphonic Regent Street and past the Kiss
of Piccadilly with its slow but passionate debauch of naked statues ...
as in dreams, the constant flow of abnormality and outrage all too soon
becomes acceptable as commonplace reality, humdrum and barely worthy
of attention, dangerously comfortable, and this is the particular insan-
ity of the Great When, the reason journeys here are best concluded
quickly ... near dissociative, he roams the Apogee of Pall Mall, bumps
into a silver-grey top hat as tall as he is, that tips its own brim in cour-
teous apology before continuing its shuffle ... only when he reaches the
expanded Strand and Arthur Machen's emerald epiphany does Dennis
cloudily remember that he's Dennis; does he inexactly piece together
how he comes to be in this excruciating landscape, or recall that he is
trying to get out ... concussed by solid poetry, he makes his dizzy way*

*down to the folded-paper counterpart of Fleet Street and, there at the base of Fetter Lane Unchained, is disconcerted to find something waiting for him ...*

   *on her ossuary charger, the preliminary gesture drawing of a woman limned in moving light still occupies the same spot she did earlier, but with her and her boneyard horse now faced the other way ... although there is no sign of her black handkerchief – perhaps explaining why time is not stopped on this occasion – she is holding the iron key up in one lightly pencilled hand, the moving traceries that are her mini-malist features flickering into what seems to be a smile as she regards Dennis's numb and vacant-eyed approach ... he shuffles past her like a wandering patient who no longer recollects which ward he's come from, peering quizzically up from time to time at the half-finished rider without demonstrating more than the most foggy recognition ... when he stumbles closest to her, the horsewoman lowers her arm in a tumbling cascade of undecided lines and then extends her key to him, the hasty pen strokes of her lips continually revised and rubbed out as she speaks, the voice like showering radio rain, blown in from elsewhere and then swishing off into the long-wave distance ... 'For the quick' ... he distantly recalls Jack Neave identifying Slenderhorse as an Arcanum capable of speech, and reaches up to take the proffered prize out of her flip-book fingers, mostly motivated by the vague sense that to not do so would in some way be impolite ... 'Yeah, thanks' ... he struggles on in fits and starts, the key now clasped forgotten in one hand, until he is once more amongst implausibly tall flowers, voluptuous glassware, and the crumpling smudge of Her Train still maintaining a safe distance, hovering cautious in the astral pallor ... wading through the wavering grass, he traipses down the now familiar incline, following a dreamy instinct rather than a conscious plan ... he's barely conscious ... when at last Dennis identifies the Doric-column stems that hold between them a more serious blackness, he at first looks for some mechanism, knob or handle by which means he might unlock this 'Fisbo entrance', although nothing of that nature is apparent ... he is slowly inching his way forward in the worse-than-dark when he*

landed with bruising force on the deserted pavement of Bride Lane, where was the sound of something weighty swinging shut behind, and where the jarring pain of impact, the unlit sky and the sudden, bitter cold were all real things. A kicked sandcastle of a man, after some several minutes grovelling and gasping, he contrived to lever himself up into a seated posture on the front steps of what he would later notice was a printer's institute. He sat there for the next hour, trembling and staring, while the six or seven passers-by who happened on him in that time assumed he was perhaps a shell-shocked veteran. In a way, he was.

Identity came back to him, but only in confused instalments. Dazedly, he reconstructed who he was and what had led him to this chilly, lightless doorstep: he was Dennis Knuckleyard, he thought, and since his mother's death four years ago, had lived with Coffin Ada Benson at her bookshop. She had sent him on an errand that had led through tipsters, gangsters, hawkers, artists and wooden men, into a shining town that relegated bricks-and-mortar London to a shadow it was casting. He supposed he was in love with Grace, though she was too grown-up and beautiful for him to stand much of a chance; would probably end up with someone more her own age, someone with a car and a career and their own place to live. In this way, with the background colours of his life at least roughed in, Dennis reluctantly came to address the foreground detail of his last two hours.

Although he desperately needed to regard his travels in the other London as those in a dream, a random sequence of unsettling but blameless incidents, he knew that wasn't true. For all of its fantastic trappings, Dennis's assistance with the killing of Clive Amery had really happened. Clive was really dead, and Dennis really had arranged for that to be the case. However justified or necessary it had been, he had a feeling that the evening's events had ushered something dangerous and new into his inner life, his personality. He couldn't talk to anybody in material London about what he'd done, not Grace or Tolerable John or Ada, because in material London, what he'd done was murder, punishable by the rope. Nor could Dennis tell anyone acquainted with the Great When, because in the Great When, what he'd done was to commit an act of treasonous betrayal,

punishable by an intestinal extroversion. He could dimly appre-
hend the loneliness of his new situation, knowing that in the
attempt to understand or to assimilate what had just happened,
he would be completely on his own. After a while, he opened
his clenched fist and gazed down blankly at the iron mortice key
that rested in his palm, without the first idea of what it meant.
Eventually, on his third try he managed to stand up and, thrust-
ing both hands and the tightly clasped key deep into the pockets
of his coat, commenced the long, refrigerated walk back home
to Shoreditch.

When he found himself outside Lowell's Books & Magazines
an indeterminate while later, all the lights were off and, mercifully, Ada herself had evidently already retired. Braving the
dead-nettles that were the bookshop's only neighbours, Dennis
fumbled with the latch of the back gate, tripped over Ada's
inconvenient flowerbed – or perhaps premature grave, he really
wasn't bothered any more – and entered by the back door
before going straight up to his excuse for human accommodation, taking off his clothes and lowering himself down into
his two-inch-thick mattress and oblivion. Where he remained
for almost the next thirty hours, left undisturbed by a landlady
who'd deduced that whatever was wrong with him was almost
certainly her fault. He finally woke, massively disoriented and
bewildered, on November 2nd, Wednesday, only to discover that
his fingers were still wrapped around the key, his cryptic and
upsetting keepsake. Dennis placed it in the top drawer of his
bedside cabinet, got dressed, and then got on as best he could
with his unsatisfactory life.

All that day and the next, both Dennis and the world surrounding him seemed hollow as a blown egg. He performed his duties
adequately with a shift or two behind the counter, but attended
to his customers without a word, without a noticeable change
in his expression. Even when the woman with a funny eye and
fondness for a titillating murder tried to carry out another of

her lightning raids, he only had to meet her frantically rotating glance with the charred abyss of his own to send her hurrying away, without so much as a beguiling strangled nudist for her troubles.

To her credit, other than enquiring if he'd like a cup of tea, Ada took care to leave Dennis alone, at least until the Thursday evening, by which point he was at least partially reassembled. They were both sat at the kitchen table, finishing the pig's liver and onions that she'd made for dinner, when he noticed that Ada was giving him a long, appraising stare, as if at a new sofa that she wasn't sure she liked the look of. Although, when at last she spoke, her tone was barely even hostile.

'Dennis, cough cough cough am I to take it you've been in a bit of cough cough cough cough bother? Since you come out of yer cough cough coma, you've been knitted out of fucking steam.'

He supposed he had been. That was certainly how it had felt.

'Yeah. Yeah, I had a spot, you know, a spot of trouble. Thanks for asking.'

Ada slithered a reptilian tongue tip around lips of bacon rind while she considered.

'Cough cough cough I see. And am I cough cough cough to understand that this, shall we say, spot of trouble, it's all cough cough cough cough done with now?'

He glanced up at the pub-piano ivory of her eyes, then ducked his head and looked back at his plate, where he was studiously scraping up the last few scraps of liver, mash and onion gravy.

'Yeah. Yeah, that's all finished. That's all done with now.'

She stared at him for a few seconds more, in silence, before leaning forward and delivering her next remarks in slightly lowered tones that were at once more urgent and more intimate.

'Yes, cough cough cough but are you sure? You say it's done with, but are you as sure of that as I'm sure of my cough cough cough cough flowerbed, for example?'

He put down his knife and fork and looked up into Ada's level and unblinking gaze, his own eyes full of nothing save for startled disbelief. She knew. Not names or even the most rudimentary details, but she knew that there was only one thing which could put that look on someone's face, the look that Dennis had on his. She knew because she was a member of the same exclusive club, had guessed what it took thirty hours of deep sleep to recover from. As somebody who'd staked their future on a body never being found, she evidently knew the signs. Still eye to eye with her unwavering scrutiny, he answered in a calm voice that surprised him, one he hadn't heard before.

'I'm sure. It's like your flowerbed. Nothing will be coming up.'

She gave a nod of satisfaction that was almost imperceptible.

'That's cough cough cough cough what I thought.'

Haltingly, Ada raised herself out of her chair with grunts and groans that made her seem like a forgotten triumph of nineteenth-century engineering. Gathering up their dirty plates and mash-scabbed cutlery, she slippered her way past him to the rough stone sink, and as she did, she briefly rested one dried-leaf hand on his shoulder, patted it and said, 'Good cough cough cough cough lad.' It was so unexpected, so precisely what he needed, that it almost made him cry. He *was* a good lad, even if the only other person to have ever called him that had been his mum. He blinked hard, having not foreseen the touching sympathy of murderers.

After she'd left the washing-up to soak in half a sinkful of cold water, Ada scuffed and spluttered to the cupboard, from which she retrieved a bottle of Bell's whiskey and two small glass tots about the size of eyebaths. Earlier that afternoon she'd splashed out on a spitting, crackling conflagration in the kitchen fireplace, and although it was now down to hot coals of translucent orange in a powdery encroachment of grey ash, its light and warmth still conjured up a close facsimile of cosy. On returning to the woefully abraded table, she poured both of them a generous measure, raised her brimming eyebath in the firelight and said, 'Cough cough cough cough cheers.'

They drank and talked for hours about everything except the dreadful things they'd done, which was more difficult for

Ada who'd done very few things that weren't dreadful. Mostly she regaled him with hair-raising stories of her brief career on stage and screen, including an informative classification of her fellow thespians as either 'cunts' or 'alright if you cough cough cough cough like that sort of thing'. By the time she'd recounted fraught affairs with both sides of the house during Ramsay MacDonald's coalition government, Dennis perceived her raddled features and her rigid hairdo in a mythic glow that didn't seem to be wholly occasioned by the whiskey.

'Ada, honestly, all of the things you've done in your long life, they're great. They're really, really great. I only hope that, if I live as long as you, I've notched up half of your experiences.'

She put her empty glass down and regarded her pie-eyed employee with a puzzled frown.

'Dennis, I'm cough cough cough cough cough cough fifty-one.'

By Friday evening, when he met with Tolerable John down at the Cheshire Cheese, Dennis was almost normal. If, after the horrifying business of the Monday night just gone, Dennis's psychological condition could be likened to a smouldering bombsite, then his thirty hours of sleep were a bulldozing of the rubble, and, come Guy Fawkes Night eve on Friday, he had managed to erect a personality equivalent to a substandard block of flats – shoddy but functional.

They mused upon this, that, the other, and the only noticeable symptom of his recent danse macabre was a persisting tendency to tune out from what John was on about, in favour of his own interior broadcasts. In the main, these focussed on the over-whelming notion that wherever Dennis was in London, there was, too, another world that occupied exactly the same space. Although he hadn't seen it, he was confident that, somewhere off its Upper Scandals, the Great When must have its own outland-ish version of Ye Olde Cheshire Cheese. Its clientele, he hazily conjectured, perhaps sitting right where he was now and yet a universe away, would be the shades of Dickens, Robert Louis Stevenson, Sir Arthur Conan Doyle and all the rest, content amid the smoky gossip of eternity. As a poetic fancy this had been a comforting idea, but as a point of fact it was disturbing, bringing to mind as it did the final line of Arthur Machen's 'N': 'It is possible, indeed, that we three are now sitting among desolate rocks, by bitter streams ... And with what companions?' Stifling an inadvertent shudder, Dennis tried to pay attention to what Tolerable John was saying.

' ... so I had a think about your situation, being stuck up there at Ada's with no expectation of parole. It seems to me that what you need's a proper job, so that you could afford to look for lodgings somewhere else, and if it turns out you can't find a proper job, there's always journalism. I remembered you'd once said how you might like to have a go at writing. Writing stories, literary fiction, I assume, but when it comes to finding your way into a career like that, or polishing your skills, then you could do a good sight worse than working as a journalist. I often hear about odd little jobs, short features to fill up a column here or there, and if you fancied giving it a go, then I could shove some of 'em your way. Course, it wouldn't be a lot of cash at first, but it'd be a start.'

Dennis was glad he'd listened. In a dizzying twenty seconds of elation, he imagined himself in a whole new life: a junior newshound with a gripping prose style that would soon see lots of money rolling in, at least compared with intermittent five-pound notes out of the till from Ada. He could get some new clothes, buy some shoes that fitted, find a decent place to live, somewhere he could take Grace to that she'd be impressed by and then probably they'd marry. He was just considering a more suitable hairstyle to accompany his new profession when it struck him that he hadn't written anything since school and, even if he had, did not own so much as a fountain pen that he could write with. As his soaring aspirations ploughed into the runway upon take-off, Dennis looked up at McAllister and shook the haircut he was stuck with ruefully.

'Nah. Thanks a lot for thinking of us, mate, but I don't reckon I'd be up to it. I wouldn't have the first idea of what to do, and, anyway, I haven't got the kit.'

John took a gulp of his just-purchased pint, wiped a Bismarck moustache of foam on to the forearm of his coat and tipped his chin from side to side as if in a display of pensive balance.

'Yeah, I knew you'd say that, although that's what comes of living up at Coffin Ada's since you were a little kid. She's siphoned off your self-respect and confidence because, in other people, those are things that get on Ada's nerves. It's just the way she is. But I've been giving it some thought, and I can't see that you've got anything to lose. As far as writing goes, you're a smart chap who's read a couple of good books and, take my word for it, could not be any worse than the great load of rubbish I see published every day. As for not having any kit, I'm getting a new typewriter in January or February next year, so if you like, you can have my old Olivetti. True, the "e" key sticks a bit, but if you don't mind that, it ought to last you a good while. I can throw in a ream of Croxley Script, a ream of onion-skin, a pack or two of carbon paper, if that's any help.'

Out of the scattered wreckage and the burn mark it had made on Dennis's internal landing-strip, his dream defied all laws of aeronautics and miraculously lifted off into the sky again, this time as a Wright brothers model that had lowered expectations but which seemed a great deal sturdier; seemed airworthy. Dennis immediately accepted John's generous offer, thanked his dolorous friend once more and promised that he'd give it his best shot. With this resolved, they got another round in and their conversation was both livelier and of more consequence. Both men devoured a packet of potato crisps – to 'line their stomachs', a beer-inspired strategy to keep them from becoming as drunk as they obviously already were – and Tolerable John submitted what turned out to be a three-pint thesis on the state of Britain following the war, talking about the massive changes in society that Dennis, up until that point, had barely even noticed, much less understood. A good hour or so later, as the landlord rang his bell and called last orders, John's political analysis approached its finish line.

'The war turned Britain into somewhere else. It had to. When it was still going on, everyone knew that this would have to be a different country when the war was finished, that it couldn't just go back to being for the benefit of wealthy toffs who claimed that poverty was what the poor deserved for being lazy, stupid and incapable. You can't say that to the people who've just saved us from a century or two of Nazi Europe, can you? Not when they've come home victorious to find jobs gone, and family members dead, and miles of rubble where their houses used to be. No, in the wartime coalition, even the Conservatives like Churchill knew that there was going to have to be a change, a serious attempt to sort out all the miseries of class and inequality, once and for all. They'd had Clem Attlee there in the war cabinet, and good old Ernie Bevin for the unions, and they could see the working classes weren't just going to let this lie. They had to feel they'd fought a war for *something*.

'And, to be quite fair, society's a lot more equal now. The main proposals in the Beveridge Report have been put into practice, we've been promised full employment, there's Nye Bevan's health service, there's proper education for all walks of life, and even with the rationing we're better fed now as a nation than we've ever been. This new Britannia's looking good, but where I think we're going to have a problem is in letting old Britannia go. It's clear the empire's had its chips, with India ready to abandon ship, but what's the betting that we'll try to hang on to our status as a grand world power, up there with Russia and the Yanks, despite the fact we're in debt to our eyeballs? We can have the decent country we've been guaranteed, or we can keep up the illusion that we're still a great one, but I can't see that we'll have the money to do both. And knowing us, we'll probably decide that destitution's not too bad, so long as you can dress it in a Union Jack waistcoat.'

Dennis, who'd been wondering if characters that had enjoyed the Cheshire Cheese in fiction – Sydney Carton, Hercule Poirot

– might be occupying nearby tables in the world next door, had missed a lot of the foregoing argument, although he thought he'd caught the gist of it.

'So, given what you're saying, what's the outlook for this next ten years? What do you think the fifties will be like, all things considered?'

Tolerable John regarded him with tired, lugubrious eyes beneath perpetually regretful brows.

'What, in a word?'

Guy Fawkes Night came and went with no more than the usual amount of maiming or disfigurement, but as Dennis walked down to Grace's around sunset on the Sunday after, the debris was everywhere. Spent banger casings littered the smashed flag-stones, while strewn over the adjacent ruins were half-pint milk bottles still full of smoke, dead sparklers, the martyred stubs of Roman candles and the blackened thumbprints left by last night's fires. He would have thought that everybody'd had enough of loud bangs in the dark, of sparks and flames and rockets, but then Dennis wasn't a psychologist; had barely a psychology to call his own when it came down to it.

He got to Folgate Street just as it started to get dark and Grace seemed pleased to see him, grinning as she asked him in. She made them both a cup of tea, and conjured a Victoria sponge with jam and buttercream from somewhere, probably her mixing bowl and oven. Her apartment, Dennis noted, looked a lot more spacious without razor-wielding thugs and timber golems. Grace was wearing some variety of Woolworth's perfume, perhaps Lily of the Valley, and, remembering the swift kiss on his cheek she'd given him when last he'd seen her, Dennis wondered if tonight might be the night. She asked him how his week had been and, while avoiding any mention whatsoever of its first three days, he told her. When he got to Tolerable John's admittedly inebriated offer of a typewriter with nearly a whole alphabet of working keys, she was almost beside herself.

'Dennis, that's champion. Now you can be a writer, like you said that you were going to be. And as it happens, I've come a bit nearer to achieving some of my ambitions, too. There's this new pitch I'm working up in Soho, not far down the road from where some of the clubs are. I've got friendly with a couple of the strippers, and they say there's always work for anybody decent-looking who can dance. It's not a job that I'd want to end up in, but I'm thinking it could be a step up on the way there, and it's better than the work I'm doing now. Oh, I'm so happy, for the both of us.'

At this point, following an amorous instinct that he did not actually possess, Dennis thought it was now or never and leaned forward with his eyes closed to kiss Grace full on the lips, but, as it turned out, it was never. Forcefully but not unkindly, she placed both hands on his chest and firmly pushed him back. He blushed and started stuttering an apology, which she dismissed with a faint shake of her vermilion locks.

'No, you don't need to say you're sorry. You just tried to have a snog, you didn't grab my tits or anything. But, Dennis love, you have to get it into your thick head that I'm not going to have it off with you. For one thing, I've a fair idea I'd be your first time, and I don't want that responsibility. You'd fall in love with me or something daft like that, you know you would. No matter what you said, give it a month or two, you'd try to rescue me. I'm sorry, Dennis. No.'

He shook his head in pained denial, although Grace's rescue in a month or two had in fact been his plan. Attempting to retrieve his dignity, instead he squandered its last shreds.

'It's not like I'm completely inexperienced. When I was four-teen, this girl pulled me off.'

Grace gave him a pained look of understanding and compassion.

'Susan Garrett?'

Slack-jawed and incredulous, he nodded. She did, too, then went to make another cup of tea. While they were sipping that in awkward silence, Dennis tried to salvage his romantic fantasies by framing what had been a flat refusal as a mere postponement. 'Look, I know there's an age gap between us, but perhaps in a few years, when I've grown up a bit, it won't seem such a big one.'

She was looking at him now with a bewildered frown, trying to get his measure.

'Dennis, I'm fifteen.'


He didn't have the heart to see Grace after that. He'd done the miserable sums to figure out how old she must have been when she took up her trade, and felt sick to his marrow. Yes, he'd known that these things happened, heard of kids as young as nine out on the game, but those were stories in the foggy, grey newspaper distance and weren't sat on a collapsing sofa next to him. He thought about the horrors that she must have gone through – she'd have only been eleven, twelve, it was unbearable – and, worse, he felt that he'd come very close to being one of them. She was the nicest, most substantial person that he'd ever met, somebody that he clearly needed as a friend, and, just as clearly, Dennis knew that he was never going to manage that. It wouldn't be real friendship, would it, if one party was forever hoping, secretly, to get the other into bed? He couldn't be the pal that she deserved and, with that being so, he thought it better that he wasn't any kind of pal at all. They parted on good terms later that evening, but with an unspoken sadness gathered on the Spitalfields front doorstep, both aware this was to be their last goodbye without it being said. No farewell kiss.

The year's concluding months were mostly empty for him, following that painful Sunday. Dennis drudged his days away in Ada's shop and only thought about Grace every half an hour or so. His musings on the other London or what had become of Clive were far less frequent, and confined to those occasions when he found himself bolt upright on his clammy bedroll, terrified, with his heart doing a quick march. He couldn't even find a book in which to lose himself, and had to be contented with the thought that Orwell would be sure to have another corker out in the new year.

Beyond the listing walls of Lowell's Books & Magazines, the country licked its wounds and went on, uneventfully, with its recovery. In mid-November, he heard how there were less miners dying since the coal industry had been nationalised a year or two before, and at the month's end, Winston Churchill gave a speech at Kingsway Hall in Holborn, in which he suggested that a union of European countries might not be a bad idea, although he wasn't sure if Britain should be in it. By December, there was an announcement that the BBC would be transmitting TV signals to the Midlands, and his Orwell-prompted vision of a population bent beneath their strapped-on walnut-finished sets crept ever closer. Christmas was, predictably, a washout, and left Dennis feeling that the whole of 1949 had been a personal disaster that he couldn't wait to put behind him.

It was possibly this fervent wish that found him staggering through London on the last night of the month, making a futile stab at celebrating the new year while hopefully extinguishing the old one. Stubbornly determined not to drink too much, he limited himself to just a solitary pint in every pub he visited and, after five of these, convinced himself that it would be a fine idea to venture into Soho and to demonstrate, once and for all, that he was over all that nonsense now. Admittedly, the thought that he might catch a glimpse of Grace was almost certainly there somewhere in the slosh of his unconscious half a mind, but this was not his main objective and, anyway, didn't happen.

New Year's Eve in the notorious district turned out not to be the best idea he'd ever had. Jostling through the steep streets clogged by cheery revellers, he couldn't stop his inner slide show flashing up bright, garish snapshots of the Soho hiding behind this one, couldn't help but wonder what, if anything, would be left of Clive Amery on the teeming, breeding, feeding gold expanse of a superior Bateman Street. Dennis had scanned the newspapers since the end of October without finding any mention of a dead or disappeared young legal brief. He hoped things stayed that way, but knew his footsteps from then on would always have a guilty echo; something following him at a discreet distance that he'd be forevermore afraid might catch him up.

It was in this beer-sodden and obscurely anxious state that Dennis found himself emerging from the press of opportunist gropes and noisily unfurling paper squeakers into the celebratory embrace of Berwick Street where, at the bottom, he bumped into Jack Neave and Gog Blincoe. They were stood together in the middle of the vehicle-free road, amongst the weaving conga lines and other terminal convulsions of the 1940s, both appearing to be slightly drunk despite the fact that only Ironfoot, swigging from a flask, seemed to be drinking. Both of them cheered heartily at Dennis's unsteady, stumbling approach. Gog Blincoe slapped him on his back and nearly broke it.

'Why, Jack, look who we've got here! It's our young Mister Knuckleyard, come by to see the old year out with us! Give him a pull on that there flask o' yours, so that he don't go thirsty.'

Grinning, Neave held out the metal canister and brushed aside Dennis's protests that this wouldn't leave enough for Jack and Gog. 'Don't worry about this great pile o' lumber. 'e don't touch a drop, because 'e can get plastered manufacturin' a sort o' turpentine in what 'e's got instead of innards. When 'e's pissed, 'is knot'oles 'ave a faraway look, if you 'adn't noticed.'

Not wishing to appear less than fellowly, Dennis obligingly knocked back enough of the flask's contents to deduce, from a scorched larynx, that it must be rum. The three fell into boozy conversation, swaying slightly in the tilted street, bumped into by a tipsy tumbril mob turned out to witness the beheading of a tyrant decade. Ironfoot passed on the news that things were looking up for 'Awstin' following his exhibition at the Temple Bar and that, at this rate, he might soon be raking in enough to move upstairs, out of that rotten basement in Wynne Road. Their talk, despite being conducted at the centre of a raucous hokey-cokey, grew more downcast when it turned to Monolulu, who'd apparently meant what he said about avoiding the Great

When after his brush with Charming Peter. Blincoe sighed and shook his huge stump of a head.

'I have impressed upon him that the London Cat may break a man with words to spare his claws the effort, but the Ras Prince will have none of it. It is the creature's mention of black magic that has done for him, I fear, this being something he is mightily afraid of.' Caught up in the bass creak of the market-trader's voice, Dennis ventured a question that he might have hesitated to submit had he been sober.

'Gog, look, no offence, but … Gog, what are you?'

Blincoe's rumbling laugh, when Dennis thought about it, definitely smelled of turps.

'Huhur. I'm carved out of a gatepost, lad, and my old mum, she's carved out of another.'

Dennis was about to ask the apron-clad colossus what he meant by this unusual metaphor, when everything was interrupted by some sort of a commotion at the lane's top end, a susurrus of gasps that seemed to move down Berwick Street towards them, awestruck merrymakers falling back to open up a path for the phenomenon, whatever it might be. At last, just as a nearby church began to sound its midnight chimes and shook the crowd from their brief hush into a slurred cacophony of 'Auld Lang Syne', a thing unprecedented stepped from out the caterwauling throng and opened its immaculately tailored arms in greeting to Neave, Knuckleyard and Blincoe. It was a blue rectangle held up by twig-thin legs which terminated in big, heavy shoes with crêpe soles almost thicker than their mock-croc uppers. It had several feet of keychain looping from its waistcoat, and upon its head a glistening wedge of moulded gelatine, coal black, that overhung the pallid forehead in a slippery twizzle. It was Maurice Calendar. He'd hatched.

'Get with it, dad! I got the drape shape, powder blue, long as me fingertips, wi' raindrop spots, Huddersfield worsted silk this is, an' pepper in the pockets. Three-inch lapels, velvet collar, an' the lining's by Gillette. Four buttons and a link, fifteen-inch bottoms on me drainpipes, it's Edwardian! I'm slashin' seats an' creepin' in the brothels, wi' white socks on an' a slim jim round me shirt neck. You can stick yer frothy coffee! Giddy-up a ding-dong! Sharpened up me comb an' got me clever stick, I'm fit to rock around the clock. Shakin' all over, mate, know what I mean?'

Nobody knew what Maurice meant, or, at least, not for a few years.

By the time that he'd veered and zigzagged back to Shoreditch, Dennis's protective alcoholic haze had almost dissipated, shrivelled up to nothing after no more than an hour or two of 1950. In the dusty silence of his room, he sat there on the edge of the pretended mattress, in his underpants, lit by the parchment aura of a too small bedside lamp. Shivering from the cold at intervals, he stared, without even a half pint of illusion, into the bare hallways of his future.

For a moment there, he'd thought that he had possibilities. He'd felt like he was on the brink of a new world, with life's big secrets opening before him, but all that had done was nearly send him mad. He'd had a new career in mind, he'd nearly had a girlfriend, but John might have been too generous about his prospects as a writer, and, as for the girlfriend, Grace was gone. He wasn't ever going to sit and talk with her again, and that alone was more than he could take. In fact, his situation now was worse than it had been before he'd laid eyes on *A London Walk*, when he'd at least believed he'd got two friends, before he'd had to murder one of them. The only person he had standing between him and homelessness, grim unemployment or conscription, was his dreadful landlady.

Despite the fact she dominated and controlled his life, for all of the grey slavery she represented, she was all he had. She was his only option, and the sooner he accepted that, the sooner he learned to surrender all hope and ambition to her greater will, the better it would be for him. He made his mind up there and then to drown his dreams in an insensate servitude, happy and willing.

He loved Coffin Ada.

## The Old Man at the End

Across the street, down on its wind-scraped corner, sodium lamps have wrapped the night with yellow cellophane. A hoarding board is colonised by handbill barnacles, blink-and-you'll-miss-them venues starring last-but-one big things as paste-up palimpsest, torn wallpaper of the millennium. Framed in the upstairs window opposite, this small-hours urban vista is deserted, motionless save polystyrene beakers scuttling in gusty gutters, looks submerged and drowning in the piss light.

Turns away from a reflection in the double glazing that seems worryingly spectral, creaks back to the leather chair and paper-back biography of Joe Meek resting open on its arm, and makes the usual alarming outcries in the course of sitting down. At this age, the career arc stands revealed as a V-2 parabola, its many questions now reduced to time and place of impact. Functions of the body once as unremarkable as waking in the morning are made hard-fought victories and thus a cause for celebration, like, for instance, waking in the morning. Every day, the future seems a shorter street, just as the lists of gone acquaintances and things that won't be done again seem longer. Even though this outcome is the one that everybody, surely, was expecting, it appears to always come as a surprise, like snow in February, or long nights in October.

Personally, this isolate condition – banishment for the last twenty years without hope of reprieve – is probably no worse than that experienced by any individual at the business end of their existence, where the times and world that were their birth-place are demolished so that everyone ends up an exile, cast up half-dead and uncomprehending on the shores of countries they don't recognise. On the way up by cab from Blackfriars Bridge the other afternoon, out through the grubby glass, there – at the bottom of New Bridge Street – was an eight-floor office complex, sprouted from the city's last remaining bombsite which, last August, had been finally cleared for development. Getting on half a century, then, it's taken the metropolis to heal the scathes of Hitler, to rise tall and confident from ruin while its older population execute exactly the reverse trajectory. This is the major difference that exists between the lives of buildings and the life of beef and bone.

Picks up the Meek biography but then remembers why it had been put down in the first place, in a spasm of anxiety caused by the anecdote about a Bible and a mortice key in chapter five. That had been what provoked the groan-fraught crossing of this cosy room, the nervous peering at the Lucozade cascade outside. More moments like that all the time these days, jumpy and fearfully expectant. Perhaps better read by light of day, *The Legendary Joe Meek – The Telstar Man* returns to its position on the chair arm where the dead producer grimaces from its front cover, trapped eyes shiny with amphetamines.

Once more considering that extinct bombsite down at Blackfriars Court, the thought occurs that London wears her rubble on the inside now: behind a smooth white concrete and black glass façade, the city's themes and ideologies are broken into irrecoverable pieces. A decade of Thatcher has hamstrung the unions and dismantled the post-war consensus on a fairer England; Blair has swept to power by renouncing socialism and rebranding Labour as the Cool Conservatives; both church and monarchy look to be self-destructing, then that inexplicable convulsion when Diana died. Kensington Palace had been buried in bouquets, improvised tributes and stunned messages that were all asking the same thing, asking, 'Where are we?' London's underlying landscape of ideas and visions, the essential character and meaning of the place, all this is wreckage tangled up in bunting from forgotten jubilees.

Sits upright for a while, reclines, but either way, the backache doesn't care. Maybe a Lemsip later, a requirement of this current life stage and this new, old body; this pre-carcass with its surprise catalogue of bruises, burns, and yet no tactile memory of where they came from. And the mind, of course, the mind is worse. Denied recourse to crutches, splints or plaster casts, it can at last collapse into whatever crumpled shape it wants, its memory a string bag, panic button jammed continually down by rust of habit, an increasing inability to differentiate between real life, TV and dreams. Imagination doesn't work the way it used to, with those threads of speculation that were once so pleasurable to pursue become a sticky spider silk of paranoia, each thought leading to a worse one.

Twenty long years of exclusion, since the fatal blunder and the fall from grace. The futile hope, back then, that contact might one day resume has been replaced by a devout wish that it doesn't, that it mustn't. Far too vulnerable to fight, with the idea of running anywhere patently laughable, insistence that the bad thing isn't going to happen is the only strategy available, a papier mâché last line of defence that's no defence at all. Denial isn't any kind of barricade, is too easily punctured by occurrences that call to mind whatever is least wanted there; the unexamined awfulness dredged up by nudges and reminders out of a blue sky. Only a week ago there'd been that young Brazilian woman at the door, waving her bulky, complete paperback edition and enquiring plaintively if Richard Ramsey was at home. 'No, sorry, love. Can't help you. There's no Richard Ramsey here.' All true enough, but that does not displace the sinking guilt which comes with watching as, dejectedly, they walk away. One every month or two, it seems like, bearing intimations that this isn't over yet; this isn't done.

Restless and shifting in the squeaky seat, unable to get comfortable despite a constantly downgraded definition of that term, there comes the thought of slipping a prismatic coaster in the CD player's elegantly gliding tray, as if to bring a change of air by lacing it with music and so possibly arrest the threatened mood slide. Although what is there to listen to that won't just emphasise this feeling of estrangement from a past no longer reachable? Maybe some Prefab Sprout but, no, that would be taking refuge in heroic modern heartbreak; dressing up in a world-wise persona that no longer fits around the waistband; wallowing in brave, tear-stained relationships that are, at this age, never going to be relatable. It's not the album's fault, but rather that of the decrepit listener with a scratched vinyl soul that crackles, sticks, repeats and has disturbing messages recorded backwards in its lead-out groove. The only discs to hand are old ones anyway, and it's the year 2000 in a few months' time. So, then, silence it is, Cage's 4'33" on infinite repeat, which, basically, has been this place's playlist for the last year and a half, a soundtrack ambient in its absence.

Drums impatient fingers on the chair arm, on *The Telstar Man*'s back-cover blurbs, nothing to read, nothing to hum along with tunelessly. Anxiety adores a vacuum. Over on the room's far side, from the neglected workplace with its empty swivel seat, the jilted word processor glares accusingly, a half-completed essay on the poet David Gascoyne still up on its screen after the listless, unproductive stab at editing attempted earlier. Seen from this far away, through failing eyes and conjoined lashes fused by optic glue, the text becomes unreadable, its paragraphs made dot-screen blocks of solid grey. Left-justified and single-spaced – a quirk left over from those long-gone manual days – the essay's right-side margin is delinquent and uneven, some lines cut off prematurely by a last word that's too long to fit and has been relegated to the line beneath. With distance and myopia, the white ground to the page's right becomes the side-on skyline of a ghostly, negative-space city, having office blocks and A-frame roofs and even smoothly curving domes, with here and there a phantom skyscraper to mark the abrupt ending of a paragraph. Once seen, the spectral urban outline doggedly persists, a lexical Fata Morgana raised up from the emptiness where words run out, a blank Byzantium beyond the ragged edge of language, reminiscent in its way of—

What was that?

A noise from outside in the street, a clattering, it sounded like, and straight away the night turns into something different. Cold, wet fish wake up, flopping and gasping in the abdomen. The whole apartment cringes, where the uplighter flings tall noir shapes against the ceiling. Oh, God, please don't let it happen now. Don't let it happen ever, but especially not now. Heart fluttering like a budgie, every atom going 'no no no no no' beneath its breath. Rocks back and forth to gain momentum and then manages to stand up on the third attempt, one veiny hand on the chair's rear to keep from falling down. Reluctantly, the carpet slippers find their own way back towards the window without the volition of their quaking passenger.

Five years of pining, desperately afraid that it was finished, and then fifteen desperately afraid it wasn't, and now, finally, it's here. Something has been despatched. Something has come. Sweat, sudden on both palms and on the webbing between trembling fingers, as the curtain is pulled back. Erectile nerve ends prickling at the nape and sour heat rising in the throat, gummy eyes blinking, squinting out into the bilious lamplight. On Columbia Road's far corner, the three-in-the-morning junction steeps in topaz, still deserted. Weathered barriers, psoriatic with ripped posters, are a silent war memorial to fallen gigs, and then, behind an overflowing skip, there's something moving.

Oh, no. No no no no no. An inner scrabbling is commenced, casting around the flat in memory for any object that might be repurposed as a lethal instrument to use against the adversary or, if it should come to it, the self. Serrated bread knife, heavy ashtray, something, anything, and down across the street a mobile clot of shadow is unwinding from the radiance and the rubbish ...

But it's just an ordinary cat.

Alan Moore, David J and Her Train – The Bridewell Theatre, Bride
Lane, 16 July 1994 – photograph by Melinda Gebbie

# Acknowledgements

Foremost amongst these acknowledgements, despite no longer being here to receive it, is the late but continually present Brian Catling, whose ultimate performance piece occurred during this book's composition. With Professor Catling's stunning *Vorrh* trilogy, I feel that a new benchmark for fantasy was established, and it's one that has been my preoccupation while embarking on my first series of fantasy novels: the need to attempt something as imaginative, as original and as committed as Brian's masterpiece. Sleep well beneath the peat with the Erstwhile, maestro.

Someone else who clearly couldn't be bothered to wait around for me to finish the book and thank them properly is my immaculate collaborator, Kevin O'Neill. It was Kevin who first introduced me to Ironfoot Jack Neave by way of a murky background cameo in our *League of Extraordinary Gentlemen* story *Century: 1969*, and it was Kevin, sharing his memories of a bombsite London childhood, that provided the anecdote about a second-hand-bookshop proprietor tearing a book to shreds as a disincentive to haggling that I appropriated for Coffin Ada. I told him I'd send him this first volume as soon as it was finished, but unfortunately Kevin finished first and lit out for the Blazing World. I hope he'd have appreciated its balance of coarseness and refinement.

Staying with the influential departed for a moment, it was Steve Moore, forever the presiding spirit of Shooters Hill, who was my entrance into London and its mystique back when we were both teenagers. This book couldn't have been written without the table-tilting interventions of these three immortal presences who, wherever they are, have my eternal love and gratitude.

And so to the quick and the living. It would have been impossible to write a fantasy about London without an awareness of intruding on the turf of writers who've made the imagined city their own, most prominently Iain Sinclair and Michael Moorcock. Iain has been massively encouraging in both our infrequent conversations and through his inspiring work, notably *My Favourite London Devils*, and any metropolitan fantasy commencing in the 1940s is inevitably going to be constructed in the shadow of Mike's stupendous *Mother London*. Thank you both. You're my favourite London devils, even if you're in Texas or Hastings. And I'm hugely grateful to the sublime Stewart Lee for sharing his obsessive Stoke Newington archive with me; the actions of a gentleman, I feel.

Thanks are also due to Mark Valentine, and to anyone involved with the Friends of Arthur Machen and their journal *Faunus*, for providing constant fresh insight into that fascinating author, and especially for providing access to Thos. Kent Miller's essay on Machen's enigmatic short story when I plaintively asked, 'Does anybody know why he called it "N"?' Keep up the exemplary work, ladies and gentlemen, and know that my continuing subscription is safe.

Also, thanks to George Orwell for my brilliant opening sentence.

As ever, thanks to everyone at Bloomsbury on both sides of the Atlantic, and to my agent James Wills and his colleagues at Watson, Little. You are my co-enablers.

Closer to home, the mighty Joe Brown has continued his vital support for both my physical existence and my literary activities. Sir, I salute your indefatigability.

The same goes for the wonderful Michelle Newton and the insurmountable Lindsay Spence for keeping the wheels of my creativity lubricated, and, indeed, to all of my friends, including my fellow gang members from Arts Labs present (Ali, Robin, Yoshe, Cavan, Tom C., Jess, Donna, Josh, Tom J., Steph and anyone I've forgotten) and past (Ian Fleming, Andy Cooper, Mick Bunting, Brian Ratcliffe and the late lamented George Woodcock). Wherever I am, I wouldn't have got here without you.

Closer still, keeping it in the family, there is the constant love, energy and enthusiasm of those who are related to me and can't really get away. Thanks to my brother Morry – who, if you look at him, isn't *that* much better looking than I am – for listening to me babble about whatever chapter I happened to be working on, and for looking forward to the finished result so earnestly. Then there's my astonishing daughters, Leah and Amber, their partners, John and Reen, and their ever-expanding offspring Eddie, James, Joey and Rowan. You are all dearer to me than I can say.

Closest of all, my sincerest thanks go to my lovely wife, the author and visionary Melinda Gebbie. Melinda has been the only person to listen to *The Great When* as it's emerged hot off the keyboard, and her enthusiasm and encouragement have been a lifeline on the many occasions when I've been unsure of the directions that the volatile narrative was taking. Thanks, sweetheart. Going to sleep and waking up next to you is my desert island luxury.

Oh, and thanks to whichever misfiring synapse woke me up laughing at two in the morning with the ridiculous name 'Dennis Knuckleyard'.

# A Note on the Author

**Alan Moore** is widely regarded as the best and most influential writer in the history of comics. His seminal works include *From Hell, Lost Girls,* and *The League of Extraordinary Gentlemen.* He is also the author of the bestselling novel *Jerusalem* and the story collection *Illuminations.* He was born in Northampton, England, and has lived there ever since.

## A Note on the Type

The text of this book is set in Bembo, which was first used in 1495 by the Venetian printer Aldus Manutius for Cardinal Bembo's *De Aetna*. The original types were cut for Manutius by Francesco Griffo. Bembo was one of the types used by Claude Garamond (1480–1561) as a model for his Romain de l'Université, and so it was a forerunner of what became the standard European type for the following two centuries. Its modern form follows the original types and was designed for Monotype in 1929.